THE CRITICAL RESPONSE
TO THOMAS CARLYLE'S
MAJOR WORKS

Recent Titles in
Critical Responses in Arts and Letters

THE CRITICAL RESPONSE TO THOMAS CARLYLE'S MAJOR WORKS

Edited by
D. J. Trela and Rodger L. Tarr

Critical Responses in Arts and Letters, Number 27
Cameron Northouse, Series Adviser

GREENWOOD PRESS
Westport, Connecticut • London

Library of Congress Cataloging-in-Publication Data

The critical response to Thomas Carlyle's major works / edited by D. J.
  Trela and Rodger L. Tarr.
       p.   cm.—(Critical responses in arts and letters, ISSN
  1057–0993 ; no. 27)
    Includes bibliographical references and index.
    ISBN 0–313–29107–1 (alk. paper)
    1. Carlyle, Thomas, 1795–1881—Criticism and interpretation.
  I. Trela, D. J. (Dale J.)   II. Tarr, Rodger L.   III. Series.
  PR4434.C75   1997
  824′.8—dc21   96–50242

British Library Cataloguing in Publication Data is available.

Library of Congress Catalog Card Number: 96–50242
ISBN: 0–313–29107–1
ISSN: 1057–0993

First published in 1997

Greenwood Press, 88 Post Road West, Westport, CT 06881
An imprint of Greenwood Publishing Group, Inc.

Printed in the United States of America

The paper used in this book complies with the
Permanent Paper Standard issued by the National
Information Standards Organization (Z39.48–1984).

10 9 8 7 6 5 4 3 2 1

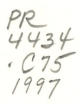

Copyright Acknowledgments

The editors and publisher gratefully acknowledge the following authors and publishers for permission to use copyrighted materials:

DeLaura, David J. "Ishmael as Prophet: *Heroes and Hero-Worship* and the Self-Expressive Basis of Carlyle's Art." *Texas Studies in Language and Literature* 11 (Spring 1969): 705–32.

Grierson, Sir Herbert. "The Hero and the Führer." *Aberdeen University Review* 27 (March 1940): 99–105. By kind permission of the Aberdeen University Alumnus Association.

Kusch, Robert W. "Pattern and Paradox in *Heroes and Hero-Worship*." *Studies in Scottish Literature* 6.3 (January 1969): 146–55. Copyright, G. Ross Roy. Reprinted by permission.

Manlove, Colin N. " 'Perpetual Metamorphoses': The Refusal of Certainty in Carlyle's *Sartor Resartus*." *Swansea Review* 2 (November 1986): 19–36.

Sorensen, David R. "Carlyle's Method of History in *The French Revolution*." *The Carlyle Society Occasional Papers* 9 (1982–83).

Williams, Stanley T. "Carlyle's *Past and Present*: A Prophecy." *South Atlantic Quarterly* 21:1 (Winter 1922): 30–40. Copyright, Duke University Press, 1922. Reprinted with permission.

Every reasonable effort has been made to trace the owners of copyright materials in this book, but in some instances this has proven impossible. The editors and publisher will be glad to receive information leading to more complete acknowledgments in subsequent printings of the book and in the meantime extend their apologies for any omissions.

To

K. J. Fielding

and

G. B. Tennyson

in appreciation

CONTENTS

Contents

Critical Response to *On Heroes, Hero-Worship, and the Heroic in History*

Critical Response to *Past and Present*

SERIES FOREWORD

Critical Responses in Arts and Letters is designed to present a documentary history of highlights in critical reception to the body of work of writers and artists and to individual works that are generally considered to be of major importance. The focus of each volume in this series is basically historical. The introductions to each volume are themselves brief histories of the critical response an author, artist, or individual work has received. This response is then further illustrated by reprinting a strong representation of the major critical reviews and articles that collectively have produced the author's, artist's or work's critical reputation.

The scope of *Critical Responses in Arts and Letters* knows no chronological or geographical boundaries. Volumes under preparation include studies of individuals from around the world and in both contemporary and historical periods.

Each volume is the work of an individual editor, who surveys the enitre body of criticism on a single author, artist, or work. The editor then selects the best material to depict the critical response received by an author or artist over his/her entire career. Documents produced by the author or the artist may also be included when the editor finds that they are necessary to a full understanding of the materials at hand. In circumstances where previous, isolated volumes of criticism on a particular individual or work exist, the editor carefully selects material that better reflects the nature and directions of the critical response over time.

In addition to the introduction and the documentary section, the editor of each volume is free to solicit new essays on areas that may not have been adequately dealt with in previous criticism. For volumes on living writers and artists, new interviews may be included, again at the discretion of the volume's editor. The volumes also provide a supplementary bibliography and are fully indexed.

While each volume in *Critical Responses in Arts and Letters* is unique, it is also hoped that in combination they form a useful, documentary history of the critical response to the arts, and one that can be easily and profitably employed by students and scholars.

Cameron Northouse

INTRODUCTION

Thomas Carlyle was born on 4 December 1795. Now that his bicentenary year is past, a thorough reassessment of one of the most enduring and pre-eminent figures of Victorian letters is in order. One of the more productive ways to accomplish this reassessment is to consider what has already been written. This volume presents some of the most inaccessible and some of the best critical opinion dealing with four of Carlyle's major works that are arguably most representative of his thought. These works include *Sartor Resartus* (1833-1834), *The French Revolution: A History* (1837), *On Heroes, Hero-Worship, and the Heroic in History* (1841), and *Past and Present* (1843). Although the inclusion of these four works needs little justification, the exclusion of criticism of Carlyle's other important works and of more general assessments of his life does perhaps need some explanation.

The initial impression one gets of Carlyle is of his utter indifference to criticism. However, a more accurate picture emerges in his correspondence and *Reminiscences* where he evinces strong interest in how people respond to his works, greatly appreciates sensitive reading and understanding of his message, and rather defiantly execrates those who disagree with or misinterpret his writings. A brief overview of Carlyle's response to his reviewers is therefore instructive in showing his lively engagement with the critical and literary establishment of his day.

It is not surprising that Carlyle would be concerned about the reception of *Sartor Resartus* (1833-1834), a work that he later came to see as his most important. Now generally regarded as Carlyle's most artistic and crafted work, the periodical publication of *Sartor Resartus* in *Fraser's Magazine* barely caused a ripple in the critical sea. The reviewer in the *Sun*, obviously distressed by its novelties, called it a "heap of clotted nonsense," a book that could be read "backwards and forwards" with much the same effect. If Carlyle was disappointed, he did not show it in his letters, but soldiered on firm in the knowledge that he had done his best. He noted in a letter to his brother John, 21 January 1834, that James Fraser tells "me that Teufelsdreck meets with the most unqualified disapproval," which Fraser thinks is "extremely proper" (*CL* 7:81). In a later letter to his wife, 21 May 1834, Carlyle writes in a bemused, yet still defiant tone: "*Teufelk* beyond measure unpopular; an oldest subscriber came in [to Fraser] and said, 'If there is any more of that d--d stuff,

I will &c'; on the other hand, an order from America (Boston and Philadelphia) to send a copy of the Magazine *so long* as there was anything of Carlyle's in it" (*CL* 7:175). In Great Britain, *Sartor Resartus* did not begin its rise to popularity until after its first trade publication in 1838, largely the result of the sensation created by the appearance of *The French Revolution* in 1837. Even then it was not very widely reviewed, while one of the most favorable estimates smacks of puffery: it appeared in *The Metropolitan* (excerpted in this volume), a magazine produced by *Sartor*'s first publisher in book form, Saunders and Otley.

A curious feature of this first trade edition is Carlyle's inclusion, in the front matter of the book, of a section titled "Testimonies of Authors," a collection of three negative reviews of *Sartor*, joined by portions of Emerson's laudatory "Preface" to the first American edition of 1836. Why include this? On the eve of the edition's appearance Carlyle wrote to his brother John that "a few pages called 'Testimonies of Authors' stand by way of Preface, beginning with John Murray and his *Taster* (which stage of it you remember well, seven years back), and ending with Emerson's Preface to the Yankee edition; it gives covertly a history of the poor Manuscript & publication, and embraces the wisest and stupidest, the worst and best, that can be said of it" (*CL* 10:121-22).

The first three references are indeed stupid, especially as Carlyle excerpts them, but make fascinating reading today. They consist of excerpts from John Murray's reader's report that led to his rejection of *Sartor* for publication in 1831. Calling the author "a person of talent" who "displays here and there some felicity of thought and expression," and is intelligent, the reader nonetheless claims that the "Author has no great tact; his wit is frequently heavy." The bookseller (Murray) suggests that Carlyle should try to produce something "popular" and "able." Excerpts from the second review in the *Sun* are included in this volume while the most imbecilic of the three is Alexander Everett's *North American Review* piece, which goes to great lengths to prove the characters of *Sartor* are fictional: "If the Clothes-Philosophy and its Author are making so great a sensation throughout Germany . . . how happens it that the only notice we have of the fact is contained in the few numbers of a monthly Magazines published at London?" Everett adds ponderously that "we doubt a little the propriety of offering to the public a treatise on Things in General, under the name and in the form of an Essay on Dress"! He does, however, conclude his review favorably, noting that *Sartor* contains "a great deal of deep thought, sound principle, and fine writing," praising Carlyle's earlier essays, and ensuring him a warm welcome in the United States should he make his contemplated visit. But this praise Carlyle omits. Emerson's more judicious preface notes the rough style of the work, but nonetheless praises its "mastery over all the riches of the language," a shrewd observation it would take decades to become more generally accepted. Although the book would likely have limited appeal, it possessed "an earnest meaning," significant insight into human nature and a "purity of moral sentiment."

Aside from Carlyle's brief explanation to his brother, what can account for this virtually unique occurrence: an author's reprinting of negative reviews of his own work? At the very least, their inclusion shows Carlyle's concern for and sensitivity to criticism. Also, we cannot rule out Carlyle's own playfulness, often forgotten by modern readers who see only a stern Victorian Sage. *Sartor*, as Colin N. Manlove will argue below, is a *funny* book, based on fictional authors, editors, and philosophical treatises. Negative reviews by real reviewers carry on that hoax. Yet it was too early in the history of *Sartor* for Carlyle to conclude the work was going to be a success. On the contrary, his letters of 1838 suggest the opposite. The edition published by Saunders and Otley was of only 500 copies, 300 of which had to be subscribed for before printing would take place. Carlyle repeatedly stressed he would make no money from it. Yet he recognized the value of his work and would stand by it even if the public did not.

Carlyle's defiance is confirmed by reference to the *Reminiscences*. Writing in March of 1867 Carlyle recalls sending six copies of *Sartor* bound from plates from *Fraser's Magazine* to "Edinburgh literary friends." The result was silence: "from not one of whom did I get the smallest whisper even of receipt—a thing disappointing more or less to human nature, and which has silently and insensibly led me never since to send any copy of a book to Edinburgh, or indeed to Scotland at all, except to my own kindred there and in one or two specific unliterary cases more." Carlyle concludes by acknowledging his own unpopularity with the "Plebs of literature," but ruefully notes "the conscript fathers" with the exception of Southey and his future endorsement of *The French Revolution*, "declined to vote at all" (2:322). Here Carlyle is writing over thirty years after the events he describes; his bitterness at his lack of recognition by his literary peers is still palpable, which in turn suggests his epistolary indifference in the 1830s was more than a trifle feigned.

A considerably more favorable response to *Sartor Resartus* had come from America, where in 1834 Carlyle had sent Emerson several *Fraser's* copies of the work. He noted the work's unpopularity in Britain, but gratefully acknowledged its warm reception in America. "Nothing ever was more ungenial," Carlyle reports, "than the soil that poor Teufelsdreckhish seedcorn has been thrown on here; none cries, Good speed to it; the sorriest nettle or hemlock seed, one would think, had been more welcome. For indeed our British periodical critics, and especially the public of Fraser's Magazine . . . exceed all speech." While from Britain Carlyle notes "simply *one* intelligent response," he enjoins his "Transoceanic Brothers" to "read earnestly" that which he had "earnestly meant and written" (12 August 1834; *CL* 7:264-65). However, it was not until the first American edition of 1836, with Emerson's Preface, that the true impact of *Sartor Resartus* began to become evident. Emerson's glowing endorsement, referred to above, of both the work and the author signaled clearly the impact that it was already having upon the American Transcendental Movement.

It is ironic that over one hundred and sixty years later, *Sartor Resartus* remains the single *essential* work of Carlyle's, at once laying out the major strands of his thought and doing so with seemingly inexhaustible wit, energy, and artistry. Although the initial reception of *Sartor Resartus* was inauspicious in Great Britain, it was to become Carlyle's most influential work, anticipating eloquently the spiritual crisis of the Victorian period. Froude in his biography of Carlyle speaks memorably of the age of doubt ushered in by scientific advances and Utilitarian theories, of "the intellectual lightships . . . broken from their moorings," of "lights all drifting, the compasses all awry, and nothing left to steer by except the stars" (*Life* 1:174). Although Froude does not, at this point, refer specifically to *Sartor Resartus*, this is the book he has in mind as the new "intellectual lightship" guiding a generation of young men. In Froude's judgment, Carlyle and Tennyson were the men who taught "how much and what we could honestly regard as true, and believe that and live by it." "Carlyle stood beside [Tennyson] as a prophet and teacher; and to the young, the generous, to every one who took life seriously, who wished to make an honourable use of it, and could not be content with sitting down and making money, his words were like the morning *reveillée*" (*Life* 1:174)

It would be fair to say that Carlyle's histories are not much read today, although in their day they were consistently praised for their vigorous style, their vividness, and, surprisingly, their accuracy. *Oliver Cromwell's Letters and Speeches*, for example, had the additional virtue of spearheading a rather radical revision of that much-maligned military and political leader. It was *The French Revolution*, however, that made Carlyle famous and gave him some financial independence. It was almost immediately recognized as an unsurpassed work of historical literature by the leading critics of the day, among them Thackeray, Mill, and Southey. In his *Reminiscences*, Carlyle recalls completing *The French Revolution*, then going off to Scotland for a long visit to recover from the "wild excitation of nerves" the writing of it had cost him. An unnamed "young neighbour," from London sent Carlyle a review that had appeared in the *Athenaeum*, "in which I was placidly, with some elaboration, set down as a blockhead and strenuous failure: the last words were, 'Readers, have we made out our case?'" The offending number was used as a makeshift teacup. Carlyle further recalls that Thackeray's "laudation in the '*Times*'" produced no "ray of exultation" (*Reminiscences* 2:319-20). However, Southey's approbation did gratify him:

> Such being my posture and humour at that time, fancy my surprise at finding Southey full of sympathy, assent and recognition of the amplest kind, for my poor new book! We talked largely on the huge event itself, which he had dwelt with openly or privately ever since his youth, and tended to interpret, exactly as I, the suicidal explosion of an old wicked world, too wicked false and impious for living longer; and seemed satisfied and as if grateful, that a strong voice had at last expressed that meaning. My poor "French Revolution" evidently appeared to him a good deed, a salutary bit of "scriptural" exposition for the public and for mankind; and this, I could perceive, was the soul of a great many minor approbations and admirations of detail, which he was too polite to speak of. (*Reminiscences* 2:321-22)

About ten days after the work appeared Carlyle wrote to his mother, 19 May 1837, that "what the critics say of the work I take no pains to know, or rather would take pains not to know. . . . I rather conjecture that all the small fry of critics (a set of the despicablest mortals living) will be afflicted at the thing; and the better kind of critics on the whole pleased: which is exactly as it ought to be." Yet he knew that Mill was at work on a review and seemed pleased (*CL* 9:206). In a more expansive letter to his brother John, 30 May, he writes he can "say almost nothing" of his book's reception, but then proceeds to say a great deal. He notes Fraser was not advertising it much, alludes to some condemnatory reviews, some "hearty, even passionate" praise, a favorable estimation in a letter from Jeffrey, and the review then being written by Mill (*CL* 9:214).

The notion of Carlyle's "indifference" to criticism is again challenged when other letters of 1837 are examined. Over a period of months his regular reference to reviews he has seen, read, been informed of, or been sent copies of is noted. To his brother John, 7 July, Carlyle notes Thackeray's review in the *Times*, other notices of his completed series of lectures on literary history, and a likely review of *The French Revolution* in the *Chronicle* (*CL* 9:243). A later letter to John, 21 September, asks: "Did you get the *Times* review I sent? There were since then three (very shallow, laudatory) articles in the *Glasgow Argus* that I saw; several others that I heard of: on the whole, a well-received Book. . . . The critic in that *Examiner* is one Fo[r]ster as I learn" (*CL* 9:312). This was John Forster, friend and later biographer of Dickens, and soon to become a close friend and advisor of Carlyle's. He would later favorably review *Past and Present*. There are more references in the correspondence to reviews, all of which suggest a substantial interest in the reception of the book, an engagement with the literary establishment of the day and little or none of the airy indifference Carlyle often professed.

The French Revolution is generally credited as the work that secured Carlyle's reputation. This fact may help to explain the falling off in Carlyle's attention to reviews of his later books. *Heroes and Hero-Worship* appeared in March of 1841. In early April Carlyle went on an extended holiday in the north of England and in Scotland, not returning to London until late September. Before his departure he took pleasure enough in Mill's laudatory letter about *Heroes and Hero-Worship* to forward it to his family in Scotland. Carlyle thanked Mill, then added typically that "No Book of mine ever looked more insignificant to me" (*CL* 13:63). Such a reaction is typical of Carlyle who seldom has anything good to say about his own work immediately after its publication. Carlyle was after all a critic himself. His instincts were seldom to praise, even his own work.

Jane Welsh Carlyle took an active part in informing her now-absent husband what London opinion was saying. She wrote him on 7 April about three reviews, one in the *Times*, a second in the *Morning Chronicle,* and a blistering third in the *Weekly Dispatch* which Jane summarized as "prov[ing] that you have not one idea in your head." One sentence of that review sets its tone: "Mr. Carlyle is the very worst lecturer and writer in the English language amongst men, at least, who pretend to any station in literary society. His style is most offensively affected . . . unmusical, harsh and clumsy, totally un-English" (*CL* 13:84). Carlyle duly forwarded portions of the last two reviews to his mother, referring to the *Weekly Dispatch* report as "a slip of abuse out of the chief blackguard Newspaper in England." He added that "no praise I have got is like what Jean tells me, of your *greeting* [weeping] to read my account of Luther and Knox My dear Mother. It is *you* that taught me to lecture in that way; — really so" (*CL* 13:93). Writing to Jane on 12 April after having received her copies of the noted reviews, he remarked with what appears to be satisfaction, "And now, at last, I do think we are very sufficiently applauded and approved; — and ought if possible to go and do something *deserving* a little applause" (*CL* 13:94).

Applause and approval—Carlyle certainly sought them, but also at times regretted seeking them. This is the side of his personality that denied interest in reviews of his own work. He felt that a work would ultimately be judged by the truth it possessed. In such a context reviews were worth little unless they captured and evaluated the truth of both the author and his works. Experience had taught Carlyle that most reviewers did not rightly judge his work, and so it was better not to regard what they said. A comment of Carlyle's in his journal, 4 June, reflects this point of view: "Lectures published *before* I went with Milnes: babble, babble about them; a thing I take *no* interest in, a thing I am almost ashamed of" (*CL* 13:138-39). The fact was, however, that Carlyle *did* take some interest in what people said about him. It is probably *this* interest that he was ashamed of showing.

By the time he published *Past and Present* in April of 1843, he was somewhat more successful at conveying the impression of avoiding interest in reviews of his work, but his actual lack of interest must remain a matter of some doubt. He also had to contend with Jane supplying reviews to him when they were apart, and did not seem to object when she sent them. Further, at the time of the publication of *Past and Present*, Carlyle took some pains to have review copies distributed. Although his letter to Chapman & Hall, his publisher, feigns indifference at this procedure, his words bely this attitude. He begins by saying that "The only *reviewer* I remember at present to whom I am under special promise is 'Thomas Ballantyne,'" but he notes that John Forster "has already got a copy." The April review in the *Examiner*, though anonymous, has been attributed to Forster. Carlyle then remembers another editor, Thomas Aird of Dumfries, to whom a copy should be sent and adds peremptorily, "I shall probably bethink me of several others by and by. . . . You will of course lose no time in despatching these parcels according to their address" (*CL* 16:133). On 6 May he wrote his mother of general responses to his work: "The people are considerably astonished with it here, I imagine, and were not altogether expecting such a thing" (*CL* 16:159).

Jane had become a fierce defender of her husband's work. In her letter to Jeannie Welsh, 9 May 1843, she recounts her angry response to Anthony Sterling's "most monstrous impertinencies about" *Past and Present*, "which *I knew that he had not read.*" "I gave him of course as good — or a pretty deal *better* than he brought," she concluded with some satisfaction (*CL* 16:162). Jane also wrote her husband, 22 July 1843, of John Ruffini's comment. This member of the Young Italy movement told her that "many persons '. . . by the reading of it have recovered their *souls*'" (*CL* 16:306) .

Carlyle also took some pains to be familiar with the response to his book. He wrote his brother John, 29 May 1843, that he had sent his sister Jean "two Newspapers . . . which contained insignificant reviews of *Past and Present*" (*CL* 17:188). On 30 November he wrote to sister Jean regarding further reviews. "The Criticisms on me," he told her, "are of small moment, all of them except one in *The Dial*, by Emerson of Boston in America: this will please you excellently. . . . There was another Criticism, which I reckoned of some moment, by a zealous and gifted Clergyman here; which also I meant to send, and will yet send; but at present, I understand, it is in Wales and so must wait. The *Dublin Review* and *Church-of-England Review* are not properly speaking *mine* at all; so pray keep them clean, if at any time they should be asked of me again!" (*CL* 17:192).

More significant, and not intended for any eyes but his own, are Carlyle's comments in his journal. On 10 October he wrote, "Seven or eight *reviews* of me out last week. *Clitter-clatter* . . . except indeed a few pages from Emerson in his *Dial*, which really contain a eulogy of a magnificent sort. A word from F. Maurice, in defence of me from some Church-of-England reviewer, is also gratifying. One knows not whether even *such* things are a benefit, are not a new peril and bewilderment" (quoted in *CL* 17:192). Carlyle would, in late December, send his sister Jean a copy of the Maurice review, calling the author "a notable kind of Puseyite Clergyman" (*CL* 17:216).

If the "Edinburgh literary friends" noted earlier remained silent, one close friend of Carlyle's did not. John Sterling's review of Carlyle in the *London and Westminster* (33 [October 1838]: 1-68) touched him deeply. It embodied the generous recognition and thoughtful understanding of his views that Carlyle received all too seldom. As David J. DeLaura notes in "Ishmael as Prophet," this acknowledgment "marked an epoch in Carlyle's conception of himself" (136 in this volume). In his *Life of Sterling* (1851), Carlyle recalled the effect the article had on him:

> What its effect on the public was I knew not, and know not; but remember well, and may here be permitted to acknowledge, the deep silent joy, not of a weak or ignoble nature, which it gave to myself in my then mood and situation; as it well might. The first generous human recognition, expressed with heroic emphasis, and clear conviction visible amid its fiery exaggeration, that one's poor battle in this world is not quite a mad and futile, that it is perhaps a worthy and manful one, which will come to something yet: this fact is a memorable one in every history; and for me Sterling . . . was the doer of this. The thought burnt in me like a lamp, for several days; lighting-up into a kind of heroic splendour the sad volcanic wrecks, abysses, and convulsions of said poor battle, and secretly I was very grateful to my daring friend, and am still, and ought to be. What the public might be thinking about him and his audacities, and me in consequence, or whether it thought at all, I never learned, or much needed to learn. (*CW* 11:191-92)

Carlyle's gratitude to Sterling is genuine. His lack of interest in the remainder of public response to his work is not. The unmistakable conclusion is that Carlyle was extremely interested in reviews of his writings in spite of recurring protestations to the contrary. He made efforts to circulate review copies when he could, shared reviews with family members, and was clearly gratified by good reviews in which critics expressed some clear idea of his message. He affected indifference to bad reviews. There is nothing wrong with this or anything all that extraordinary about it. Since most of his income came from what he earned through his writing, it would be surprising to find him completely indifferent to the likely influence good or bad reviews could have on sales of his work. The point, though, is to show Carlyle's own engagement on a practical level with the literary establishment of his day. It is this engagement that is in some conflict with the image Carlyle at times projected of being above it all, an image that in later life was itself projected onto him by others as he donned the mantle of "Victorian Sage."

II

The articles and excerpts we include here, with few exceptions, deal exclusively with four major works. Only the excerpts from Henry Larkin's *Carlyle and the Open Secret of His Life* and G. Robert Stange's "Refractions of *Past and Present*" are taken from books. Stange's fine article is reprinted from the 1976 collection of original articles *Carlyle Past and Present*, edited by K. J. Fielding and Rodger L. Tarr.

We concentrated primarily on articles because books are more difficult to excerpt effectively and are more readily accessible than periodicals. We concentrated more on earlier reviews and criticism for much the same reason: earlier material is likely to be difficult to locate. And, much of this early material is intrinsically more interesting and valuable criticism.

Our primary difficulty was in choosing what to reprint, since the volume of reviews and criticism regarding Carlyle is enormous. In his secondary bibliography, Rodger L. Tarr identifies approximately 1700 nineteenth-century and 1300 twentieth-century citations in British and American periodicals from 1824 to 1974. Two five year bibliographies by Robert Dillon bring the bibliographical record down to 1985 and add several hundred more citations to the available record. Impressive as these bibliographies are, neither Tarr nor Dillon exhausts the British and American provincial newspapers, especially important in the nineteenth century, and neither makes an effort to locate works not in English. Carlyle was undoubtedly one of the most written about men of letters during his lifetime, the more so because he worked in genres, such as the essay and non-dramatic prose, that were deemed more canonical at the time. Although opinion about him and assessments of his work have fluctuated greatly in the years since his death in 1881, interest in his myriad canon has seldom waned. Thus, the critical record is not only voluminous but varied, and, like the universe, is still expanding.

The question then becomes, how to choose what to reprint? It is scarcely possible to be representative when, in having to sift through thousands of articles one can only decide upon excerpts from thirty or forty. Space limitations alone exclude much excellent yet expansive Victorian criticism. Further, the closer textual analysis that is a hallmark of modern criticism comes from a variety of schools and theories of literature, not all of which are represented here. Our working guidelines were to concentrate on early reviews, and thus to present the initial reception of the work. Early critics often engaged in sustained and thoughtful analysis of Carlyle's ideas and so raised the same sorts of criticisms of, objections to, and endorsements of Carlyle's ideas and style that are common today.

Secondly, we sought more mature analyses of each work from later in the nineteenth century or early in the twentieth. It was in the decades after Carlyle's death that a harsh reaction against him set in, given impetus by the publication of the controversial *Life of Carlyle* by Froude and the equally controversial *Reminiscences* and the *Letters and Memorials of Jane Welsh Carlyle* edited by him. What perhaps is not well-enough known is that thoughtful criticism continued in the midst of much shrill execration, charge and countercharge. Particularly important in this regard is Margaret Oliphant's impressionistic assessment of both *Sartor Resartus* and *The French Revolution*, Vernon Lee's excellent evaluation of Carlyle's manipulation of tense in "Carlyle and the Present Tense," which must be regarded as one of the earliest and most remarkable pieces of literary criticism of Carlyle, and Henry Larkin's sensitive reading of Carlyle's overarching philosophical and religious ideas found in *Carlyle and the Open Secret of His Life*.

In the twentieth century we sought single articles, both early and more contemporary, which reflect excellence in assessment of Carlyle. In the 1930s and 1940s especially, Carlyle's reputation plummeted and writing about him reached a low point, both in the amount produced and in the quality. Although important critics like Charles Frederick Harrold, Hill Shine, and Carlisle Moore were producing groundbreaking work, this era saw major efforts, regrettably repeated today, to link Carlyle to the rise of Fascism in Germany and Italy. And, as Carlyle in many respects epitomizes some of the excesses of the Victorian age, his reputation also suffered from the general reaction against Victorianism in the early decades of the twentieth century. It is useful in this context to read a corrective article like Stanley T. Williams's on *Past and Present*, which suggests Carlyle's importance to the rise of the social welfare state in Britain. Equally significant and slightly later is H.J.C. Grierson's assessment of Carlyle's theory of hero worship and Frank A. Lea's sensitive reading of the social thought underlying *The French Revolution*.

Finally, in choosing more recent twentieth-century criticism we tried to search for the more unknown publication, such as Colin N. Manlove's evaluation of *Sartor Resartus* in the *Swansea Review*, or the more obscure, such as David R. Sorensen's consideration of Carlyle's historical method in *The French Revolution* which was published in limited numbers for members of The Carlyle Society of Edinburgh.

Both authors have graciously revised their articles for the current volume. In the end, however, our primary reason for providing less modern criticism was our belief that it is more generally accessible to readers than the older material. We intend our bibliography to be an extension of this book and a guide to additional writings that we believe serious students of Carlyle should consult.

In editing the material for this volume, we have endeavored to preserve the original. We have not, for example, regularized punctuation and spelling of British and American authors. In the British, one will find the continental convention of punctuation marks outside quotation marks, and spellings such as "honour" instead of "honor." We have silently corrected obvious spelling and typographical errors, such as "Buddah" for "Buddha" and "hte" for "the." To conserve space, we have eliminated lengthy extracts, common in nineteenth-century reviews, of Carlyle's works, indicating the excision either by ellipses or brackets, depending upon the length of the quotation. In rare instances, we have excised text that had nothing to do with the subject at hand, which also is indicated by ellipses. For consistency within essays, we have regularized Carlyle's titles: *Past and Present* replaces "Past and Present." We have been guided by the MLA style. To facilitate reference we have changed various citations of Carlyle letters to the Duke-Edinburgh Edition of the *Collected Letters of Thomas and Jane Welsh Carlyle*, and we have changed various citations of Carlyle's works to the Centenary Edition of Carlyle's *Collected Works*, unless otherwise indicated.

G. Robert Stange, David J. DeLaura, Colin N. Manlove, and David R. Sorensen revised slightly their essays for this volume.

Ann Greenseth, Publications Unit at Illinois State University, designed this volume.

D. J. Trela and Rodger L. Tarr

WORKS CITED

Carlyle, Thomas. *Reminiscences*. Ed. Charles Eliot Norton. 2 vols. London: Macmillan, 1887.

___. *Collected Works*. Ed. H. D. Traill. 30 vols. London: Chapman and Hall, 1896-99.

___, and Jane Welsh Carlyle. *Collected Letters of Thomas Carlyle and Jane Welsh Carlyle*. Ed. Charles R. Sanders, K. J. Fielding, Clyde de L. Ryals, et al. 24 vols. Durham: Duke UP, 1970-.

Emerson, Ralph W. "Preface." *Sartor Resartus*. Boston: James Munroe, 1836. iii-v.

Everett, Alexander. "Thomas Carlyle." *North American Review* 41 (October 1835): 454-82.

Froude, J. A. *Life of Carlyle*. 4 vols. New York: Harper, 1885.

CRITICAL RESPONSE
TO *SARTOR RESARTUS*

THE SUN

1 April 1834, p. 2.

ANON.

"Sartor Resartus" is what old Dennis used to call "a heap of clotted nonsense," mixed, however, here and there, with passages marked by thought and striking poetic vigour. But what does the writer mean by "Baphometic fire-baptism?" Why, cannot he lay aside his pedantry, and write so as to make himself generally intelligible? . . .

We quote by way of curiosity a sentence from the Sartor Resartus; which may be read either backwards or forwards, for it is equally intelligible either way. Indeed by beginning at the tail, and so working up to the head, we think the reader will stand the fairest chance of getting at its meaning:—

> The fire-baptized soul, long so scathed and thunder-riven, here feels its own freedom, which feeling is its Baphometic baptism: the citadel of its whole kingdom it has thus gained by assault, and will keep inexpugnable; outwards from which the remaining dominions, not indeed without hard battering, will doubtless by degrees be conquered and pacificated.

Here is a bray worthy of the most sonorous animal that ever chewed the thistle. It reminds us of another equally lucid passage, which we remember meeting with in the works of an eminent transcendental philosopher of the day, who observed (we forget on what occasion, but that is not material), that "there were some people who supposed that an unusual collocation of words, involving a juxtaposition of ideas, immediately suggested the notion of an antiperistatical paradoxology." These two scribes should be harnessed together in a donkey cart. They have both an equal length of ear.

KNICKERBOCKER MAGAZINE

9 (May 1837): 432.

ANON.

This is a collection of papers from Frazer's London Magazine, which in truth are very little to our taste. The writer walks beneath a German cloud more dense than a Scotch mist; and, in our humble estimation, the trouble of penetrating it is worth all his companionship. We cannot divest ourselves of a strong distaste to the "peculiarities," for which patience is involved in the preface by some German-loving *littérateur*; and while we disclaim any intention to flatter, we must say, that, to our poor conception, Professor Teufelsdrockh is an eminent bore. But, "*Chacun a son goût.*"

TAIT'S EDINBURGH MAGAZINE

5 (September 1838): 611-12.

ANON.

By what fatality was it that the most *radically* Radical speculation upon men and things, which has appeared for many years, would have first come abroad in a violent Tory periodical? This work, which was, but cannot always be, neglected in England, has been reprinted in America, in which land we have the authority of the late traveller Miss Martineau for saying, that the prophet has found the honour and acceptance not at first awarded in his own country. A collected edition of the papers, which went through several numbers of *Fraser's Magazine*, has, however, at length appeared in London; and we are farther promised Mr Carlyle's Miscellaneous Works, which, we presume, must include his editorial labours also, or "The Life and Opinions of Herr Teufelsdröckh," that true philosopher of the Radical school, and original expounder of "*the philosophy of Clothes.*" He is a somewhat mysterious personage this said Professor Teufelsdröckh—"a Voice publishing tidings of the Philosophy of Clothes; undoubtedly a spirit addressing spirits." His English editor cannot promise the *Discloser* "a paramount popularity in England." Apart from the choice of the subject, the manner of treating it "betokens rusticity and academic seclusion, unblamable, indeed inevitable in a German, but fatal to success with our public. . . ."

We must, however, leave the reader to discover how these singular characteristics of the Professor are unfolded in the course of his lucubrations on the
Philosophy of Clothes. These lucubrations have puzzled both the Old and the New
World. Editors and *Booksellers' Tasters* have been at a loss what to make of them,
or even to determine whether the affair presented as a translation from the German,
was not what the English call a *hoax*, and the Yankees a *hum*. The *North American*
Reviewer had been nearly fairly bitten, though his rare sagacity finally discovered
that Professor Teufelsdröckh is about as real a personage as Tristram Shandy's
father, Captain Gulliver, or Don Quixote. We can, no more than the English
translator, promise the Professor's discursive, light, profound, quaint, and humorous disquisitions, a permanent popularity in England; but this we promise: those
who can *taste* him, will not easily forget his race.

MONTHLY REVIEW

147 (September 1838): 54-66.

ANON.

Hereby hangs a tale or a tail, it matters little which way you take it, although
the latter term may under certain views be preferred; because the book is about a
tailor re-tailored, or re-patched; that is to say, clothes are the subject,—clothes, and
all that is exterior to them and within,—clothes are made the text of "Things in
General." Any one who is acquainted with Mr. Carlyle's whimsical, original,
Germanized, far-travelling, and far-travelled genius, will be at no loss to conjecture
that be it anything or nothing that he thinks and writes about, he must make a curious,
learned, and suggestive book. Under the garb of humour, levity, nonsense, or
mysticism, there is always matter for thought and speculation. He is least liked when
he is first viewed and studied: for even when he is unintelligible, to him the blame
does not attach if he do not so transcendalize you that something like a kindred
afflatus is experienced, and a taste of that wisdom and joy which must be inseparable
from his own exaltation and eye-piercing of the mysteries of time and life be not felt.
The present is surely one of Mr. Carlyle's most characteristic works; characteristic not only in regard to its matter but to the manner of its appearance, and its
pretended author, and professed editor. We presume that he enjoyed the joke of
throwing *glamour* into eyes of some folks, merely as respects the alleged parentage
of the work. It came out successively and in small divisions in Fraser's Magazine,
and its principal parts as the production of Dr. Diogenes Teufelsdröckh, Professor

of the Science of Things in General, at the University of Weissnichtwo in Germany, the subject, as already stated, being Clothes, or rather the Philosophy of Clothes. The professor's philosophizings, and the anonymous editor's enlargements, elongations, explanations, and comments make up the contents. In a word the work forms a most curious romance, partly biographical, but chiefly sentimental and philosophical,—beautiful fancies and valuable truths being, in the quaintest manner possible, yet often happily and forcibly, brought out.

Before presenting a few specimens, a sentence or two may, with the view of farther helping our readers, who may feel a curiosity about the splendid vagaries of an original mind, to arrive at a just appreciation of the performance.

As to the biographical part, it is to be understood that the Professor of the Science of Things in General at the University of Weissnichtwo (that is Nobody-knows-where) has not found life void of vicissitudes, either of fortune, condition, nor mental convictions. First of all, he appears upon the stage as a foundling; but though he falls into the hands of poor persons, he receives a deal of schooling, and in fact is educated for the legal profession. After having been called to the bar, the want of a patrimonial independence, and a paucity of briefs, render it necessary for him to bethink how he is to eke out day after day, and to support the necessities of the time being. Fortunately, at that period, at least, he forms an intimacy with an English gentleman who is travelling, and, by means of this link, gets introduced to the family of a Count, where he is sometimes entertained. In the course of his visits, Blumine, the Flower Goddess, fascinates him, in whose society he experiences a wonderful degree of happiness, and to the future union with whom he looks forward with full-blown hope. But Teufelsdröckh was not destined to be so soon set at his ease and planted in a paradise, for the fair one prefers Towgood and weds him. If our hero's embarrassments were considerable before, they become next to intolerable now; he turns his back upon the bar, leaves his home, and starts an adventurous traveller. Nor is he a lazy or limited wanderer; nether is he an idle or incompetent observer. Still the mere circumstances of locomotion, and the feasting of the eyes with sights, or the storing of the mind with knowledge when without the means for commanding necessary comforts, and without the consciousness of being beloved by the choice of his own heart, especially as the doubts and darknesses of infidelity beset him, do not suffice his immortal craving nature. At length, however, his mind gradually, and after many attempts and many arrivals at various ports, gets into a genial climate and basks under a clear and sunny sky. Comfort is simultaneous; he betakes himself to the pen to earn a subsistence, and the produce of his brain and of his acquired light and knowledge eventually secure for him a chair, as the Professor of Things in General, in the university so queerly situated as its name imports. The present speculations and moralizings on the subject of clothes, which the editor has illustrated and ably commented upon, were, there can be no doubt, the offspring of many tranquil evenings spent in the academic bowers of Nobody-knows-where; nor, so far as we know, have his lectures or any other of his writings ever since or before attracted half the notice or deserved half the admiration which has attended this production.

As to the pith, marrow and intent of the Professor's present code of philosophizings, it will be sufficient to intimate, that, although he be an original, an original, too, we venture to assert which no country but Germany could educate and foster, yet the more, as well as the less obscure spirit of the book, guides the reader's mind to certain moral and precious lessons in regard to the manner in which an inquisitive, an honest, and a sensitive mind is affected and instructed by those external influences and phases of society to which it is more immediately subjected, or of which it is made to be cognizant. Accordingly, though the titles of the various chapters of the book be whimsical and grotesque, and apparently, in as far as names go, a random jumble of words, yet there is a train of connected thought brought out from under such headings, that is concomitant with the course of events and of convictions already sketched in regard to the life of Dr. Diogenes Teufelsdröckh. . . .

Diogenes is not . . . void of spiritual pride. Indeed in the course of his life he has to pace the mental ladder, from "The Everlasting No," to the "Centre of Indifference," and thence to "The Everlasting Yea." The chapter about this last stage of conviction and principle of action, appears to us to be a very remarkable one. We are mistaken, if the author has not ... happily pointed the way, in some of the most obscure regions of philosophy and Christian doctrine, where many have stumbled or come far short of the whole truth. . . .

. . . sound as well as great principles, gathered from, and illustrated by, the spirit of the age, taking the subject of clothes, or dress, for a starting point, have been with strange force, a prodigality of imagination, and often an amazing splendour of language, made by Mr. Carlyle to bear on wide domains of social life, literature, the arts, politics, and religion.

METROPOLITAN MAGAZINE

23 (September 1838): 1-5.

ANON.

In saying that Mr. Carlyle is one of the deepest thinking and most original minded writers of the present day, we merely repeat the confirmed opinion of the most intellectual and philosophical part of London and Edinburgh society—an opinion, too, which is now gaining ground rapidly even among those who knowing him only by his writings, were at first deterred by the oddity of his manner, and the German turn of his style and language. On the latter head, perhaps, more objections have been raised by hasty and unthinking readers than the case justifies; and it would be difficult to prove, on philological principles, that Mr. Carlyle's metaphysical terms, compound words, and compound figures, are *unenglish*. For ourselves, we recognise no formal and unchangeable law in our plastic and elastic language—a rich mosaic made up of all idioms, but the grand substratum of which, together with its constitution and spirit, is essentially Saxon. Sometimes, we confess, there is a sort of mistiness in Mr. Carlyle's sentences, but this never lasts long; and however much he may delight in wrapping himself in a German-looking mantle, he has English flesh and bones, thews and sinews, and a thoroughly British heart beneath it. His thoughts and feelings are national without prejudice or bigotry. Some heresies he has both in politics and poetry; but we let them pass. We admire his bold examining for himself, his total freedom from the thraldom of mere conventionalities: we admire, even when it is at its roughest, his odd or crabbed style; in part, because we are wearied to death with the trim and measured sentences of the mass of modern writers—sentences that look as if they had been turned on a turner's wheel, and that have, too often, no thought at all, or not more than a vague generality under their silky, sliding, shiny surface.

No man is more happy in epithets, or in describing character in a word or two. We remember being mightily tickled at one of his lectures on German literature, wherein he hit off a Doctissimus of one of the universities, an antagonist of Luther's, as being *a very illustrious dull sort of a man*. We believe that Mr. Carlyle displays this faculty more forcibly in conversation than in writing. As a conversationist, indeed, his fame stands at the highest. He is esteemed by many as being equal in this way to Coleridge himself; but we believe that Mr. Carlyle sometimes lets other people talk, which Coleridge never did, though few there were but were fully satisfied with giving rest to their tongues and employment to their ears when he was holding forth. As in poor Coleridge's case, Mr. Carlyle's admirers admire him with a fervency quite rare to the English character; and as some of the brightest and purest of intellects are included in this wide and spreading circle, we are justified in assuming that he is an extraordinary man, and one (being active and industrious) that will do greater and better things than those he has hitherto produced, though upon those he may safely build an honourable reputation. We see that he announces the publication of his miscellaneous works in four volumes. His essays are not for the vulgar and the trivial: they will find no favour in the eyes of those who read running; and to circulating libraries and fashionable boudoirs they will be unknown; but we trust that there is manly sense enough in the country to appreciate and reward such writing—that there is a sufficient number of lovers of metaphysical inquiry, of original thinking, to absorb a very large edition. A small one, we should think, would be engrossed by Mr. Carlyle's personal friends, admirers, and disciples.

The history of the startling little work before us is rather curious. It was first published, in monthly parts, in "Fraser's Magazine," and did not attract a tithe of the attention which it merited; it was afterwards taken up by an American bookseller, and published as a separate volume in the United States. It is laudable in the transatlantic bibliopoles thus to discover merit which has not been puffed in England; and it is no doubt *convenient* unto them to be able to appropriate an English author's lucubrations, without reference to the substantial and vulgar consideration of dollars and cents. The book puzzled Jonathan mightily, (and it will pleasantly puzzle many of the family of John Bull as well,) but it was widely read and admired. In its American shape it first attracted the notice of Miss Martineau, who, in one of her delightful volumes about America, spoke of it as it deserved to be spoken of:— and then people at home began to inquire touching "Sartor Resartus; or, the Life and Opinions of Herr Teufelsdröckh."

To tell precisely what this oddest of odd books is, is an utter impossibility—

"Who can describe the indescribable?"

We are, however, inclined to believe that the North American Reviewer is not far from the truth in saying, that *Sartor Resartus* means, in the vernacular, "The tailor patched;" that there is in it a treatise upon clothes, their origin and influence; but that, though there is a good deal "throughout the work in a half serious, half comic style upon dress, it seems to be in reality a treatise upon the great science of things, in general, which Teufelsdröckh is supposed to have professed at the university of Nobody-knows-where." Nay, we even think that we may safely add the reviewer's advice to dandies not to purchase the volume in the expectation of finding in it any particular instruction in regard to the tying of the neckcloth and the cut of their coats. . . .

Still, however, not triangles and wrinkles, not collars and swallow tails, not waistcoats and breeches, but things in general, and everything else, are the main subjects of the book; and we rather think, with the Boston editor, that "Sartor Resartus" may be a criticism upon the spirit of the age, exhibiting in a just and novel light the present aspects of religion, politics, literature, arts, and social life.

The worthy Bostonian seems to have been rather startled at our author's advancing the gravest speculations upon the gravest topics in a quaint and burlesque style; but to our own particular taste this humour is perfectly delicious. We love to be led by a smile or a laugh to deep wisdom; and we have no doubt that many will be drawn to listen to his valuable lessons and materials for thinking, who would have turned away with a yawn if he had put them in the usual didactic shape. . . .

The man who can write poetry like this in plain, idiomatic, English prose, may be forgiven his heresies touching rhythm and verse, and his occasional indulgence in extravagances.

"The Clothes Philosophy of Carlyle"

YALE LITERARY MAGAZINE

7 (August 1842): 378-382.

J.

Whilst the heretofore intellectuality of the globe was contented to plod hoodwinked to the grave, knowing no more of things, nor caring to know, than as they were presented to those five avenues of the brain, the senses—cheated by the mere *superficies*, the varnish, the polish, the glaze—it was reserved for the illustrious Clothes Philosopher to *pierce* the universal integument with which nature had so long been clad, to strip humanity of its "three-ply" of broadcloth, and show man to be, in the utter nudity of all such false appliances, the "forked, straddling animal" he actually is.

What hand that has ever plied a goose, will not be raised in grateful benedictions upon the head of him who has elevated a cruelly berated craft to unwonted dignities, restored to unity a once fractional portion of the human race, proven beyond the shadow of a doubt, that the imperial Ottomite upon his throne has not a more extended empire than cross-legged occupant of that same shop-board.[1] This was reserved for the acumen of thy genius, Herr Teufelsdröckle!

Nor think, willing but as yet uninitiated reader, that the pryings of this sublime philosophy is confined alone to the outward envelope with which the caprice of Fashion has from time to time encased her votaries. No: under the same unobtrusive title, research is extended to the conventional forms of society, shallow articles with which "we deceive ourselves, for the truth is not in us." From the cradle to the grave, from the moment we are ushered into being, and the swaddling clothes are hurried about our persons, to hide the nakedness we all must confess, to that solemn period when the lifeless tenement is thrust into its rude charnel-house, and therein be sodded and concealed, lest the too susceptible senses of still remnant mortality might take offense at the exposure, our life, entrance and exit, is one complicated system of rank hypocrisy. But the world's *courted* fallacies are but tissues of gossamer to the analytical eye of Clothes Philosophy, where opaqueness presents no obstacle, distance no indistinctness. The every-day plodder upon this earthen ball sees stretched before him but a poor three miles of level surface—and that only under certain mathematical conditions.[2] Unsophisticated gaze, it is bounded by the earth's horizon! Our Clothes Philosopher leaps the barrier, and with a curvature in his line of vision that puts the optician's laws at defiance, comprises, in a single glance, the two Poles—ay, and the Nether Tropics. "Hail, Antipodal Brother!" he exclaims, in very recognition of some priest of Buddha, or, perhaps, the High Cham of Tartary himself: "Hail, Antipodal Brother!—are we not both attracted to the same center? are we not daily whirled around in the same infinitude of space, and do we not yearly take a tour about the same great sun—and shall we be no better acquainted?—thy hand." With that the intervening mass sinks into nihility—and behold, met together in spiritual unison, two distinct, world-separated beings.

Time, equally with space, is susceptible of annihilation. The Clothes Philosopher is thus his own scene-shifter upon the stage of life, recalling or anticipating, with the same facility, what era of the drama he please. He walks the streets of some crowded metropolis—one in this New World of ours—frequents the busy marts of commerce, and studies the wonderful antithesis of past and present. Stately edifices have upreared their marble heads from off the ground-plot of wigwams. Athwart the track of startled deer a noisy thoroughfare has stretched its course. And now trip French boots along where once strode the moccasin.

The Herr Teufelsdröckle (we are informed) was a simple-minded professor in the University of Weissnichtwo, but whose characteristic features of soul and body were so totally dissimilar, that whilst the physical proportions of the one displaced but five feet of atmospheric air—and that, too, from beneath the tiled roof of a little attic in one of the provincial burghs of Germany—the spiritual essence of the other was co-extensive with the universe. It was thus, with himself for a center and the whole habitable world for a circumference, he would, not only with the expedition of a *Diabile Boileaux*, unroof the surrounding tenements of brick and mortar, but, with a more skillful *diablerie*, unclothe the surrounding composites of flesh and fustian, and subject to an honest analysis their be-tailored nakedness.

[Excerpt from Book 1, chapter 3, "Reminiscences," the paragraph beginning "'*Ach, mein Lieber!*'"]

Nor yet again, fastidious reader, think that these researches into the outward woofings and wrappings of humanity tend only to a degradation of the species. The same celestial spark that prompts the search and aids in its fulfillment, that gives luster to the whole undertaking, still and ever advises us of an inherent dignity, to which such superficial trappings can be in no-wise accessory. The eye that can detect beneath the russet smock as true a heart as ever beat behind the breastwork of stars and garters, elevates rather than degrades. Impressed, then, with a due sense of this fact, be nothing loath boldly to push investigation there where the tide of life flows the thickest. Look upon society, not as a clown upon a puppet-show, but as a philosopher, who only seeks to discover the grand main-spring of action—the *primum mobile*; and in furtherance of thy first effort, (which shall be the explosion of three precious bubbles—Title, Wealth, and Fame,) frequent the busy haunts of men, and see where the expiring breath of the dying beggar goes to inflate the lungs of passing royalty. The multitude crowd heedlessly by, or give a tear of compassion to the one, and to the other a respectful obeisance. Were they conscious of the connecting *link*, would they have given either to either? Thus, despite an absolute conformity of physical structure—so much so that the slightest deviation is looked upon as a *lusus naturæ*, a profit to the showman—despite a perfect identity in all the mysteries of animal existence—creation and final dissolution; yet shall the trumpery of tags and tassels, a jewel-be-spattered vest, endow the wearer with else unattainable honors.

The Money-changer must be at the City Bourse by twelve o'clock;—he pulls from his breeches-pocket—from his right side—a metallic watch, the mechanism of which tells him what time of day it is. * * * Hark, in thine ear, insatiate griper of smelted ore—remove that facing of bone, muscle, and cuticle from before thee, and thou wilt find, suspended to thy left side, a less erring chronometer; consult that, and learn what *Time of Life* it is, thou man of to-day.

The *Debutante* of the opera, making every exertion of voice and limb, meets with her reward in—what? surely something adequate to the vast deal of toil and trouble spent in acquiring it—the burst of applause from the audience, a clapping together of the hands, a concussion of the air, which, striking upon the tympanum of the ear, is at once conducted to the heart, and produces all that sweet sensation and flutter of excitement exhibited in the countenance; it is that bouquet or coronel tossed from the boxes, and more highly prized than a full week's salary;—it is all those marks of approbation under which, crowding upon her, and too much for human nature to bear, she is borne fainting and drooping from the stage. Verily, the brawny hands of pit-sansculotism possess a magic they little wot of.

But is it only active life—the thronged and busy world without, that is to be subjected to this all-potent analysis? Nay, every object I cast my eye upon—myself—the very book I hold—reader, from what do these words that thou now spellest over, speak to thee?—from the shred of a wench's petticoat!—The mill hath well chewed up the rag, and so disguised the fact, that, but to the eye of Clothes Philosophy, it would appear a fair sheet of paper.

Though to the professor of Weissnichtwo belongs exclusively the honor of the first analytical disquisition upon the much neglected article of Clothes; yet, from time to time, some faint glimmerings of the same pervading idea have unconsciously emanated from the brains of other celebrated originators. Does not Shakespeare's own Hamlet, in that church-yard ramble of his, display the true

Clothes-philosophical spirit of inquiry, when he searches into the ultimate disposition of elementary particles, and finds, by a just logical inference, the dust of dead Alexander stopping the bung-hole of some beer barrel?

And now, in conclusion of this critico-essaical treatise, whilst I claim from the courtesy of each generous reader extenuation for a few discursive remarks, let me urge upon his consideration their only design—a more thorough investigation on his part into the doctrine of Clothes. And welcome the time when he shall have doffed the trammels of established prejudice, and become a disciple of that Philosophy whereby he shall obtain a touchstone mightier than the Alchimist's—a more than Mesmeric *Clairvoyance.*

NOTES

[1] Might not the adage, "It takes nine tailors to make a man," have originated from the consideration of how much of his *making* man owes to the tailor? One will not suffice him, but for his perfect completion nine are requisite; i.e. it takes nine tailors to *manufacture* a single man. Might not this be satisfactorily shown, and that, too, notwithstanding to the contrary, Queen Elizabeth's significant address to the deputation of eighteen tailors—"A good morning to you, gentlemen *both*"?

[2] If a man, standing on the level of the ocean, has his eye raised 5 1/2 feet above the water, to what distance can he see the surface? Answer, 2 7/8 miles.

CARLYLE AND THE OPEN SECRET OF HIS LIFE

London: Kegan Paul, Trench, 1886.

HENRY LARKIN

[Excerpts from Chapter One, pp. 8-10.]

It is admitted by all competent readers that "Sartor Resartus" contains, in a highly condensed, suggestive, and symbolic form, an initial utterance of all Carlyle's intellectual or speculative convictions concerning God's Universe and *Man's* position therein. Some readers even go so far in their admiration of it as to pronounce it the greatest of Carlyle's works. Such exaggerative partiality, however, means little more than that they themselves have not yet passed beyond the splendours of speculative insight into the more vital realities of ethical and spiritual conviction. It is neither the greatest nor yet the highest of Carlyle's intellectual efforts; nor does it express his own most spontaneous intuitions, or his final ethical convictions. And yet it is undoubtedly the most brilliantly suggestive of his books, and contains the intellectual germs of all that he afterwards grew to. It is the seed-plot of the future harvest of his life. But essentially it is an importation from Germany; a wonderfully successful attempt to embody in a practically suggestive form, for the use of English readers, the entire German Transcendental Literature, which centred and culminated in Goethe, and which had for some years past absorbed Carlyle's earnest attention almost to the exclusion of everything else. No wonder it is so pregnant with meaning, and so teeming with soul-awakening thoughts. Carlyle's great merit for us lies in the fact that he was the first among us to discern the almost unspeakable social significance of that great uprising of speculative insight and passionate intuition; and that he brought home to us its practical issues with such a masterly incisiveness and freshness of utterance and of illustration, as not merely to stamp it with his own overpowering individuality, but to make it a direct appeal from his own heart to the intellects and hearts of his fellow-countrymen. But he no more originated the essential thoughts which it contains, than he originated the characters in the French Revolution which he so vividly portrayed. Without his German initiation and training, and the German platform from which he finally rose to his true intellectual stature and moral strength, it is impossible to imagine what he could have grown to. The Goethean ethics and transcendental intuition were to him the beginning of all practical light and hopeful effort in his generation.

The central idea of "Sartor Resartus," and of Goethe's "Transcendent Realism," is, that the physical universe does not stand for itself; that it is neither self-sufficient nor self-sustaining; but that it is the visible clothing and sensuous ultimatum of an invisible spiritual universe. That whatever we see with our eyes is a phantasmagoric projection of its own inner reality, thus made visible and tangible to our senses. That the Inner Universe is the real universe, and determines all the issues of seemingly physical existences. That the human body, especially, is a revelation to the physical senses of the presence of a human soul. And, as a corollary from this vast conception, that he who would vitally influence the physical sphere must work from the plane of realities, and not from the plane of mere visual appearances. This also was Swedenborg's great ontological conception of God's Universe.

Thus all visible or imaginable appearances are regarded as the covering or symbolic clothing of whatever reality may be hidden within them. It was this grand and pregnant thought which suggested to Carlyle his quaint notion of the "Philosophy of Clothes," which "Sartor Resartus" (the Tailor Re-tailored, or German Philosophy with a new application) professes to elucidate. . . .

[From Chapter Three, commentary on "Centre of Indifference," pp. 36-37.]

These discoursings from the Centre of Indifference form a magnificent instance of Carlyle's method of working out his subject. The quaint, searching, kindly realistic pictures and comments, as if from one who never even knew what conventionality meant, are all strangely suggestive of Richter; while the concluding and more earnest portion, telling us "how prospered the inner man of Teufelsdröckh under so much outward shifting," seems to point no less significantly to the more sombre experiences of Goethe. Not, I must emphatically repeat, that Carlyle merely appropriated their thoughts, and wove them into his own design. I should say there is very little of such formal appropriation, without express acknowledgment, in all the pages of this singular book. If "Sartor Resartus" is not a spontaneously creative effort on the part of Carlyle, it is at least sufficiently and characteristically original. There is much nonsense often talked about originality. The man who with his whole heart strives to be *true*—true to himself, and to the facts he strives to elucidate—must necessarily be original to the full extent of his ability; but the man who consciously aims at originality will generally succeed in becoming a spinner of cobwebs and a weaver of moonshine. What Carlyle proposed to himself was, not to spin a web of new speculative ideas (however perfect in symmetry or sparkling with dewdrops), all out of his own conceit; but, first of all, to try to understand the practical purport of the German teaching; and then to embody the wisdom he had thus gained, in a form which would bring it home to English experiences and needs. It seems to me that he has done this in a manner as strikingly original as it has been practically effective. What better originality could we wish for? Richter and Goethe did not *invent* the truths they taught, any more than Carlyle did. They simply *saw* them. Saw them here and there, in all the wise books they had ever read; saw them in the experiences of their own lives; saw them in the needs and the failures and successes of others. Their originality consisted, not in starting spontaneously in new directions "with no past at their back," but in seeing just a little further, a little wider, and therefore a little more clearly than they had been expressly taught; and the wisest man can have no better said of him. Happy is he who can have as much. This note of originality and wisdom I claim for Carlyle in all that he has written, and pre-eminently in [*Sartor Resartus*].

[From Chapter Four, commentary on "Symbols," pp. 43-45.]

"Man, though based, to all seeming, on the small Visible, does nevertheless extend down into the infinite deeps of the Invisible, of which Invisible, indeed, his life is properly the bodying forth." This is the key-note of all Carlyle's ideas of "the benignant efficacies" of Symbols and of Silence. No part of his teaching has been the subject of more frequent comment, both wise and foolish, than his great doctrine that Silence is greater and more fruitful than Speech. Yet the matter is really simple, although it reaches to the deepest foundations of our being. Speech, as Carlyle says, is like Light. But what would be the value of light to us, if there were no seeing-eye and nothing for the light to reveal? The value of light depends wholly on the wonders and the splendour of the Facts it illuminates. Therefore is the Universe greater even than the Light which reveals it to us. Again, "wise speech" is humanly uttered truth; but "the Divine Silence" stands for all the unuttered, and even unutterable truth in God's entire Universe. Well then might Carlyle say, "Speech is of Time, Silence of Eternity." So, in like manner, is it with each one of us. Wise speech is that portion of our wisdom, be it much or little, which we can put into intelligible words; while Silence stands for, and covers as with a mystic veil of reverence, all the insights, aspirations, accumulating experiences, formed and half-formed purposes, and all the as yet unconscious infinite possibilities, which in their totality form the sum of our character. Who then shall say that wise Silence is not infinitely greater than the wisest Speech? But once more, speech is of two kinds, superficial and symbolic. Superficial speech is easily understood, and its interest is soon exhausted; for it tells only of sensuous things to the sensuous intellect. But symbolic speech, as in the Divine Parables, although still uttering itself in sensuous images, contains meaning within meaning, inexhaustible and ever new; and deepening in interest as the inner sight becomes more and more open to discern its inner and profounder significance; and thus connects the lowest with the Highest in one ever-living sacramental thought. This is for ever true of all intrinsic symbols, and of all extrinsic symbols while life is in them: for in every real Symbol, Speech and Silence walk hand in hand together, even though, as so often happens, the one be taken and the other left.

THE VICTORIAN AGE OF ENGLISH LITERATURE

New York: Thomas Y. Crowell, 1892.

MARGARET OLIPHANT

[From Chapter Three, "Of Thomas Carlyle, John Stuart Mill, and Other Essayists and Critics," pp. 111-120.]

The years he passed at Craigenputtock or Craig o' Putta, as it is frequently called in the letters, was the true period of incubation for Carlyle's genius, and laid the foundation of all his future work and fame. Here his beliefs, such as they were, took form and established themselves. What they finally came to be it is difficult to tell, even after all the expositions given by his biographer and by other authorities. Mr. Froude describes the revolution in his thoughts by the emblem of Galileo's discovery that the sun did not revolve round the earth, but the earth round the sun, thus making plain the fact that our world was no longer the centre of a system made for its convenience, but only an atom in the vast universe. We are obliged to say that no light to speak of is thrown to ourselves upon Carlyle's creed by this simile, though it is no doubt a fine one, and indeed originally used by himself in those interpretations which are generally but fresh whirlings and blasts of cloud, and contain no precise light whatever. There is no reason to suppose that he meant any light to be precise. His mission was to show to the world the cloud wrappings, the strange delusive vapours, the deep abysses of mystery in which our little tangible life floats, surrounded on every side by bewildering darkness, and wonders which no man can clear up. To those who saw in it a clear, comfortable, solid universe enough, the best of all possible worlds, in which man's chief end was to attain comfort and respectability, he was a great destructive, pulling down every foundation and leaving the unhappy soul weltering in mists and marshes of the unknowable.

And yet in all his scorn of the things that be, in all his wild expositions of "that stuff that dreams are made of," in all his indignant denunciations of sham and false appearances, he held fast to the great central idea of God and Providence—a Being before whom every man should answer for his deeds, a divine and miraculous system in which at the last everlasting Justice should be found supreme. This was the only thing he was sure of; but of it he was as sure as that he lived. The mists and tempests that whirled about his head, the wild quagmires which he felt to spread around him, the rolling billows of cloud which shut out except in glimpses all natural shining, never blurred for him the consciousness of one eye that penetrated all, the certainty of that power which is beyond and above all the contentions of earth. That the world was a place for a man to make his way in, to make his fortune, to attain comfort and reputation by steady climbing, catching at every twig to help himself up, was the famous gospel of respectability which he felt himself bound to trample under foot; and it is true that he had no other gospel to proclaim; that was not his business. In his mind there was perhaps little hope of any; sometimes when excited by the sight of what he considered sham religion, he was wildly and contemptuously profane: often when moved by real piety and devotion, tenderly reverent and respectful. But his faith was this only—the faith of a man conscious of God everywhere—God undeniable, all-pervading, whose ways were righteousness, and whose service was the only use of man. This was much. On other matters he pronounced according to his feelings and moods, often those of the moment only. On this he stood as on a rock. The world to him was full of the wildest phantasmagoria, the puniest atoms of living creatures playing such pranks before high heaven! performing all injustices, cruelties, intolerable perversities, storming out their little day of contradiction and blasphemy. But over all God looking on, permitting the wild tempest to work itself out, keeping ever, through all seeming impossibility, the reins in His own hands. "He that sitteth in the heavens shall laugh: the Lord shall have them in derision," most terrible words of any in Holy Writ, might have been the text upon which Carlyle's work was founded.

And yet we think amid all his consciousness of supreme thought, and a tempestuous power of intellect, and all the drawbacks of gloomy and arrogant nature with which he is credited, Carlyle was always, both as a man and a writer, subject to his heart and feelings in a way which few have been. The veriest sham and impostor denounced in burning words, once brought into contact with him, showing another personal side, the real side of nature, became at once a man and a brother. Against no voice out of a human heart could his heart steel itself. Fire and flame and the bellowings as of a volcano in labour, for the abstract, the general; for the individual once actually brought before him, instant perception of those gleams of humanity, those underlights of truth which are to be perceived in most men by the eye that can see. Coming into a London drawing-room with his intense peasant suspiciousness and distrust of his fellow-men, with his equally intense peasant expectation that here at last might be found the society of the imagination, the brilliant talk and lofty thought which he had believed in from the time of earliest musings and eager hopes conceived in his father's farmyard or among the beasts on the Annandale farm—he turned with disgust and a silent anathema, finding it all empty talk, and foolish rivalry: but once seduced into a corner with—it scarcely mattered whom—looking into a pair of unaffected human eyes, brought to bay and to conversation, the abstract opposition, so fiery, so bitter, so almost vindictive in dislike and disappointment, floated in a moment away, and the man he spoke to became tolerable, if not lovable; no thing at all to be denounced, but a fellow-creature, perhaps a friend. . . .

The chief outcome of the life at Craigenputtock was "Sartor Resartus," the great test-work and shibboleth by which the true Carlyle-lover is to be proved at all times. It was amid all the "articles" which kept the family going, and which by that time had developed from essays on German literature to such a tremendous chapter of history as the Diamond Necklace, the first real revelation of the new form in literature—that this book was produced. Its strange philosophy, its stranger tumultuous volcanic style, its extraordinary stamp of a burning earnestness and meaning which were incomprehensible to the multitude, stupefying instead of exciting the public, came out in the last form which was likely to do them justice—in successive instalments in "Fraser's Magazine" during the year 1833. And we can but honour the daring publisher who ventured to place it there, and to pay solid money for it, after its rejection by all the great firms who returned it with dumb amaze—to the dogged resignation of the author; whose determination some time or another to bring out "Dreck," as the unfortunate manuscript was called in the family, and force him upon the stupid race which had not discernment enough to see what was in him, never faltered. That "Dreck" caught here and there a listening ear, and that even among those to whom much of the rhapsody and whirlwind was incomprehensible there were a few landscapes, a few situations which could not be forgotten—there can be little doubt. The wonderful episode of childhood, the home scenes of Weissnichtwo (Kennaquhair according to Sir Walter, in the vernacular Ecclefechan, there standing for ever in ethereal light and soft visionary shadow)—the mountain path where the hero-philosopher sees love and happiness sweep past him in the carriage that bears Blumine and her lover across the Alps, were not to be passed lightly by; but the book itself was like the song of the Ancient Mariner, a thing to be delivered into the ear of the man whom the poet could discern as he passed to be the man who could hear, and whom no wedding feast or brave procession could deliver from that necessity. The public learned afterwards, from the insistence of these predestined listeners, to receive with respect and a certain awe those wild vaticinations of the new prophet, but never heartily took to "Dreck"; though by means of its power of showing in the strongest form all the peculiarities and extravagancies of its author, it was swept afterwards into the adoration of many who without much understanding always find the exaggerated gestures of the orator, the wildest tropes of the poet, most easy to mimic and to adore. . . .

"'Perpetual Metamorphoses': The Refusal of Certainty in Carlyle's *Sartor Resartus*"

SWANSEA REVIEW

2 (November 1986): 19-36.

COLIN N. MANLOVE

To read most critics of *Sartor Resartus* one would think that the work was a disguised tract, a set of Carlyle's views done up in ornamental clothes, a book that leaves style the mere garment of thought. It is true that many commentators take account of Carlyle's elusiveness, but on the whole they see it either as symbolic of his philosophy or else requiring of the reader a diligent search which will make that philosophy more penetrative of his psyche when unearthed.[1] G. H. Brookes, for instance, in an able book, describes *Sartor* as "a form of persuasive essay";[2] Walter Waring sees it as "an attack on the materialism of its day";[3] A. L. Le Quesne declares that "*Sartor* is important because it represents the first connected setting-out of the thematic ideas that run through and dominate all Carlyle's later work."[4] G. B. Tennyson caters for Carlyle's humour, but boxes it off in a separate chapter from his philosophy, and his philosophy from his style, despite his avowals that the style and the content are integrated.[5]

Even Albert LaValley, whose argument in his *Carlyle and the Idea of the Modern* is the nearest to the one advanced here, still sees the basic concern of *Sartor* as being with meaning. LaValley sees that *Sartor* is as much chaos as order, and he links this with Carlyle's view, outlined in his "Characteristics", that nature is at once unconscious and conscious, random multitude and coherent unity. But to him the aim of the book remains the serious one of arriving at a philosophy, however dialectical, however much or little of the darker side of life it is capable of admitting:

> Nothing . . . is so distinctive of Carlyle in both style and content . . . as his drive towards embracing everything, no matter how painful, confusing, humorous, chaotic, ridiculous or bleak, and his simultaneous need to reduce the multiplicities to order, plan, and harmony, to bind them into acceptance through humour and to bring them within the totality of art and a reconstructed self and society. From this drive, in its most extreme form, arise(s) the deliberate pursual of confusion, raggedness, formlessness and randomness for the sake of the new totality in *Sartor*.[6]

This line of argument has been continued in recent essays, if with more emphasis on the reader's experience of Carlyle's chaotic style as a means to apprehending his message.[7] Most recently, however, the application of postmodernist ideas on literary indeterminacy to the text has proved more apposite, even if this still leaves it as the reflection of an anti-authoritarian ideology.[8]

What will be argued here is that *Sartor* is as much a panegyric on the mysterious multiplicity of life as an attempt to make sense of it; and that the message or doctrine of *Sartor* is at once "there" and continually rendered uncertain, both earnest and jest. The "No" and the "Yea" that are applied to the changing spiritual condition of Herr Teufelsdröckh are in this reading equally applicable to every aspect of *Sartor*; every assertion is wedded to its denial. Carlyle does mean the Clothes Philosophy; he does intend to persuade, as the critics cited declare; but equally he means to do the reverse, and this from a delight in the elusiveness, the mobility of truth. For him, "all . . . is borne forward on the bottomless, shoreless flood of Action, and lives through perpetual metamorphoses."[9]

Carlyle owed much at the time of writing *Sartor* to the work of the German Romantics[10] with their stress on the unconscious imagination as the source of life and truth: and in particular to the work of Novalis and Hoffmann (whose *The Golden Pot* he first translated into English) for the view that the world is only seen aright when it is seen not by the ordering intellect but by the subconscious spirit, when it will reveal itself as a chaos. Seen thus, no single philosophy of the world can do it justice, and this is what Carlyle says in "Characteristics":

> Boundless as is the domain of man, it is but a small fractional proportion of it that he rules with Consciousness and by Forethought; what he can contrive, nay, what he can altogether know and comprehend, is essentially the mechanical, small; the great is ever, in one sense or other, the vital; it is essentially the mysterious, and only the surface of it can he understood.[11]

To try to comprehend something is to render it static and dead, where for Carlyle the condition of reality is continual change and movement (*CW* 28:37): the social order and prevailing philosophy are on course for their overthrow; the present scepticism is but the necessary feverish writings of the "conscious or Mechanical" skin of the mind which precludes the withdrawal of the principle of life inwards through "abysses of mystery and miracle" to the domain of the Unconscious, from which alone "all wonders, all Poesies, and Religions, and Social Systems have proceeded" (*CW* 28:40). Reality so conceived can be properly conveyed by art only through indirections of musical or poetical form (*CW* 28:14), or else by silence.[12]

Yet even this is only one side. Throughout "Characteristics" Carlyle has to admit, somewhat inconsistently, that the conscious mind too has an unavoidable part to play in attempting to define reality. The declarations of the final value of the unconscious are mingled with assertions that, whether through his fallen condition, or the inevitability of his subjection to time, or the essentially dualistic character of society, man must continue to formulate philosophies and systems, however empty. In a passage that seems to prefigure his treatment of Teufelsdröckh, Carlyle asks,

> Man stands as in the centre of Nature; his fraction of Time encircled by Eternity, his handbreadth of Space encircled by Infinitude; how shall he forbear asking himself, What am I; and Whence; and

> Whither? How too, except in slight partial hints, in kind asseverations and assurances, such as a
> mother quiets her fretfully inquisitive child with, shall he get answer to such inquiries?
>
> The disease of Metaphysics, accordingly, is a perennial one. (*CW* 28:25)

Life cannot then be so simply unconscious, nor can Carlyle's own "philosophy" of
it escape the duality he sees as besetting all things:

> Our being is made up of Light and Darkness, the Light resting on the Darkness, and balancing it;
> everywhere there is Dualism, Equipoise; a perpetual Contradiction dwells in us: "where shall I
> place myself to escape from my own shadow?"[13]

Elsewhere, more utopian, he shifts to a view of the workings of the unconscious
mind as eventually productive of certainty:

> Thought must needs be Doubt and Inquiry, before it can again be Affirmation and Sacred Precept.
> Innumerable "Philosophies of Man", contending in boundless hubbub, must annihilate each other,
> before an inspired Poesy and Faith for Man can fashion itself together. (*CW* 28:32-33)

We will find precisely this contradiction in *Sartor*, where the Everlasting No is both
everlasting and yet leads to the Everlasting Yea, and where there is both a plan and
none. It is fair to say that we might come away from "Characteristics" with no finally
clear philosophy either. But the point of that essay so far as *Sartor* is concerned is
clear: here is a central and contemporary "statement" which may throw light (and
darkness) on the chiaroscuro that is that work itself. Why else write a wire-drawn
philosophy of *clothes*, if not, in part, to show the preposterousness of all philosophies?

The views of "Characteristics" are reflected in the sheer exuberance of the style
of *Sartor*, an exuberance and elasticity of thought and attitude that are there from
the very opening paragraph:

> Considering our present advanced state of culture, and how the Torch of Science has now been
> brandished and borne about, with more or less effect, for five-thousand years and upwards; how,
> in these times especially, not only the Torch still burns, and perhaps more fiercely than ever, but
> innumerable Rush-lights, and Sulphur-matches, kindled thereat, are also glancing in every
> direction, so that not the smallest cranny or dog-hole in Nature or Art can remain unilluminated,—
> it might strike the reflective mind with some surprise that hitherto little or nothing of a fundamental
> character, whether in the way of Philosophy or History, has been written on the subject of Clothes.
> (3)

The first phrase here, with its pompous suspension, "Considering our present
advanced state of culture", asks demurral, and the desire to undercut is increased by
the seemingly fatuous cliche of the Torch of Science. The reader is led to desire the
removal of this rotarian smugness, and he begins to get it as the sentence bounces
in another direction and the metaphorical becomes almost literal. The Torch has
been "brandished": not quite what we would expect. Then it has been "borne about"

which suggests a much more clumsy and vague action, with no definite purpose, and this is certainly reinforced by the "with more or less effect". Then the Torch has in this generation kindled all sorts of other tapers, suggesting something of a danger of conflagration. And its effects are satirised in its illumination of the smallest crannies or dog-holes of nature and art, suggesting that it is only crannies that it does illuminate, suggesting too that it is an inquiry too vulgar that rips up the secrets, the privacy and mystery of our being, and that light may be less educative than darkness. We begin in short to object to that which strips away: and the solution is perfectly given in a proffered philosophy of clothes, an account of those things that serve to conceal in life (all this fitting with Carlyle's preference for darkness and mystery as the true character of life). But none of this has been thought out by Carlyle; the opposition of "exposure" by science and "enclosure" by clothes is something instinctually and unconsciously happened upon, as he himself believed the best things should be in nature and art.

Yet at the same time of course the Philosophy of Clothes is itself an extension of the absurdities of scientific investigation, and at this point as unnecessary as they; it has the status of Slawkenbergius's dissertation "Upon Noses" in Sterne's *Tristram Shandy*, a mere bagatelle, a satire on the preposterous and arrogant mental constructs of man. Thus Carlyle gives us a philosophy at once necessary and useless, full and empty, and enactment of that yea and no which he saw as the fundamentally enigmatic character of reality. But he also gives us an amazing sentence—a marvelous sprawl of syntax, pushing out tentacles here and retracting them there, endlessly dynamic, full of enjoyment of language and life alike. It is a wonderful start to a book, with its long stentorian opening and suspension, disintegrating into a rabble of innumerable Rush-lights, Sulphur-matches and dog-holes before it draws itself together again with the superb non-sequitur of a need amid all this flaring of science for a philosophy of clothes. The dynamic of the sentence throws our minds about as we read, until by the end we do not know quite where we stand, if such a static condition is at all possible in this work. This freedom of syntax and language testifies to Carlyle's own free delight in creation itself; one of the strongest pulses of *Sartor* is an endless pleasure in energy almost for its own sake.

This rug-pulling as regards the clothes philosophy continues throughout. Sometimes the philosophy can produce a profound insight into reality:

> "But deepest of all illusory Appearances, for hiding Wonder, as for many other ends, are your two grand fundamental world-enveloping appearances, SPACE and TIME. These, as spun and woven for us from before Birth itself, to clothe our celestial ME for dwelling here, and yet to blind it,— lie all embracing, as the universal canvas, or warp and woof, whereby all minor Illusions, in this Phantasm Existence, weave and paint themselves. In vain, while here on Earth, shall you endeavour to strip them off; you can, at best, but rend them asunder for moments, and look through." (260)

Here the clothes philosophy can serve to open our minds to the degree to which they have previously been closed in, and to give a window on to the possibly unquantifiable and free nature of being.[14] Elsewhere the philosophy can be absurd; it can lead to a worship of clothes themselves, a mistaken grovelling before graven images, in the awe-struck reverence with which Teufelsdröckh walks through the stalls of old clothes in London's Monmouth Street: "'Even as, for Hindoo Worshippers, the Pagoda is not less sacred than the God; so do I too worship the hollow cloth Garment with equal fervour'" (240). Similarly farcical-seeming is Teufelsdröckh's near-deification of tailors (289-90), and this especially after his abuse of them (56-57). And some of the extensions of the clothes philosophy are tenuous and conceited: "'How much has been concealed, how much has been defended in Aprons! Nay, rightly considered, what is your whole Military and Police Establishment, charged at uncalculated millions, but a huge scarlet-coloured, iron-fastened Apron, wherein Society works . . . ?'" (44; also 73, 289-90).

In one sense the clothes philosophy is an anti-philosophy: it refuses us a settled view. And it turns the fixed to the mobile:

> "Of Man's Activity and Attainment the chief results are aeriform, mystic, and preserved in Tradition only: such are his Forms of Government, with the Authority they rest on; his Customs, or Fashions both of Cloth-habits and Soul-habits; much more his collective stock of Handicrafts, the whole Faculty he has acquired of manipulating Nature: all these things, as indispensable and priceless as they are, cannot in any way be fixed under lock and key, but must flit, spirit-like, on impalpable vehicles, from Father to Son; if you demand sight of them, they are nowhere to be met with." (171)

Seen thus, everything is in a process of becoming, rather than a state of being. Activity and dynamism are as we have seen for Carlyle part of the essence of life: "'All things wax, and roll onwards; Arts, Establishments, Opinions, nothing is completed, but ever completing'" (247). Settled forms are for breaking, or are being broken by necessity; Teufelsdröckh reduces all different forms of church and religion to the basic and fluid church where—or wherever—two or three are gathered together (213-15); society "'through perpetual metamorphoses, in fairer and fairer development, has to live till Time also merge in Eternity'" (236). Teufelsdröckh's own life is such as to cut him loose from the forms of society; he has no ascertainable parents, rejects school and university, is barred from marriage and made a wanderer.

The true character of life as Teufelsdröckh sees it is one of wonder and miracle; we must penetrate through the dead categories and forms we have made of existence to the mobile realities beyond. Custom, he announces, would persuade us "'that the Miraculous, by simple repetition, ceases to be Miraculous'"; names, he perceives, "'are but one kind of such custom-woven, wonder-hiding Garments'" (259, 260). He goes on, "In every the wisest Soul lies a whole world of internal Madness, an authentic Demon-Empire; out of which, indeed, his world of Wisdom has been creatively built together, and now rests there, as on its dark foundations does a habitable flowery Earth-rind" (260). The purpose of the clothes philosophy, the Editor later tells us, has been to expose the demon empire beneath the rind, to show us the energies that lie behind our dulled perception of life and to lead us "into the true Land of Dreams . . . into the region of the wonderful . . . (where thou) seest and feelest that thy daily life is girt with Wonder, and based on Wonder, and thy very blankets and breeches are Miracles" (269-70). Seen thus, life becomes a fantasy or fairy-tale, and indeed Teufelsdröckh views "'Fantasy (as) being the organ of the Godlike'" (217).

This absence of the settled and the fixed is seen in every aspect of the book. Its structure seems largely chaotic, the more so because we cannot be sure that it is chaotic. If we set aside the device of an editor trying to put into order the fragmentary utterances and history of an eccentric philosopher, we are left with Carlyle himself having deliberately chosen to write a book which would frustrate attempts to organise it into clear argument, relevance and consistency. We begin with some account of the clothes philosophy, then break off to hear at length the scattered and questionable biography of Teufelsdröckh as transmitted to the Editor, the return to the clothes philosophy. Of the relation of the life to the philosophy little is said. The Editor initially claims that to understand the philosophy it is necessary to have the biography of the philosopher (11, 75), but when that biography, filling almost half the book, has been given, he is rather at a loss to see its relevance:

> If now, before reopening the great *Clothes-Volume*, we ask what our degree of progress, during these Ten Chapters, has been, towards right understanding of the *Clothes-Philosophy*, let not our discouragement become total. To speak in that old figure of the Hell-gate Bridge over Chaos, a few flying pontoons have perhaps been added, though as yet they drift straggling on the Flood; how far they will reach, when once the chains are straightened and fastened, can, at present, only be matter of conjecture. (204-05)

Within two paragraphs he follows this with a somewhat strained argument to explain the transition from Teufelsdröckh's—questionable—experiences to his philosophy:

> May we not say that Teufelsdröckh's Biography, allowing it even, as suspected, only a hieroglyphical truth, exhibits a man, as it were preappointed for Clothes-philosophy? . . . everywhere do the Shows of things oppress him, withstand him, threaten him with fearfullest destruction: only by victoriously penetrating into Things themselves can he find peace and a stronghold. But is not this same looking-through the Shows, or Vestures, into the Things, even the first preliminary to a *Philosophy of Clothes?* (205-06)

We may ask why others, who have equally suffered as Teufelsdröckh has done, be it a jilting or a dark night of the soul, and have thereby come to a further understanding of the "true" character of reality, have not themselves given rise to philosophies of clothes.

Some kind of sequence is followed with the biography of Teufelsdröckh, from infancy to school, university, rejection in love, despair, travel, spiritual renewal and the commencement of work on the clothes philosophy. The organisation and sequence of presentation of that philosophy itself however are more obscure. The

account of the tyranny of time and space which is to form the climax of the
philosophy in the late chapter "Natural Supernaturalism" (254-67) is in fact
anticipated (55). Throughout we are moved from one context to another which does
not clearly follow from it. A history of fashions in clothes entitled "Miscellaneous-
Historical" (Book 1, ch 7) is followed by one on their spiritual significance; the
Editor admits that while the one comes from the "Descriptive-Historical portion"
of the clothes philosophy, the other comes from the "Speculative-Philosophical"
portion (51). Chapters on the mystical import of clothes are apparently interrupted
by one on Teufelsdröckh's homage to actual cast-off clothes during his walk
through Monmouth Street market (Book 3, ch 6). The heights of the chapter
"Natural Supernaturalism" shrink to the comparative trivia of the succeeding
humorous chapter, "The Dandiacal Body", on the different clothing of rich men and
beggars (Book 3, chs 8, 10). There is often a sense of irrelevance: the chapter on
"Helotage", with its opposed comments, now Marxist (avant la lettre), now
Malthusian, on the relative dignity of the common man, seems scarcely related to
the clothes philosophy; and similarly oblique is the following chapter, "The
Phoenix", on the eventual destruction and renewal of the present social order. There
are frequent sharp changes of subject within chapters, as from speaking of
superannuated symbols to discussing over-population (226), or when in describing
the numerous "organic filaments" that bind society together Teufelsdröckh suddenly switches, first to talking about society's extinction and eventual restoration,
and then to a dissertation on the value of titles of honour such as Duke, Earl, Marshal,
and King (246-49).

The other side of the dualism is that, as the Editor claims, the book is "a mighty
maze, yet, as faith whispers, not without a plan" (52). There is amid the deliberate
chaos some steady penetration, from the early chapters on the outward forms of
clothes, to the later ones that deal with the more or less empty forms of society. Or,
as the Editor himself puts it, "Long and adventurous has the journey been: from
those outmost vulgar, palpable Woollen Hulls of Man; through his wondrous Flesh-
Garment, and his wondrous Social Garnitures; inwards to the Garments of his very
Soul's Soul, to Time and Space themselves!" (267). There is, with numerous
irrelevancies, back-trackings and switches of subject, something of a developing
topic throughout. This, as we saw in the first paragraph of the book, is mirrored in
the style itself, with its elastic syntax. What we see here again is a mixture of clarity
and obscurity, so that we are refused the certainty of either one: a plan and no plan,
a yea and a no.

The book works to make us continually uncertain. Two—or if we add the
comments of Hofrath Heuschrecke, three—voices present the material to us, and
nothing is finally any more certain in any of them than the name Weissnichtwo,
Know-not-where, Teufelsdröckh's place of residence. Sometimes we do not know
which is speaking, as one voice slides without announcement into another—for
example in the switch without warning from the Editor to Hofrath between chapters
one and two of the first book (14), or in the frequent shifts between Teufelsdröckh

and the Editor which only the presence or absence of a single quotation mark at the beginning of a paragraph conveys. Nor are the characters themselves always simply recognisable by their tone. We might think of the Editor sometimes as a plain roast-beef Englishman trying to pin the airy speculations of this metaphysical Teuton down to hard specifics and plain common sense, but in fact he is often to be found passionately concerned to give to the English nation a high mystical insight into life which he is as ready elsewhere to condemn as a piece of chaotic nonsense. Commenting on a particularly fervent passage of Teufelsdröckh's on how man stands "'at the centre of Immensities'", the Editor remarks,

> In such passages, unhappily too rare, the high Platonic Mysticism of our Author, which is perhaps the fundamental element of his nature, bursts forth, as it were, in full flood: and, through all the vapour and tarnish of what is often so perverse, so mean in his exterior and environment, we seem to look into a whole inward Sea of Light and Love. (66)

What at one point the Editor can call "this grand Theorem" he elsewhere sees as "close-bordering on the impalpable Inane" (52, 74; cf. 80, 292). And if we feel drawn to the Editor's commonsensical side, we will find that at the opposite extreme from mysticism such sense becomes merely boorish or stupid, as when he mistakes Teufelsdröckh's eulogy on George Fox for a prescription to all classes to dress themselves in suits of leather (212-13), or, when Teufelsdröckh looks to that destruction of society that will bring about a new age of truth, rebukes him for being ungrateful to his own society which has given him a job, food, clothes, "books, tobacco and gukguk" (237).

As for Teufelsdröckh himself, it is far from always clear to the Editor whether he may not be as readily in jest as in earnest with his philosophy. The Editor asks, "Is the whole business one other of those whimsicalities and perverse inexplicabilities, whereby Herr Teufelsdröckh, meaning much or nothing, is pleased so often to play fast-and-loose with us?" (202; also 94, 185, 213, 274). Again, "with a Teufelsdröckh there ever hovers some shade of doubt" (287):

> Gleams of an ethereal love burst forth from him, soft wailings of infinite pity; he could clasp the whole Universe into his bosom, and keep it warm; it seems as if under that rude exterior there dwelt a very seraph. Then again he is so sly and still, so imperturbably saturnine: shows such indifference, malign coolness towards all that men strive after; and ever with some half-visible wrinkle of a bitter sardonic humour, if indeed it be not mere stolid callousness. (32)

Even in his response to his sufferings Teufelsdröckh shows "the strongest Dualism: light dancing, with guitar-music, will be going on in the forecourt, while by fits from within comes the faint whimpering of woe and wail" (186-87).

The mere fact of having two contrastive views, realistic and idealistic, whether in Teufelsdröckh himself or in the contrast between him and the Editor, throughout the book, adds to our uncertainty as to what is going on and what attitude to take. If Teufelsdröckh himself does not afford some ironic perspective on his own experiences and often high-flown diction, that is provided by an Editor who continually pulls away from his protagonist to make comments at least partly tongue-in-cheek. "To our less philosophical readers, for example, it is now clear that the so-passionate Teufelsdröckh, precipitated through 'a shivered Universe' in this extraordinary way, has only one of three things which he can next do: Establish himself in Bedlam; begin writing Satanic Poetry; or blow-out his brains" (146). "'Man,' says the professor elsewhere, in quite antipodal contrast with these high-soaring delineations, which we have here cut-short on the verge of the inane, 'Man is by birth somewhat of an owl'" (220): we are left to wonder whether the inane in another sense has been avoided in that last pronouncement.

Nor are the supposed events of the story unambiguous either. The biography of Teufelsdröckh, with its dubious origins and its chaotic presence in the six paper bags, is far from providing definite facts. The Editor wonders whether the biography is a hoax by Teufelsdröckh: "What if many a so-called Fact were little better than a Fiction: if here we had no direct Camera-obscura Picture of the Professor's history; but only some more or less fantastic Adumbration, symbolically, perhaps significantly enough, shadowing-forth the same!" (202). And of course there is the larger "fact" that the entire book, the supposed creation of a German professor whose philosophy is communicated to an assiduous English editor, is itself a hoax on the public, since Carlyle is the sole author and begetter. But other factors make us doubt the autobiography. For one thing, the Editor is continually remaking it, imposing spiritual significances that may not have been present in the events themselves, or else commenting ironically on Teufelsdröckh's life and philosophy, thus making it more difficult to take them at face value: for instance, at one point, knowing nothing of Blumine's appearance and worldly circumstances, he simply invents some (135-36). And then the autobiography itself, seeming to bear out the Editor's suspicion of the veracity, sometimes sounds like cliche: as in the idyllic pastoral picture of Teufelsdröckh's childhood, which could have come straight from Goldsmith's *Deserted Village* (91-92; also 137).

But the centre of doubt and uncertainty in the book comes with that account of Teufelsdröckh's spiritual pilgrimage from loss through the Everlasting No and on to the Everlasting Yea. Commentators have almost without exception seen this as the keystone of Carlyle's faith, presented with unquestionable gravity and commitment. It cannot be gainsaid that Carlyle did mean the process as he describes it; and it is certainly one that is rehearsed in his later work also. Who can deny the intensity of Teufelsdröckh's despair when it finds language such as this:

> "To me the Universe was all void of Life, of Purpose, of Volition, even of Hostility: it was one huge, dead, immeasurable Steam-engine, rolling on, in its dead indifference, to grind me limb from limb. O, the vast, gloomy, solitary Golgotha, and Mill of Death! Why was the Living banished thither companionless, conscious? Why, if there is no Devil; nay, unless the Devil is your God?" (164)

Yet the passage from which this comes contains the more comic and banal observation of Teufelsdröckh that "'In such cases, your resource is to talk little, and that little mostly from the Newspapers'" (163); and it is immediately followed by the Editor's concern lest "such corrosions" work on Teufelsdröckh to such an extent as to make him sick (164). Such oscillations permeate the whole of Teufelsdröckh's spiritual autobiography.

Here we shall consider the more comic side, since the other has received sufficient attention in the past. As a lover Teufelsdröckh must have cut a comic figure, from what impressions we have of his appearance, whether as seen by Hofrath Heuschrecke as a diminutive figure with long, lank hair (16), or as pictured by the Editor at North Cape in a blue cloak "like a little blue Belfry" (179), or in Monmouth Street as "the little philosophical figure, with its steeple-hat and loose flowing skirts, and eyes in a fine frenzy" (242). Certainly Teufelsdröckh's dwarfishness seems at variance with the gigantic impression we get of him from his philosophic outpourings. By no means is he the figure of Werther, handsome, dark-eyed and passionate: indeed, his romance, such as it is, with Blumine, is perhaps something of a parody of *The Sorrows of Young Werther*. Teufelsdröckh's pains in love are described in terms of combustion, his nature being of so passionate and inflammable a kind that the least spark may set it off:

> Without doubt, some Angel, whereof so many hovered round, would one day, leaving "the outskirts of *Aesthetic Tea*," flit nigher; and, by electric Promethean glance, kindle no despicable firework. Happy, if it indeed proved a Firework, and flamed-off rocket-wise, in successive beautiful bursts of splendour, each growing naturally from the other, through the several stages of a happy Youthful Love; till the whole were safely burnt-out; and the young soul relieved with little damage! Happy, if it did not rather prove a Conflagration and mad Explosion; painfully lacerating the heart itself; nay perhaps bursting the heart in pieces (which were Death); or at best, bursting the thin walls of your "reverberating furnace", so that it rage thenceforth all unchecked among the contiguous combustibles (which were Madness); till of the so fair and manifold internal world of our Diogenes, there remained Nothing, or only the "crater of an extinct volcano"! (134)

Our capacity to take seriously this comparison of Teufelsdröckh's love to a squib is as much reduced by the pursuit of the conceit to these elaborate lengths as by its inherent incongruity. As for Teufelsdröckh's meeting with Blumine, this is how he and then the Editor describe it:

> "It was appointed," says our Philosopher, "that the high celestial orbit of Blumine should intersect the low sublunary one of our Forlorn; that he, looking in her empyrean eyes, should fancy the upper Sphere of Light was come down into this nether sphere of Shadows; and finding himself mistaken, make noise enough."

> We seem to gather that she was young, hazel-eyed, beautiful, and some one's Cousin; highborn, and of high spirit; but unhappily dependent and insolvent; living, perhaps, on the not too gracious bounty of monied relatives. (136)

Teufelsdröckh's high-flown style, with its preposterous amorous geometry, is self-deflating, but the Editor adds something of a *coup de grace* (rather as Fielding does after his first lyrical description of Sophia in *Tom Jones*). In *Werther* there is only one perspective, that of Werther; one passionate voice and feelings fully conveyed to us, and pains the sharpness of which we continually sense:

> Oh, how wildly my blood courses through my veins when, by chance, my hand touches hers or our feet touch under the table! I start away as if from a fire, a mysterious power draws me back, and I become dizzy . . . I feel I must sink to the ground as if struck by lightning.[15]

It is hard, too, to take Blumine, who is a mere name to us, though the universe to Teufelsdröckh, entirely seriously, especially when she so clearly has her bourgeois feet sufficiently on the ground to marry the more monied and unscrupulous Towgood. The picture of this final turning of the knife in Teufelsdröckh is also not without its comic side. After the tearful farewell with Blumine he becomes a wanderer, and while one day on a mountain road meditating on the peaks around him he is moved to rapture; "'He gazed over those stupendous masses with wonder, almost with longing desire; never till this hour had he known Nature, that she was One, that she was his Mother and divine . . . he felt as if . . . the Spirit of the Earth had its throne in that splendour, and his own spirit were therewith holding communion'" (151). But then,

> "The spell was broken by the sound of carriage-wheels. Emerging from the hidden Northward, to sink soon into the hidden Southward, came a gay Barouche-and-four: it was open; servants and postillions wore wedding-favours: that happy pair, then, had found each other, it was their marriage evening! Few moments brought them near: *Du Himmel!* It was Herr Towgood and—Blumine! With slight unrecognising salutation they passed me; plunged down amid the neighbouring thickets, onwards, to Heaven, and to England; and I, in my friend Richter's words, *I remained alone, behind them, with the Night.*" (151)

The events are sad enough; but that "to Heaven, and to England" is inescapably funny; and that Teufelsdröckh should draw on a literary quotation to describe his feelings rather undermines them. But most of all, the vulgar clash of marriage realities and the "slight unrecognising salutation" of these preoccupied dolls as they drive abruptly past the rejected suitor in the midst of his sublime musings does tip into the comic. Comic too is the discrepancy of the previously deified Blumine being associated—and till now that association has not been known—with someone of the name of Tough-gut.

Overall, this rather intense enamourment of Teufelsdröckh over "Aesthetic Tea" and his love for the anonymous Blumine as the source of his subsequent bottomless despair seem rather comically disproportionate. Throughout the whole subsequent account of Teufelsdröckh's torment, we are placed sufficiently far outside it, and feel its source potentially petty enough, not to be able to take it with seriousness alone. The language seems often overpitched. When he is in the darkness of unbelief Teufelsdröckh wishes that "'the Arch-Devil himself, though in Tartarean terrors, [could] but rise to me, that I might tell him a little of my mind'"; and sees the Heavens and the Earth as the "'boundless jaws of a devouring monster, wherein I, palpitating, waited to be devoured'" (166). In context these phrases serve partly to deflate. Similarly Teufelsdröckh's deepest emotions and convictions are often rendered in terms of comic figures or schemata, as when the Editor describes his romance as like the descent of an exploded Montgolfier balloon in a confusion of tatters and sandbags (144-45), or when Teufelsdröckh himself likens the attainment of happiness to arithmetic; *"the Fraction of Life can be increased in value not so much by increasing your Numerator as by lessening your Denominator"* (191).

Sometimes there is even question of how much Teufelsdröckh is really suffering. As he wanders Europe after his rejection and Blumine's marriage he seems often unmixedly happy to enjoy what is before him, and the Editor remarks that his tone at this time "has more of riancy, even of levity, than we could have expected" (186). Certainly, many of the observations made on his travels, whether on towns, wars, or great men (148-49, 170-79), have no evident connection with his supposed spiritual condition or development, and the Editor draws attention to this: "thus can the Professor, at least in lucid intervals, look away from his own sorrows, over the many-coloured world, and pertinently enough note what is passing there" (175).

The culminating discrepancy in the account of Teufelsdröckh's spiritual history comes from the product of his final ascent to the Everlasting Yea and his sudden perception that the great way forward is through work and action:

> "I too could now say to myself: Be no longer a Chaos, but a World, or even Worldkin. Produce! Produce! Were it but the pitifullest infinitesimal fraction of a Product, produce it, in God's name! 'Tis the utmost thou hast in thee: out with it, then. Up, up! Whatsoever thy hand findeth to do, do it with thy whole might. Work while it is called Today; for the Night cometh, wherein no man can work." (197)

In the midst of ringing assertion and sublime biblical imagery the words "Worldkin" and "out with it, then" strike a discordant note. And what does Teufelsdröckh produce? A clothes philosophy, or rather fragment of a philosophy, a possible bagatelle. Of course it is not all simply useless, but there are many occasions in which we feel, like the Editor, that the whole life and works of Teufelsdröckh are a "farrago" (193). Once again we are left in ambiguity and uncertainty: the clothes philosophy seems at once to be worth the high rhetoric and significance with which it is endowed, and yet at the same time quite useless and ludicrous.

Throughout *Sartor* we find Teufelsdröckh taking opposed attitudes, one undercutting another. Just as he can condemn tailors in one place and laud them in another (56-57, 287-91), so he can see clothes now as accidental, now essential, as rags and as glorious insignia, as concealments of truth or revelations of the divine. Thus on the one hand, arguing that clothes obstruct reality, he can say "'The beginning of all Wisdom is to look fixedly on Clothes, or even with armed eyesight, till they become *transparent*.... Shall we tremble before clothwebs and cobwebs?'" (67). On the other hand he can maintain that the revelation of truth is to be found within clothes themselves:

"Matter exists only spiritually, and to represent some *Idea*, and body it forth. Hence Clothes, as despicable as we think them, are so unspeakably significant ... all emblematic things are properly Clothes, thought-woven or hand-woven: must not the Imagination weave Garments, visible Bodies, wherein the else invisible creations and inspirations of our Reason are, like Spirits, revealed and first become all-powerful? ... what is Man himself, and his whole terrestrial Life, but an Emblem; a Clothing or visible Garment for that divine ME of his, cast hither, like a light-particle, down from Heaven? Thus is he said also to be clothed with a Body." (72-73)

Contempt for clothes has shifted to reverence for them as manifestations of the divine; and though Teufelsdröckh still speaks of looking through clothes to the truth, it is here in no rejectionist view of them as obstructions, but rather in the belief that only through them can the divine be communicated. Here truth is as much immanent as transcendent.[16] Teufelsdröckh's dual stance on clothes, of rejection and embracement, no and yea, is present throughout the entire clothes philosophy, and provides some of the fundamental uncertainty of the whole book: "Nothing that he sees but has more than a common meaning, but has two meanings: thus, if in the highest Imperial Sceptre and Charlemagne-Mantle, as well as in the poorest Ox-goad and Gypsy-blanket, he finds Prose, Decay, Contemptibility; there is in each sort Poetry also, and a reverend Worth" (66).

Other inconsistencies abound. At one point, applying the "unclothing" side of his thought, Teufelsdröckh can argue that kings are no more important than carmen, indeed of less value, since they do not understand draught cattle or know how to construct wagons: "'Whence, then, their so unspeakable difference? From Clothes'" (64). Yet later he can state with equal assurance his belief that kings are chosen for men by heaven, and that obedience to these "heaven chosen" is the sole source of freedom (249). Again, Teufelsdröckh can attack warfare and its hideous consequences (173-75), and yet see Napoleon as an evangel: "'The man was a Divine Missionary, though unconscious of it; and preached, through the cannon's throat, that great doctrine, *La carrière ouverte aux talens* (The Tools to him that can handle them), which is our ultimate Political Evangel, wherein alone can liberty lie'" (178-79). Here we can if we like see Teufelsdröckh as playing with ideas, whether in order to add wonder to the world or to kick us out of our complacency, but the contradiction is nonetheless being entertained. Sometimes the contraries can clash still more nearly against one another, as when Teufelsdröckh is praising the worship of symbols by men and passes on without pause seemingly to eulogise "'five-hundred living soldiers sabred into crows'-meat for a piece of glazed cotton, which they called their Flag; which, had you sold it at any market-cross, would not have brought above three groschen'" (222). Or again, he can despair at how the bane of utilitarianism and mechanism is sweeping its soul-destroying way over Britain (232-35), and yet proceed to argue that this process is an essential and indeed glorious part of spiritual history, whereby mankind will emerge more wondrous for its sufferings: "'would Destiny offer Mankind, that after, say two centuries of convulsion and conflagration, more or less vivid, the fire-creation should be accomplished, and we too find ourselves again in a Living Society, and no longer fighting but working,—were it perhaps prudent in Mankind to strike the bargain?'" (237). Here the horror at the way things are turns to joy at the way they will become; there are two views, one static, one evolutionary.

It is this duality, between the static and the evolutionary, that informs Teufelsdröckh's whole view of time and death. On the one hand he sees no-one as dead: only that their "'Time-shadows have perished,'" leaving their essential being, which will be "'forever'" (262); and says that the actions of an Orpheus or a Christ, seemingly so divided from us by time, are in fact for ever present:

> "The stroke that came transmitted through a whole galaxy of elastic balls, was it less a stroke than if the last ball only had been struck, and sent flying? O, could I (with the Time-annihilating Hat) transport thee direct from the Beginnings to the Endings, how were thy eyesight unsealed, and thy heart set flaming in the Light-sea of celestial wonder! Then sawest thou that this fair Universe, were it in the meanest province thereof, is in very deed the star-domed City of God; that through every star, through every grass-blade, and most through every Living Soul, the glory of a present God still beams. But Nature, which is the Time-vesture of God, and reveals Him to the wise, hides Him from the foolish." (264)

Yet Teufelsdröckh at once goes on to paint a picture of humanity as an assemblage of evanescent ghosts. "'Are we not Spirits, that are shaped into a body, into an Appearance; and that fade away again into air and Invisibility?'"; "'These Limbs, whence had we them; this stormy Force; this life-blood with its burning Passion? They are dust and shadow; a Shadow-system gathered round our ME; wherein, through some moments or years, the Divine Essence is to be revealed in the flesh'"; "'we emerge from the Inane; haste stormfully across the astonished Earth; then plunge again into the Inane'" (264-66). It would be possible to reconcile the two views here, but the sharpness of their juxtaposition bids defiance to the attempt.

"'Thinkest thou there is aught motionless; without Force, and utterly dead?'"; "'all . . . lives through perpetual metamorphoses'" (71-72). What is at the centre of *Sartor*, more than any doctrine or *Weltanschauung*, is a sense of the wonder and movement of life. Who else but Carlyle could have written a passage like this, which surges forward and yet shoots out tentacles in every direction:

> "Laplace's Book on the Stars, wherein he exhibits that certain Planets, with their Satellites, gyrate round our worthy Sun, at a rate and in a course, which, by greatest good fortune, he and the like of him have succeeded in detecting,—is to me as precious as to another. But is this what thou namest 'Mechanism of the Heavens', and 'System of the World'; this, wherein Sirius and the Pleiades, and all Herschel's Fifteen-thousand Suns per minute, being left out, some paltry handful of Moons, and inert Balls, had been—looked at, nicknamed, and marked in the Zodiacal Way-bill; so that we can now prate of their Whereabout; their How, their Why, their What, being hid from us, as in the sightless Inane?" (257)

There is a delight in words here perhaps, but what is behind that is an exuberance in living itself. It is that which is the strength of *Sartor*, for it is that which gives its force to Carlyle's fundamental belief, that everything about us is miracle.

In the end *Sartor* is panegyric, a praise of being.[17] To create such a work Carlyle has not allowed his meaning to solidify into some dead object, but has left it shifting and elusive, something both there and not. For Carlyle, in *Sartor* at least, whatever the mind formulates is subject to manipulation, alteration or destruction by time, and every mental castle we make also lights a keg of gunpowder in its cellars. Yet even here the paradoxes and oppositions are not complete. Here is a work which glorifies being and yet shows how evanescent and ghostly that being is; which tells us that darkness and silence are the roads to truth and yet delights in words, noise and multiplicity; which produces a clothes philosophy supposed to be the key to all the multifariousness of life, and yet also leaves us with that life more manifold and complex and chaotic than ever before. Being and nothingness, darkness and light, conscious and unconscious, speech and silence, centripetal and centrifugal: those are all true and yet self-defeatingly neat ways of encapsulating the oppositions of the book. Best finally to end with the simple No and Yea, with a "No" that can develop through suffering into a "Yea" and yet at the same time is not an evolutionary stage only, but no less everlasting than its opposite.

NOTES

[1] See Leonard W. Deen, "Irrational Form in *Sartor Resartus*", *Texas Studies in Literature and Language* 5 (Autumn 1963): 439; George Levine, *The Boundaries of Fiction: Carlyle, Macaulay, Newman* (Princeton UP, 1968): 62; G. H. Brookes, *The Rhetorical Form of Carlyle's Sartor Resartus* (Berkeley: U of California P, 1972): 118-19.

[2] Brookes, 8.

[3] *Thomas Carlyle* (Boston: Hall, 1978): 47.

[4] *Carlyle* (Oxford UP, 1982): 23.

[5] *Sartor Called Resartus* (Princeton UP, 1965): 273, 281, 283.

[6] (New Haven: Yale UP, 1968): 12; see also 56-118.

[7] See Lee C. R. Baker, "The Open Secret of *Sartor Resartus*: Carlyle's Method of Converting His Reader," *Studies in Philology* 83.2 (Spring 1986): 218-35; Charles A. Beirnard, "Rebelling from the Right Side: Thomas Carlyle's Struggle Against the Dominant Nineteenth-Century Rhetoric," *Studies in Scottish Literature* 22 (1987): 142-156.

[8] See Vivienne Rundle, "'Devising New Means': *Sartor Resartus* and the Devoted Reader," *Victorian Newsletter* 82 (Fall 1992): 13-22; D. Franco Felluga, "The Critic's New Clothes: *Sartor Resartus* as 'Cold Carnival,'" *Criticism* 37.4 (Fall 1995): 583-99.

[9] *Sartor Resartus: The Life and Opinions of Herr Teufelsdröckh*, ed. C. F. Harrold (New York: Odyssey, 1937): 72. Page references in the text are to this edition.

[10] On Carlyle's debt to the German Romantics, see C. F. Harrold, *Carlyle and German Thought: 1819-1834* (New Haven: Yale UP, 1934); LaValley, 17-56.

[11] *Centenary Edition of the Collected Works.* 30 vols. Ed. H. D. Traill (London: Chapman and Hall, 1899): 28:3. (Hereafter cited in text by volume and page).

[12] *CW* 28:16; Compare *Sartor*, 219: "Speech is of Time, Silence is of Eternity."

[13] *CW* 28:27. On the contradictions in Carlyle's own thought, see David Daiches, *Carlyle: The Paradox Reconsidered*, Thomas Green Lectures 6 (Edinburgh: The Carlyle Society, 1981).

[14] On Carlyle's distorted debt to Kant and others for this view of space and time, see Harrold, 87-95.

[15] Goethe, *The Sorrows of Young Werther and Selected Writings* (New York: Signet, 1962): 51.

[16] For some background to this duality, in Fichte and Novalis, see Harrold, 76-119, esp. 112-14. "Carlyle regarded the two points of view as readily reconcilable, as they were also regarded by Novalis, who held that the outer world, though relatively a shadow, was a means of *Selbstverständnis*. The particular steps in the logic of such a reconciliation did not trouble the primarily intuitive thinking of Novalis and Carlyle" (113).

[17] In this and in its glorification of wonder *Sartor* is close to the genre of fantasy, which it portrays as "the organ of the Godlike" (217); see Colin N. Manlove, *The Impulse of Fantasy Literature* (London: Macmillan, 1983).

CRITICAL RESPONSE
TO *THE FRENCH REVOLUTION*

LITERARY GAZETTE, AND
JOURNAL OF THE BELLES LETTRES

No. 1062 (27 May 1837): 330-32.

ANON.

Of this strange work we hardly know how to speak. To treat of it seriously is impracticable; and yet there are portions of it of such an order, that we find it equally impossible to laugh at it. Caricaturing the worst manner of the worst part of the worst German school, Mr. Carlyle out-Richter's Richter, and robs Paul to the last farthing without satisfying Peter, or any body else, with the plunder. He calls his performance "The French Revolution;" but it is more than that: it is a triple revolution:— 1st, allowing the French Revolution itself to be *one*; 2d, there is the Revolution of Mr. Carlyle, *two*; and 3d, the Revolution of the English language, *three!*

The volumes, also, are quaintly divided into "The Bastille," "The Constitution," and "The Guillotine;" and, especially when relating to the most horrid and sanguinary matters, so worded, that we cannot tell whether the author is in earnest or in jest. "Life is a jest," said Gay, and "Murder in jest," says Hamlet; but with Mr. Carlyle, not only life, but death, is a standing jest; not only murder, but fusillades, nayades, and massacres, the merries of jocular descriptions. The very titles of his chapters are like grinning and hideous laughs at mortality and mortal sufferings. Thus, the chapters giving an account of the fall of the Gironde and the Reign of Terror, are headed, "Culottic and Sansculottic," "Growing shrill," "Sansculottism accoutred," "In death grips," "Sword of sharpness," "Death," "Destruction," "Carmagnole complete," "Like a thunder-cloud," "The gods are a-thirst," "Mumbo jumbo," "To finish the Terror" go down to "Grilled Herrings," and "The Whiff of Grapeshot." Surely this is sad trifling with such scenes as those of the French Revolution, and altogether revolting to taste and feeling: but it is the same with the narrative throughout. There is nothing like a history of the events which took place; but, instead, there is a series of rhapsodical snatches, which may remind readers acquainted with the facts, from previous histories and memoirs, what it is that the author is really writing about. By itself, his book is unintelligible.*

. . . we have heard as sound sense and as meaning language in a large house called Bedlam. . . .

His sort of poetical jargon is sometimes relieved by queer anecdotes, picked up in the course of much miscellaneous reading and liberally sported by our author. . . .

One cannot help lamenting the perversity which has marred all the better qualities of a writer like this. . . .

It is, we have to repeat, difficult to make head or tail of this history. . . .

Classical absurdities; multitudes of new-coined words; and concocted phrases; illustrations which darken, and expositions which perplex; and a hundred other bewildering follies crush the sense of this work in every page. It is only a literary curiosity, and rather a tiresome one. . . .

---

*The author's peculiar style of punctuation, and strange system of commencing certain words with capital letters, have been retained in our extracts.

MONTHLY REVIEW

N.S. 2 (August 1837): 543-48.

ANON.

Whatever may be the merits of this work, one thing is certain—they have been, and will be, very differently estimated by different individuals. The impugners say that a new history of the French Revolution was not yet called for—that these volumes, at any rate, are misnamed, when laying claim to the dignified title they have assumed, for that they are unintelligible to any one who has not previously made himself acquainted, and minutely too, with the records of the period here embraced, and meant to be depicted—that in point of thought, or the philosophy that pervades and sustains them, the most extravagant German transcendentalism is offensively apparent—and that in as far as regards language or style, the worst of the worst German school is merely caricatured. On the other hand, it is even more strenuously maintained by a party, that though the philosophy and spirit of such men as Kant, Schiller, and Goëthe, have passed into Mr. Carlyle, with all that is most poetic in the system of the transcendentalists, yet that therein is to be found the only true or safe principles and method which ought to be followed in a historical composition. It is also by the same party asserted that here is the best, in fact, the only history of the French Revolution that has yet been written, as well as a model for all histories—nay, that it comes nearer the manner which has been observed by the inspired writers than any other, in as far as the vividness with which it brings the actors and the scenes described before the reader's eye; and even the decided ground is taken that the strength of a man's understanding, the warmth of his imagination, and the purity of his heart, are to be gauged by his mode of estimating this work.

Now, we believe that most of our readers do not care very much for the mere *dicta* of those who set themselves up for critics, unless specimens of the work under consideration be also presented, by which these opinionative statements may be tested. On this occasion, therefore, we, to a certain extent, vary our accustomed order of proceeding, and give our extracts before offering a criticism, so that when the readers of the Monthly Review have finished the perusal of the former, they will be enabled at once, and without any prejudice occasioned by us, to judge of them as well as of ourselves. The only thing we request *in limine* is, that it may be borne in mind that a writer's performance cannot be correctly or adequately pronounced upon, unless a steady attention be paid to the following points:—unless the reader every now and then asks himself, or be made unconsciously to yield an answer to these questions—Have I obtained any distinct ideas from what I have now read?— are these ideas numerous or rich?—are they original?—are they just?—and, lastly, are they expressed in a way that is agreeable, natural, or in the manner of a man who is in possession of a sober mind that yet has been highly cultivated? To afford means whereby these things may be ascertained, it is not necessary to do more than quote certain passages from different parts of Mr. Carlyle's volumes, without any regard being paid to their connected arrangement in the course of a chronological order. It is proper to mention, however, that the volumes are severally designated in an historically emphatic manner—"The Bastille," "The Constitution," "The Guillotine;" and that the chapters are still more singularly headed; some of them thus— "Culottic and Sansculottic," "In death grips," "Like a thunder-cloud," "The gods are a-thirst," "Mumbo jumbo," "Grilled Herrings," "The Whiff of Grapeshot," &c. . . . .

[Three pages of extracts.]

Now, are our readers, or are we to be deterred from expressing an honest opinion concerning this extraordinary work, of which the above extracts are fair specimens, by any dogmatic or dictatorial member of a crazy clique, who having been seized by that mania for German Mysticism and affectation, threatens to throw everything to the clouds, by mistaking unintelligible jargon, and adulterated English for profundity, and originality of thought and speech? Has not the reading of almost every one of these extracts, instead of impressing the mind with any new or precise ideas, induced a doubt whether they are better calculated to excite laughter or sadness? It is not to be said however, of Mr. Carlyle, that he is not a man of original powers of mind, or denied that he is a master of German literature. But what would be the consequence to the English language, and as relates to our English classics, if such quaint, deformed, whimsically affected, and bastard modes of expression should become fashionable amongst our sober-minded countrymen, not to say any thing of the strange and obscure system of *philosophism*, as Mr. Carlyle has it, which would also therewith be imported? It is well known that he is deeply read, and that he must be master of his native tongue; and can any one be so ignorant as to suppose that that tongue is too poor and so destitute of signs for the most subtle or exalted thoughts as to require the monstrous coinages, specimens of which we have just seen? But then it is alleged that the mental idiosyncracy of the man is extraordinary, and we have heard persons labour in a manner as mystic as his own, to define it and to laud it to the skies. According to our opinion, however, the very fact that his mind is singularly constituted must remove him for ever from having a right to be held as a model; for the generality of mankind must necessarily be incapable of fathoming such an out-of-the-way genius, and cannot safely venture to imitate him. We, therefore, while yielding to this History of the French Revolution, the right which it undoubtedly possesses of being regarded as one of the curiosities of modern literature, must set it down as a work that never can be useful, and, which ought to be shunned by every one who desires to cultivate a pure and rational style of writing, as well as to acquire an intelligible system of political ethics.

"New Books. Briefly Noticed, but After Thorough Perusal"

MONTHLY REPOSITORY

N.S. 11 (September, 1837): 219-20.

ANON.

There is no account of the French Revolution that can be in the slightest degree compared with this for intensity of feeling and profoundness of thought. We cannot help thinking it a pity, for the sake of the popularity of the book, that Mr Carlyle, who is an original thinker, should have made the style of it so uncompromisingly German; though the complaints against him of unintelligibility on that score are very shallow and ridiculous; and he should not have called it a "History;" for it cannot be said to tell the story to those who are unacquainted with it, so as to enable them to dispense with others; though a reader of as exquisite perception as the writer might gather it. But if a man wishes to go through the Revolution with feelings analogous to those who suffered in it, who wept in it, who hoped in it, who were driven deeply to reflect in it, and who ended by concluding that there was good in its worst evil, and a tear due to every sufferer, but not virtue or settled manhood enough in the light and joyous French character to bring the question to its noblest close, here let him suffer, and be exalted, and be depressed, and awakened into the widest thoughts upon the nature of himself and his duties with the most thoughtful heart now speaking among men.

THE EXAMINER

17 September & 1 October 1837, pp. 596-98, 629-30.

[JOHN FORSTER]

. . .—consider [*The French Revolution*] as the intense outpouring of the heart of a great thinker made in the manner of a soliloquy as of one thinking aloud—do anything that will reconcile you to a style which is at first very strange and unusual—reckon it worth some labour, and be content to make some sacrifice of leisure and of taste—rather than throw down one of the most remarkable books of our age in an ignorant, short-sighted, and despicable disgust. We repeat that we wish the style altered in many places, as in matters of quiet and level consideration; but in the major portion of the book, we would not have the alteration of a word. It is the very language of the season and the men—riveting breathless attention, and, in the midst of scenes of the sorest inflictions on humanity, stirring the deepest yearnings of the affections. It is like Sterne, but with a far superior power, as the various scenes elicit it. The finest eloquence or the most ruthless logic relieve in their proper seasons the grotesque, the pathetic, the ludicrous, or the horrible. What reader deserves to have Genius think and toil for him, that, weighing such characteristics as these, does not hold a few somewhat repulsive mannerisms, an offensive Germanism here and there, or occasional assumptions that the said reader is better informed than he really is, to weigh very light in the balance! . . .

And so, says our philosophic historian, that there be no second Sansculottism in our earth for a thousand years, let us understand well what the first was; and let rich and poor of us go and do OTHERWISE.

Most wise advice, and deeply to be considered. The world has a great account to settle yet. The body of man calls for replenishments and enjoyments, and so does his mind; and till these two possess in justice their proper food in every individual, and no mass of men be sacrificed to any other mass of men, the world will be more or less uneasy and restless, and be making perpetual experiments and undergoing pains and misgivings—symptoms, not of a disease remediless (otherwise the very restlessness would have died ere this and a dull mortification ensued), but of the necessity of getting rid of the disease. And this is a necessity which surely should not, in any case, make us hopeless, seeing that we know but little of the Past, and have all Eternity before us.

. . . The excesses of the days of September, before the commencement of the Reign of Terror, are philosophically treated by Mr Carlyle, because of the simple circumstance that he portrays the chief actors in them as men with some ultimate hope and purpose, and not mere mad or wanton shedders of blood. . . .

In painting the most terrible scenes of the French Revolution Mr Carlyle is always careful to keep one important consideration in view—which is in fact the moral of the history—that while the shrieks of units and hundreds told over Europe the tale of their frightful sufferings, *dumb millions* had felt for the first time in their silence the sense of safety— . . .

BLACKWOOD'S

42 (November 1837): 592-93.

[JOHN WILSON]

Burke's book about the French Revolution is the greatest Prose Work, out of all sight—since when? Ay! name its equal. It is Truth. But who of mortal kind, if not inspired directly from Heaven, ever spoke the Truth, the whole Truth, and nothing but the Truth, respecting any one era of this world's destiny, any one chapter in the history of the fate of man? Destiny! Fate! Dark words and dreadful—yet may the Christian use them—for the mystery they denote is not cleared up by Revelation—and finite intelligence strives to take refuge from terrors unendurable and not to be overcome, in any creed that seems to afford any shelter, though it hears God Himself driving it forth in thunder, or drawing it with "a still small voice" within the shadow of His love. That what was written might be fulfilled! That is—decreed—announced—come to pass. Of all human agencies man may speak, so far as they can be known to him; how far that may be the case of whole nations, let him think who has all his life-long been baffled in the attempt to know one individual—himself! Thomas Carlisle seems to care little for Edmund Burke, but Christopher North cares much for Thomas Carlisle. We must speak out erelong on "The French Revolution, a History in three volumes." He assumes as facts, somewhat too scornfully, the ignorance and incapacity of all other historians, somewhat too haughtily his own knowledge and his own power. Many terrible truths he utters, but the terror assuredly lies not in their being new to this generation; while he paints pictures of many "an ugly customer," as if they had been among his familiars, and he had been hand and glove with the men of blood. Nor murderer nor murdered comes amiss to this critic of pure reason. He understands *intus et in cute* each cut-throat as he tramps by on his vocation with tucked-up shirt-sleeves, and looks after him with a philosophic smile. Danton is one of his darlings, chiefly on account of his huge bulk, vast voice, hideous aspect, and prodigious *tout ensemble;* Mirabeau, whom he knows better, he is never weary of describing, by his physical qualities, and stands with open mouth and uplifted palms, "wondering, and of his wonder finds no end," at that black bushy fell of hair. Now, here are two sets of stanzas, which we venture to prefer to all he has written about the same personages in his portentous prose—

prose that may defy the world. The one set are simple, the other elaborate, but both effective; and our excellent Carlisle must admit that our New Contributor, and Christopher too, knows Louis XV., and what is more, Mirabeau, every whit as well as himself, without either of us making as much fuss about the matter as if we had found a mare's nest, with a brood of foals just chipping the shell.

CHRISTIAN EXAMINER

23 (January 1838): 386-87.

ANON.

We welcome the appearance in this country of this extraordinary work. It is by far the largest, the most elaborate, and the best work which Mr. Carlyle has yet attempted, and although an accurate and extended history, not a whit less original and eccentric than any of his earlier productions. One thing has for some time been becoming plainer, and is now quite undeniable, that Mr. Carlyle's genius, whether benignant or baleful, is no transient meteor, and no expiring taper, but a robust flame self-kindled and self-fed, and more likely to light others into a conflagration, than to be speedily blown out. The work before us indicates an extent of resources, a power of labor, and powers of thought, seldom combined, and never without permanent effects.

It is a part of Mr. Carlyle's literary creed, "that all history is poetry, were it rightly told." The work before us is his own exemplification of his doctrine. The poetry consists in the historian's point of view. With the most accurate and lively delineation of the crowded actions of the revolution, there is the constant co-perception of the universal relations of each man. With a painter's eye for picturesque groups, and a boy's passion for exciting details, he combines a philosopher's habitual wonder as he stands before the insoluble mysteries of the Advent and Death of man. From this point of view, he is unable to part, and the noble and hopeful heart of the narrator breathes a music of humanity through every part of the tale. Always equal to his subject, he has first thought it through; and having seen in the sequence of events the illustration of high and beautiful laws which exist eternal in the reason of man, he beholds calmly like a god the fury of the action, secure in his own perception of the general harmony resulting from particular horror and pain. This elevation of the historian's point of view is not, however, procured at any expense of attention to details. Here is a chronicle as minute as Froissart, and a scrupulous weighing of historical evidence, which begets implicit trust. Above all, we have men in the story, and not names merely. The characters are so sharply drawn that they cannot be confounded or forgotten, though we may sometimes doubt whether the thrilling impersonation is in very deed the historic man whose name it bears.

We confess we feel much curiosity in regard to the immediate success of this bold and original experiment upon the public taste. It seems very certain that the chasm which existed in English literature, the want of a just history of the first French Revolution, is now filled in a manner to prevent all competition. But how far Mr. Carlyle's manifold innovations shall be reckoned worthy of adoption and of emulation, or what portion of them shall remain to himself incommunicable, as the anomalies of a genius too self-indulgent, time alone can show.

BOSTON QUARTERLY REVIEW

1 (October 1838): 407-17.

W. H. CHANNING

"What induced Thomas Carlyle to select such a subject as the French Revolution," we have heard asked by those, who, having read only the "Sartor," think him a poetical mystic. "Did he write for bread, or from sympathy with that social movement?" To those who know him it is plain enough, that our good friend, however pinched by want, could not let out his mind to do job-work. His Pegasus would break down at the plough. Carlyle's heart is always, must always be, in what he does.

He selected this subject then, because to him there came a voice out of the Chaos, we may be sure. But farther, to any one, who will review his literary course, the explanation will be clear enough of his interest in that ruin and recreation of a social world. The gradual progress of his studies through Voltaire and Diderot led him to the observation of this unparalleled phenomenon. But his taste, his instinct guided him also. Like his master Goethe, he has been always hunting for a "bit of Nature." Whether he is writing of Burns or Richter, of Novalis or Elliott, of the Spirit of the Age or its Characteristics, or finally of Mirabeau, he everywhere shows the same longing after the genuine product of Nature. Hypocrisy however self-deceived and respectable is his horror, and is greeted with nothing more civil than an "anathema maranatha." This is his "fixed idea," his creed; and he clings to it with an unquestioning *bigotry*. Yes! bigotry;—for noble as the creed is, it is yet a *creed*; and, though he might deny it, a "formula;" and his range of sympathy, his candor of judgment, and even truth of moral sentiment are narrowed by this notion. In consequence he is prejudiced. He trusts to his first impressions. He casts his eye on a man with cutting penetration, and is satisfied that he knows him. He takes him by the arm, and by the feeling of the iron or flabby muscle judges instantly of his vigor. Truly he seldom seems much deceived by this instinctive love of Nature. Shams vanish before his glance, as gauze would in the fire. Yet even this love of Nature seems to us a kind of Cant after all. But we check ourselves; we do not like to say even thus much in the way of fault-finding with one of the truest, honestest of critics and of men.

Our student of Nature had already picked up rare specimens here and there as he found them; and now at last he has arrived at this grand volcanic outbreak, and sits down amid mighty heaps of most indisputable genuineness, to learn what is in man. And truly he is nowise repelled by stench of sulphur and dreads not burns. But there was another reason for the study of the French Revolution. Carlyle loves man, loves the men he lives among. He is not indifferent to the temper of his own age, and thinking it, in its philosophy and professed maxims, a peculiarly mechanical, self-conscious, and artificial one, he cannot but obey the inward behest to sound his prophecy in men's ears, whether his fate be Cassandra's or not. He doubtless feels as if a sick generation needed a sanative; and what better than the pure crystal of natural feeling? His text is certainly a healthy one, and his homilies have a freshness, as if he had dipped with a leaf from the bubbling spring. In a word, our author probably anticipates, as many others do, that the *matchless* British constitution may be rent asunder by some larger growth of the social germ; and meanwhile, he may think it would be well for us not to hinder but to aid, as we can, the process.

Carlyle, we feel sure, has dropped all conventional spectacles, and opened his eyes to the true characteristic of our times,—which is, that the "better sort" are being elbowed more and more for room by the "poorer sort," as they step forward to gather a share of the manna on life's wilderness. Perhaps he thinks it high time, that they who are clad in decencies and good manners should busy themselves in teaching their brother "sans-culottes" to wear suitable garments. We believe then that our author was led to a study and history of the French Revolution, because he saw it illustrating in such characters of fire the irrepressible instinct of all men to assert and exercise their natural rights;—and the absolute necessity which there is, therefore, that man's essential equality with man should be recognised.

Mr. Carlyle has evidently done his work like a man. He appears to have read most voraciously, and sifted most scrupulously. And when one thinks of the multifarious mass which he must have digested in the process of composition, we cannot but equally admire his sagacity, and respect his faithfulness. Add the consideration, that the first volume, when fully prepared, was by an unfortunate accident destroyed; and that the author, without copy or plan, was thus forced to tread over when jaded the path he had climbed in the first flush of untried adventure; and that yet with this additional labor he has been occupied only some two years and more upon the book, and our estimate of his ability, his genius, his energy, cannot but be great.

And now what has he produced? A history? Thiers, Mignet, Guizot forbid! We for ourselves call this French Revolution an Epic Poem; or, rather say the root, trunk, and branches of such a poem, not yet fully clothed with rhythm and melody indeed, but still hanging out its tassels and budding on the sprays. And here, by the way, may it not be asked whether Carlyle is not emphatically the English poet of our epoch? Is he not Shelley and Wordsworth combined, and greater than either? Thus far indeed we have seen this luminary in a critical phase chiefly. But is it not because he has read, in the life of the men he has apotheosized, true poems, incarnations of that ideal he worshipped? It seems to us an accident, that prose and criticism, not odes and positive life, have been his vein. Had he but form and tune what a poet was there! This book we say is a poem, the most remarkable of our time. It is not like a written book; it is rather like the running soliloquy of some wonderfully living and life-giving mind, as it reads a "good formula" of history;—a sort of resurrection of the dry bones of fact at the word of the prophet. Marvellous indeed! It seems as if, in some camera obscura, one was looking upon the actual world and sky and moving forms, though all silent in that show-box. Of all books this is most graphic. It is a series of masterly outlines *à la Retzch*. Oh more, much more. It is a whole *Sistine Chapel* of *fresco à la Angelo*, drawn with bold hand in broad lights and deep shadows. Yet again it is gallery upon gallery of portraits, touched with the free grace of Vandyke, glowing with Titian's living dyes, and shining and gloomed in Rembrandt's golden haze. And once more, let us say in our attempt to describe this unique production, it is *a seer's second sight of the past*. We speak of prophetic vision. This is a *historic vision*, where events rise not as thin abstractions, but as visible embodiments; and the ghosts of a buried generation pass before us, summoned to react in silent pantomime their noisy life.

The *point of view*, from which Carlyle has written his history, is one which few men strive to gain, and which fewer still are competent to reach. He has looked upon the French Revolution, not as a man of one nation surveys the public deeds of another; nor as a man of one age reviews the vicissitudes of a time gone by. Still less has he viewed it, as a religionist from the cold heights, where he awaits his hour of translation, throws pitying regards on the bustling vanities of earth; or as a philosophist, from his inflated theory of life, spies out, while he soars, the battle of ideas. And it is not either in the passionless and pure and patient watching, with which a spirit, whose faith has passed into knowledge, awaits the harmonious unfoldings of Heaven's purposes, that he has sent his gaze upon that social movement. But it is as a *human spirit*, that Carlyle has endeavored to enter into the conscious purposes, the unconscious strivings of *human spirits*; with wonder and awe at the mighty forces which work so peacefully, yet burst out so madly in one and all at times. He has set him down before this terrible display of human energy, as at a mighty chasm which revealed the inner deeps of man, where gigantic passions heave and stir under mountains of custom; while Free-will, attracted to move around the centre of holiness, binds their elements of discord into a habitable world. As a *man* Carlyle would study *man*. It is as if he were ever murmuring to himself; "Sons of Adam, daughters of Eve, what are ye? Angels ye plainly are not. Demons truth cannot call ye. Strange angelic-demoniac beings, on! on! Never fear! Something will come of you." Carlyle does not pretend to fathom man. His plummet sinks below soundings. We do not know a writer, who so unaffectedly expresses his wonder at the mystery of man. Now this appears to us a peculiar and a novel point of view, and a far higher one than that of the "progress of the human race." Not that he does not admit progress. The poor quibbles of those, who see in one age only the transmigration of the past, do not bewilder him. But he feels how little we can know, and do know, of this marvellous human race,—in their springs, and tendencies, and issues. This awe of man blends beautifully with reverence for Providence. There is no unconscious law of fate, no wild chance to him, but ever brightening "aurora splendors" of divine love. Enough, however of this point of view. We will but add that its effect is to give the most conscientious desire of seeing things exactly as they are, and describing them with scrupulous truth. Hence we suppose his intense effort to transfuse his soul, and animate the very eyes and ears of the men, who lived in that stormy time, and mingle up his whole being with theirs. Hence, too, the pictorial statement of what he gathers by that experience; and hence, in fine, a mode of historical composition, wholly original, which must revolutionize the old modes of historicising, so "stale, flat, and unprofitable," do theories and affected clearness appear, after we have once seen this flash of truth's sunlight into the dark cave of the buried years.

Of the *spirit*, in which this book is written, we would say that it breathes throughout the truest, deepest sympathy with man. Wholly free from the cant, which would whine, and slap its breast, and wring its hands, saint-like, over the weaknesses, which the canter himself is full of,—it yet is strict in its code of right. Most *strict* indeed, though somewhat peculiar. It is not the proper or decorous, which he prizes, but it is the true. And of all writers he is the most unflinching in his castigations of pretence. He never flatters, he never minces; but yet he speaks his hard truth lovingly, and with an eye of hope. He does not spare men, because he sees more life in them than they wot of. While he says to the moral paralytic, "sin no more, lest a worse thing befall thee," he adds, "rise, take up thy bed and walk." He is kind, and pitiful, and tolerant of weakness, if it only does not affect to seem what it is not, and paint the livid cheek with mock hues of health. This leads us to say a word of his irony and humor, and he is full of both, though chiefly of the latter. No man has a keener eye for incongruities. It is not the feebleness of men, or the smallness of their achievements, which excites his mirth;—for where there is humbleness in the aspiration, he is of all most ready to see the Psyche in the crawling worm. But what appears to him so droll is the complacence and boastfulness, with which crowds build their Babel to climb to heaven, and the shouts of "glory" with which they put on the cap-stone, when their tower is after all so very far beneath the clouds. He loves so truly what is good in man, that he can afford to laugh at his meannesses. His respect for the essential and genuine grows with his success in exposing the artificial. Under the quaint puffings and paddings of "vanity fair" he does really see living men. He joins in the carnival. He looks upon it as a masquerade, and it is with real frolic that he snatches off the false nose or the reverend beard, and shows the real features of the dolt who would pass for a Solomon. He evidently does enjoy a practical joke on primness. But if he would, like the doctor in the tale, make his gouty patient hop on the heated floor, it is only for his *cure*. Carlyle seems to us full of true benevolence. He loves everything but insincerity. This he cannot abide. It is the very devil, and he has but one word, "Apage Satanas." He stands among the Pharisees with the indignant words bursting from his heart, "Ye Hypocrites." In this relation it is too true our friend is nowise angelic, but only too much a man. His contempt is too bitter. We do not readily tolerate in a frail mortal the scornful mirth, with which Carlyle sometimes shows us the cloven hoof under the surplice. Not that the indignation is not merited. But is a man ever pure enough from all taint of falsehood himself, thus to wield the spear of Michael against the dragon? Yet honor to this brave and true man. It is because he has struggled so hard, and withal so well, to disentangle himself from the last thread of cant, that he has so little patience with the poor flies yet buzzing in the web. This loathing of the formal, which a vigorous nature and a bold effort have freed him from, is, we take it, the true and very simple explanation of that occasional rudeness, and even levity, with which, it must be confessed, he speaks of so called worshippers and worship.

And this introduces us to a consideration of his religious spirit. Some perhaps would say, have said, that Carlyle's writings are not baptized into that "spirit of adoption which cries Abba Father." But to us no writings are more truly reverential. It surely is from no want of faith in the fullness of divine love, from no insensibility to the nearness of almighty aid, from no doubt as to the destiny of the soul and its responsibilities and perils, that he uses so little of the technical and prescribed language of piety. Oh how far, far from it. But he will not name the Unnamable. He will not express more than he feels, or desecrate by familiarity what he does feel, yet knows not how adequately to utter. His sense is so abiding of our present imperfect development, his hope is so vast in that good which Providence has in store in its slow but harmonious processes, that he will not "enter the kingdom of God by violence." To him the Infinite is ever present. That holy and eternal life is his life,—the soul of his soul,—the love of his love,—the wisdom of his wisdom, the power of his power,—the Father. But he strives not so much to look upon the dazzling glory of this central source, whence all of good and fair streams forth;—rather with lowly eyes would he drink in the beauty rayed abroad from each object which its light vivifies and hallows. He would *worship* in the longing to be true and pure, in the dutifulness, the cheerfulness, the humble joy, the patience, and the charities of daily life. His devotedness should be his devoutness; his joy should be his thanks; his progress his confessions; his hopeful energy his prayer; and his offering of the First Fruits a full developed, genial healthiness of nature.

But it would carry us too far to say the half of what we feel about this noble soul, whom we love, not for being the "healthiest of men," for that he is not; but for the pure instinct and reposing confidence, with which being sick, as the most are, he gives himself up to the "mighty mother" to be nursed on her bosom.

With a few words on his style we must bid Mr. Carlyle for the present farewell, only hoping for that rich fruitage of his autumn years of which this summer flush is the promise. Of his later writings it would not be far from the truth to say that we like them, not by reason of the style, but in *spite* of it. They are so savagely uncouth by the side of his former classic gracefulness. It is a savage crowned with ivy though, and crushing luscious grapes as he dances. But the Life of Schiller and the early essays had all this naked strength and free play of movement, and yet were decent. They wore their garland of imagery like a festive wreath; and though bright and cheerful, with the melody of pipes, they had no lawless friskiness. He has always been remarkable for the picturesqueness of the metaphors which clothed his thoughts. But this growth of the symbolic has become ranker and ranker, until, in this last book, the very trees in full foliage are fringed with mosses. It seems as if the axis of his mind had shifted, and the regions of fancy had been brought from the temperate zone beneath the tropics, and hidden germs were bursting prodigally into life. With this teeming fruitfulness and gorgeous wealth we associate the thought of miasm and disease. One feature of this style though we do like much, it is its freedom, its conversational directness, its point and spirit, its infinite variety. How far preferable to the dandy precision of so called elegant styles, and to the solemn dryness of so called clear styles. Is it a delusion however that something of that old bewitching melody of his earlier speech has been sacrificed? There is less to our ear of that rhythm which used to charm us, of that sound and sweep like the bursting of long swelling billows on the broad beach. But we have no notion meanwhile that there is any degeneracy in the artist. We believe that there has been a progress even. We think this present style a transition one. It is a struggling for some adequate utterance, for some word of power which should open the deaf ear; for we must remember his countrymen have been deaf comparatively, and perhaps for the want of some free, hearty speech, less prim than suited the scholar's garb. Will not this Apollo find one day the murmuring shell? Some, wiser than we pretend to be, settle this matter of style summarily. They will have it that Mr. Carlyle is "*affected*." We commend to all such for candid consideration these few sentences of his own. "Affectation is a cheap word and of sovereign potency, and should not be rashly applied. Its essence is that it is *assumed*: the character is, as it were, forcibly crushed into some foreign mould, in the hope of being thereby reshaped and beautified: the unhappy man persuades himself that he is in truth a new and wonderfully engaging creature, and so he moves about with a conscious air, though every movement betrays not symmetry, but dislocation. This it is to be affected, to walk in a *vain show*. But the strangeness alone is no proof of the vanity. Many men who move smoothly in the old established railways of custom will be found to have their affectation; and perhaps here and there some divergent genius be accused of it unjustly. The *show*, though common, may not cease to be *vain*; nor become so for being uncommon. Before we censure a man for *seeming* what he is not, we should be sure that we know what he *is*."

AMERICAN BIBLICAL REPOSITORY

N.S. 7 (January 1842): 233-34.

ANON.

To one who has never read any of Mr. Carlyle's writings we should despair of success in attempting to convey an adequate idea of his peculiarities. His style of thought and expression are not only his own, but they are so unlike those of any other writer of the English tongue, that they are incapable of being illustrated by example in the whole range of our literature. His productions have exceedingly puzzled the critics both of the old and the new world. That his style is faulty in a high degree,— that it outrages all the laws of rhetoric, as established by the usage of the best writers, and that no man can attempt to imitate it but at the expense of his reputation for good sense and correct taste,—is now universally admitted. Yet Carlyle himself is an original, and as such he commands the toleration of the literary public, and even the admiration of many who would wage relentless war against the eccentricity, the affectation and the mannerism of his style, were they found anywhere but in the writings of this one man. But here they belong to himself. They are perhaps essential to the filling up of his character; and if these exuberances could be destroyed, it would probably be with greater loss than gain; and so both readers and critics are beginning to adopt the conclusion that, in this case as in many others where remedy is impracticable, it is wise to

> "Do as they do in Spain,
> Let it rain."

The reader may of course expect to find, in this history of the French Revolution, a singular, an eccentric production. It is unlike all other histories in prose. It is a prose epic, the plan of which was suggested by the thrilling and fearful events and transactions of that "reign of terror." He accordingly groups his materials by a different law from that of their succession in time, and thus, by connecting the more trivial details with the prominent events, he clothes the whole story with an interest, which the ordinary style of narrative never produces. And the conception is not only epical, but the plot is developed with wit and irony, which to a reader somewhat familiar with the events referred to will appear to be well sustained. And, withal, Mr. Carlyle is a serious writer. In the language of an English reviewer, "Duty,—the duty of acting,—in however small a sphere, it is his perpetual task to preach;" and he preaches it too with an earnestness, with which the wildest playfulness in details seldom interferes. On the whole, then, we strongly recommend the reading of this "great work" of Carlyle,—not as a history, but as an epic description of the French Revolution. It will wake up the mind to new and more vivid impressions of the scenes of that age of confusion than any history we have read. . . .

THE VICTORIAN AGE OF ENGLISH LITERATURE

(New York: Thomas Y. Crowell, 1892), pp. 120-23.

MARGARET OLIPHANT

Carlyle's first work in London was the "History of the French Revolution,"
... One of the first literary distinctions of Queen Victoria's reign was the publication
of this book, which took place in the year of Her Majesty's accession, 1837. The
perfection at once of that new grandiose yet rugged voice, which broke every law
of composition and triumphed over them all, which shocked and bewildered all
critics and authorities, yet excited and stirred the whole a slumbrous world of
literature, and rang into the air like a trumpet,—and of a new manner altogether of
regarding the events of history, a great pictorial representation, all illuminated by
the blaze, sometimes lurid, sometimes terrible, of the highest poetic genius and
imagination,—were fully displayed in this astonishing work. Histories enough of
the French Revolution had been given to the world, and have been since—personal
experiences, formal documents, fictitious narratives, all the collections of material
possible, showed forth in almost every setting that could be thought of,—but none
which conveyed the very sound and uproar of that wild orgie of the fates; none that
showed the unhappy confused workings of those blind guides and leaders, of those
still more blind opponents of the national frenzy, with such living force and power.
If they are all perhaps too much like wild shadows running thither and hither against
a background of flame and smoke and ever-blazing fire, that is the very bitterness
of the truth with which the genius of Carlyle seized the reality of the most
lamentable, the most awful, the most influential of recent epochs. It is no mere
record, but a great drama passing before our eyes. We are made spectators rather
than readers of the terrible developments, one after another, of each successive act.
A drama working blindly towards a *dénouement* of which its actors had neither
conception nor intention, through which they blindly stalk, stumble, fall, each in his
turn bringing numerous and unthought of complications, new turns and twists of
fate, as veritably happened, as happens continually, though to most generations
there is no Seer to perceive how these strange new openings and closings succeed
each other, and how the great thread of destiny rolls on. . . .

. . . There can be little doubt that it was his "French Revolution" which turned
the scale [in favor of his popularity]—a book more interesting than any romance,
which those who took it up could not lay down, and which was far too impressive
in its general character, too powerful and novel in its art, to be mistaken or
overlooked. . . .

"Studies in Literary Psychology III. 'Carlyle and the Present Tense'"

CONTEMPORARY REVIEW

85 (1904): 386-92.

VERNON LEE [VIOLET PAGET]

Persuaded as I was . . . that the greatest differences in literary effect are due mainly to different treatment of the verb, I set about an examination of the present tense, as it has been employed in our language.

It seems an idiotically obvious remark, yet one is apt to feel a little shock of surprise when its truth is brought home to one: *the present tense makes things present;* it abolishes the narrative and the narrator. This can be verified, as the relation of relief and colour is best verified in pictures, by a process of reversing, like standing a picture on its head. The ballad gives us this. For in the ballad the bulk of the telling is sometimes in the present tense. . . .

I have said that the present tense abolishes the fact of narration. This has a most important result, that of doing away with the sense of cause and effect. For we cannot feel any causal connection without projecting ourselves into the past or the future. The present tense, constantly pushing us along, leaves no leisure for thinking about *why*; it hustles us into a new *how*. The present, in this case, never becomes a past, the thing which we can keep and look into; it simply drops off into limbo, vanishes entirely, as it probably does in the case of many children and thoughtless, uneducated persons.

Moreover—and this is obvious—the present tense can bring the event before us, or us before the event, forcing us into a kind of sham belief. I say of *sham* belief, because this special kind of condition, that of dramatic illusion, is often totally different from the genuine kind of belief, what William James would probably call the "warm, familiar acquiescence" which belongs to the sense of reality. We may sit in a theatre and be hurried, bullied into interest and sympathy with something which we do not seriously believe possible. And here I should like to distinguish very clearly between this kind of realisation, due to presentation on the stage or to presentation by the present tense and similar devices, and realisation by such fulness and harmony, such organic synthesis of co-ordinated detail, as is produced by only the very greatest novels or poems. After watching a Sarah Bernhardt play, or reading a chapter of Dickens even with breathless interest, I am by no means haunted by a certainty that something is going on, that certain people are contriving to live, struggle and suffer, such as I have after reading Thackeray, or Stendhal, or Tolstoi; on the contrary, there is often, as one lays down the book or rises from one's seat, a feeling of abrupt breaking off, of blowing out the lights. For once lapsed into silence, Lady Dedlock, Snagsby, Jo, Tulkinghorn, Chadband, cease to exist, cease therefore to develop, even like the personages of a Sardou drama after the curtain has fallen. But the Newcomes, the family of Del Dongo, and Katia, Levine, Anna, Vronsky, Natacha, Princess Mary or Pierre are just as living and active when I am not reading about them as when I am; and the poisoning of Othello's mind takes place, as a matter of fact, between as much as during the acts. Why? Because all these great creations have an organic, inevitable existence of their own, and once in contact with our thoughts, they must alter and act on one another even like real things; whereas the others are mere cleverly-painted puppets, whose movements catch and arouse our attention; but which, once the band hushed and the lights out, collapse into heaps of wood and wire.

By this hangs the fact, often puzzling in the extreme, that "thrilling" stories are so often very poor and so often forgotten as soon as read; also that pathetic effects can be produced by third rate talent. The difficult, the unique thing to produce is such fascination as continues when the reader is surrounded by different impressions, and submitted to contrary influences, the fascination given by the life organic, which is also the life everlasting! I have spoken of Dickens' use of the present tense. It is accompanied by several dodges converging towards the same effect. First, the dodge (the essential factor of theatrical illusion) of making the characters say their whole say, instead of telling us what they said; with the result that the most unlikely thing is accepted because, in a way, you are made to hear it, and speeches are listened to with acquiescence which would revolt our sense of probability if their substance were merely retailed. Again, and more efficacious still, the dodge of undoing the wrappers one by one, taking the boxes one out of the other, and thereby producing, like the conjuror, a spurious belief in the reality underlying these deliberate proceedings. I will not lay impious hands on Dickens, whose greatness exists despite such glaring drawbacks; so I will invent a passage after his manner, burn him only in effigy: "In that street there is a house; in that house there is a room; in that room there sits a woman." Each affirmation (impossible to negative because there is no real connection with any) builds up a certainty in the reader's mind. So that when we come to "and that woman is sewing a shroud," the certainty is positively crushing. How sceptical we should remain if the passage ran as follows: "In a certain house of a certain street, a woman sat sewing a shroud."

This undoing the wrappers is, as I hinted, a frequent accompaniment of the use of the present tense; it exists in most ballads, and in the popular recital (as one may still hear it in certain countries) of fairy tales. And all such processes—or all processes so employed—present tense, dialogued narrative, reiterative development of unrelated facts, or, if you prefer, elaborate peeling away of one fact and showing the next, and take the place of the power of persuading the reader by intellectual or emotional evidence that things really have happened in that particular way. They have the advantage of saving, not merely the skill or genius which the writer has not got, but the intelligence and imagination, the sympathy, nay, the mere attention which the reader may not be able or inclined to give. We are all of us at times too poor in spirit or nerves to meet the artist half way, and help him to build his magic cities and plant his enchanted woods in our soul. It is on such occasions that a good thumping on the drum, or a good flaring of Bengal lights is highly welcome. And for this reason such aids to interest and to tears are indispensable to a large number of persons, those who happen to be tired, or were never anything else.

In amazing contrast to what, let us say, Dickens contrives by means of the present tense, is what Carlyle employs it to achieve. The contrast is between melodrama and the highest lyric, the lyric of prophecy. Here—say in "The French Revolution"—we become witnesses no longer of juggler's tricks, but of miracles. Let us watch and wonder.

The intellectual process is wholly different from the one we have been examining in Dickens. Carlyle's present tense does not oblige us to witness the taking of the Bastille or the death of Louis XVI. in the manner in which Dickens' present tense has obliged us to witness the death of the Man from Shropshire, or the interview of Lady Dedlock and Guppy. Louis XVI., Mirabeau, Danton, and the rest are seen but vaguely, as from a distance, recognisable on the whole by some constantly recurring attitude easily identified from afar; nay, by some quite superficial peculiarity like "Dusky D'Esprimenil," "Gyrating Maurepas," or "Sea Green Robespierre," Carlyle's "Revolution" affording in this a curious contrast to Michelet's, where we learn so well the actual features, the marks of underlying temperament, the very visceral life, in many cases, of all the *dramatis personæ*. No; in Carlyle the illusion is not in the least of the dramatic kind; it is of the lyric. What the present tense does here is to transport us perpetually, to hustle us unceasingly into the presence of Carlyle himself. It forces us, without allowing a pause to think or glance over our own shoulder, to look down on the revolution from the skyey post of observation where *He* sits, like some belfry gargoyle overlooking a flattened city and a mapped out country, among the storms and sunsets; a kind of cosmic, archangelic dæmon, seeing the molehill-upsettings, the ants' processions and tumults of this world, and this world as but a tiny item of the swirling universe around him; seeing it all with comprehension of the how and why, with pity and disdain. It sounds ridiculous to say (something like the anti-climax of a nostrum advertisement) that it is the present tense which allows Carlyle to do and be all this; but that seems to be the case. For the present tense dispenses with all question and answer, all explanation; and it gives continuity not to the things he speaks about, but to what he says about them, with the result that what we are witnessing is not the drama down below in streets and fields, nor even the drama in human hearts (there is wonderfully little fellow-feeling with anyone); but the drama up here in the soul of this strange, marvelous prophet, Stylites-like among the forces of Nature, calling out what he sees in the little earth, in the vast infinity, like Jeremiah muttering and shouting of the past and future, "Therefore I am full of the fury of the Lord; I am weary with holding in. . . ."

There is no difference, save in length, in subject and in philosophic attitude, between the "Revolution" and a poem like "Abt Vogler," or the "Grammarian's Funeral." The doings of Jacobins and Girondins, the September Massacres or the War in Argonne, hold the same place as the Illumination of the cupola or the uphill procession; they are episodes, illustrations, metaphors almost, bringing home the eternal laws of Being and Becoming, of Death and Revival; and they are for Carlyle, as for Browning, what they were for the "Chorus Mysticus": alles Vergängliche ist nur ein Gleichniss.

Take a chapter of the "French Revolution" and transpose it into the past tense; you will get the same effect as by similarly transposing "Abt Vogler" or the "Grammarian": all cohesion, all co-ordination will disappear; the transition from one subject to another will become senseless; the action, which is that of the Prophet holding forth, will come to a stop. But the consecutiveness of cause and effect, the intelligibility of history will not have been attained. For what will those sudden vocatives, invectives, prophecies become in a mere past tense narrative of sublunary events? And what connection will there be among those historical affairs, stranded in bits, if we no longer feel their connection in the travailing or transfigured spirit of the Seer?

But I will take an example. I open the "French Revolution" literally at random, at the beginning of the 4th chapter of the last book. And, substituting the past tense for the present, I produce the following half page:—

> The Convention, borne on the tide of Fortune towards foreign victory, and driven by the strong wind of Public Opinion towards Clemency and Luxury, rushed fast; all skill of pilotage was (or *being*) needed, and more than all, in such a velocity. Curious to see how it veered and whirled, yet had ever to whirl round again, and scud before the wind. If, on the one hand, it re-admitted the protesting Seventy-Three, it had, on the other, to consummate the apotheosis of Marat; it had to lift his body from the Cordeliers' Church and transport it to the Pantheon of Great Men; flinging out Mirabeau to make room for him. To no purpose: so strong did public opinion blow. A Gilt Youth-hood, in plaited hair tresses, tore down his busts from the Theatre Feydeau; trampled them under foot; scattered them, with vociferation, into the cesspool of Montmartre. His chapel was swept away from the Place du Carrousel; the cesspool of Montmartre was to receive his very dust.

I should add that in making this slight alteration in a few verbs, I have found it inevitable to alter the pronouns also: it is impossible, for instance, to speak of the Convention as *we*, once it is a thing of the past it becomes *it*; and thereby the interrogative passages become more or less childish.

This one travesty should suffice to show that in this book the present tense is not in the least a device (as people sometimes imagine) for making the narrative rattle on. As a fact the narrative never does rattle on; anything but that! The use of the present tense answers on the contrary to Carlyle's very personal attitude in what is really the world of contemplation; and it is, I believe we should find, only one of the inevitable literary expressions thereof; for no man's style was ever so organically personal as his, so intimately interwoven with individual habits of thought and feeling; at all events, I think, among English prose writers. But if my reader is not convinced we will try again, but this time purposely selecting one of the pieces of purest narrative, one, therefore, which ought, on the fact of it, rather to gain than lose by transposition into the past tense. Here it is, made a hash of by that simple alteration of tenses.

> On the morrow morning, she delivered her note to Duperret. It related to certain family papers which were in the Minister of the Interior's hand . . . which Duperret was to assist her in getting; this, then, had been Charlotte's errand to Paris? She had finished this in the course of Friday, yet said nothing of returning. She had seen and silently investigated several things. The Convention in bodily reality, she *had* seen; what the Mountain was like. The living physiognomy of Marat she could not see: he was sick at present and confined to home. About eight on the Saturday morning she purchased a large sheath knife in the Palais Royal; then straightways, in the Place des Victoires, took a hackney coach: "To the Rue de l'Ecole de Médicine, No. 44." It was the residence of the Citoyen Marat! The Citoyen Marat was ill, and could not be seen; which seemed to disappoint her much. Her business was with Marat, then? Hapless beautiful Charlotte! hapless squalid Marat! From Caen in the utmost West, from Neuchâtel in the utmost East, they two were drawing nigh each other; they two had, very strangely, business together. . . . No answer. Charlotte wrote another note, still more pressing; set out with it by coach, about seven in the evening, herself. *Tired day labourers had again finished their work*; huge Paris was circling and simmering, manifold, according to its wont; this one fair figure had decision in it, drove straight, towards a purpose. . . . And so Marat, People's Friend, was ended; the lone Stylites had got hurled down suddenly from his pillar; *whither?* He that made him does know.

I have italicized the passage about the workmen, because the result of the altered tense is particularly bad here. This passage deals with the general, the universal, the always happening, and that cannot be adequately given by the historic tense. For the same reason no large generalisation can be formulated in the past tense. Compare the difference between "all men have died," and "all men are mortal."

The present tense, therefore, which is a rough and ready dramatic trick in the ballad, and a vulgar dodge for realisation in a writer (for all his genius) of the superficial psychology of Dickens; the present tense is also the natural form of the lyric or the prophecy. For men like Shelley, Browning or Carlyle, it is the tense of the eternal verities, which, from their very nature, have not *been*, but, like all divine things, always *are*.

"Carlyle and the French Revolution"

THE ADELPHI

n.s. 18 (November-December 1941): 20-24, 36-38.

FRANK A. LEA

"All they that take the sword shall perish with the sword."

Thomas Carlyle was born in the same year as Keats—1795; three years after Shelley and seven after Byron. We think of him as one of the great Victorians; yet in fact he belongs to the second generation of the English Romantics. He was the only one of that generation who lived to maturity. Keats died in 1821, Shelley in 1822, and Byron in 1824; Carlyle lived on until 1881. Small wonder that he seemed, and felt, out of place in Victorian England.

The Romantic Revolution was, like all revolutions, at once a protest and an affirmation: a protest against formulas and institutions that no longer corresponded to the deepest reality in men; an affirmation of that reality in all its profundity and aspiration. The Romantic Revolution in England was the counterpart of the French Revolution on the Continent. A counterpart and not, as it is often claimed, a consequence. That it expressed itself in cultural rather than in political forms was due more to the objective historical situation than the subjective content of the movement: the same forces were at work in both. Hence, in part, the deep sympathy which all the Romantics felt for the Revolution. It became an integral part of their experience, which every one of them would sooner or later have been driven to comprehend.

That Wordsworth was the man appointed by Destiny to comprehend it seems obvious. He had been more intimately involved in the Revolution than any of his contemporaries or successors. But Wordsworth shrank from the duty. The defeat of his revolutionary hopes had been too bitter for him to bear; he drove it and them from his memory: and Destiny forsook him in consequence—like Hercules forsaking the camp of Anthony—to ally itself with one who had never known the Terror but grown up under the threat of Napoleon. Wordsworth's vision was never turned to illuminate

> "the fierce confederate storm
> Of sorrow barricadoed evermore
> Within the walls of cities."

It was left to Carlyle to complete his work.[1]

That Carlyle did not succeed in disclosing a beauty in the storm of the French Revolution as Wordsworth might have done is true. And yet, to reveal a necessity and meaning in the event, to which beauty of some wild kind cannot be denied, is an achievement not far removed from that. Carlyle was no poet; yet his *French Revolution* has many of the qualities of a great epic poem. Even in its structure it resembles one. Nobody reading it can have failed to have been struck by the magnificent manner in which he turns to account the Procession of the Estates General in Volume I: making of it an opportunity to introduce all the outstanding figures of his narrative: and this design and presentation, as of a great work of art, is maintained throughout. But that is only the outward and visible sign of an inward and spiritual grace. This architectonic, like the unique style of Carlyle's prose, is only the form in which his imagination naturally clothed itself. The imagination is the miracle. In the *French Revolution* history transpires, so to speak, in three dimensions. It becomes something more than a "record of successive stages of finitude"; it takes on the depth and mystery of eternity.

There are some who deny that it is history at all, who would even deny to Carlyle himself the right to be called an historian. Certainly if accuracy of detail is the only test, then he must take second place to Madelin. But one suspects that it is not really the inaccuracy of his record that provokes the envy of these dons; it is this very power of uncovering the abyss over which humanity plays—which they feel, and feel rightly, to be a judgment upon their own limited perception, against which they have to defend themselves. To submit to it would mean undergoing a revolutionary enlargement of consciousness: a third dimension of consciousness is needed to respond to the third dimension in history. And as a matter of fact Carlyle was not inaccurate. Such mistakes as he made were due solely to the poverty of the documents at his disposal. Carelessness or "subjectivity" in dealing with events of this importance would, by such a mind, have been felt as a betrayal of conscience or God. This revelation of the depth and mystery of human existence is not attained through the indulgence of subjective whims and artistic licences. On the contrary, it is the product of an unwavering loyalty to the truth. As Tillich has observed, it is only "when methodical severity combines with pure devotion to matter that the understanding of the past becomes a living, creative deed, re-creating the past—an achievement of great historians."

Such an achievement was possible to Carlyle because the French Revolution had become a crucial part of his experience, which he was driven to comprehend. Had he been born in any other generation than the Romantic it is possible that he would have been within reach of a far greater number of documents, and have produced a far more accurate chronicle of events, but it is doubtful whether he could so have transmuted them. In this connection it is interesting to contrast him with Gibbon. Gibbon's *Decline and Fall* stands in the same relation to Carlyle's *French Revolution* as Goldsmith's *Deserted Village* does to Wordsworth's *Leech-Gatherer*. Gibbon and Goldsmith stand apart from their material; Carlyle and Wordsworth are united with it. We might say that Carlyle had achieved a conscious reintegration into history analogous to Wordsworth's conscious reintegration into nature.

In common with the other Romantics, Carlyle has fallen into disfavour of late years. He is little read. As Havelock Ellis once remarked in *The Adelphi*, "we recognise his right to a pedestal, and there leave him". But it is doubtful whether this neglect can last much longer. Now that we are faced, for the first time since he wrote his history, with catastrophes on a scale commensurate with those of 1789-1815, we find ourselves turning instinctively, in our effort to comprehend them, to the works of one who was in a very real sense the consciousness of the French Revolution. The crises and catastrophes of the last three decades in Europe are, indeed, still too near for us to attain anything like the same finality as made his epic possible. But some sense of a meaning, some detachment, we must reach, or else be abandoned helplessly and hopelessly to the flux of events. Carlyle can once again speak to us as he spoke to those who had grown up with him through the *Stürm und Drang* of the Napoleonic wars.

What was the meaning that Carlyle discerned in the French Revolution? A meaning not easily to be defined. He saw in it an apocalypse within history, a judgment passed by society upon itself—and Berdyaev rightly numbers him among the prophets. The Revolution demonstrated, on an all but cosmic scale, that "a Lie cannot endure forever"; it was "the explosive confused return of Mankind to Reality and Fact, now that they were perishing of Semblance and Sham". But, more subtly than that, it demonstrated that the True is indestructible. "Alas, does it not still sound strange to many of us, the assertion that there *is* a God's-truth in the business of God-created men; that all is not a kind of grimace, an 'expediency', diplomacy, one knows not what?"

The prophetic spirit in Carlyle reached out to that same spirit in Mirabeau, the first Hero of the Revolution. For Mirabeau had perceived long before 1789 the falsity of the State to which he belonged: a State no longer true either to the material or spiritual desires of the people. That it was no longer true to their material desires was manifest for all who had eyes to see in the universal starvation of the peasantry, their repressed fury and indignation. But very few had the eyes to see—"the true man is needed to discern even practical truth"—and he had been almost alone in feeling the tremors of the oncoming earthquake that was to engulf monarchy, aristocracy, and a decaying feudalism together. The effort to which he devoted all his powers, the superhuman effort which eventually killed him, was to arrest decay at the eleventh hour: so to harness the pressure from below as to revolutionise the State in time to avert catastrophe. "Had Mirabeau lived, the History of France and of the World had been different."

So at least Carlyle believed, and he cannot easily be refuted. It is impossible to prove that Mirabeau's struggle was foredoomed to failure. Cromwell (and Cæsar before him) had succeeded through no less a crisis in keeping the forces of anarchy in check: using them just so far as they served his purpose, never allowing them to get the upper hand; so that, even to-day, it is possible for historians to deny that the Great Rebellion was a revolution at all, or Cromwell a revolutionary. And assuredly if we equate revolution with the uncontrolled, volcanic outburst of anarchy, then there was no such thing in England: moreover, the whole effort of every great revolutionary is to prevent revolution.

But Mirabeau died before he could fulfil his purpose, and there was none to succeed him. The Girondins had no sense of the forces at work—"They and their Formula are incompatible with the Reality; and, in its dark wrath, the Reality will extinguish it and them". And Danton, "Mirabeau of the Sansculottes," though he had such a sense, and strove manfully to give an order to chaos, did really come on the scene too late, when the insurrection had gone too far to do other than burn itself out. The breaking of Mirabeau's bust in the Jacobin's Church and the ejection of his remains from the Pantheon, to make room for Marat's, were symbolic. Mirabeau's death cleared the way for the emergence of a different kind of revolutionary altogether, of whom Marat and Robespierre are the archetypes: men born not to harness and check the ambitions of the mob, but to spur them and whip them on, and be carried by them to the supreme positions of power.

For this sort of revolutionary Carlyle had the utmost loathing: "The man had a heart-hatred of anarchy", as he once remarked of Napoleon. Not that he could not sympathise with it; he could, and did. He himself had witnessed at close quarters the deprivation of the Scottish proletariat during the Peterloo period, and shared their indignation; he had even succumbed (like Wordsworth and Shelley) to the materialism of Hume and Voltaire. Indignation of this violent sort was, he felt, itself a kind of assertion of Reality, a swallowing of formulas. (The comparative dullness of Volume II of the *French Revolution*, "The Constitution", as contrasted with Volume I, "The Bastille", and Volume III, "The Guillotine", can be attributed to the fact that Carlyle was not interested in constitutions that were merely formulas; they did not deserve "that loving minuteness a Menadic Insurrection did".) But there was not implied in this, as there was in the direct perception of Mirabeau, any corresponding affirmation of the Truth. It was a Negation pure and simple.

The proof of this is in the ideology with which it clothed itself. Jacobinism proclaimed openly as its principles those very ones by which its opponents had lived surreptitiously. It enthroned the Goddess of Reason, and declared that expediency was the only morality. In somewhat the same way, a century later, Marx-Leninism was to expose the sham religion of the bourgeoisie, and then, instead of going on to enunciate a true religion in its stead, proclaim the motives that had actually governed the bourgeoisie—class-interest and the pursuit of material wealth—to be the sole motives of human endeavour. Again, in Hitlerism we see the Christian piety and international law professed by the democracies rudely exposed, and the principle of power-politics, to which they had always done obeisance, adopted openly as the be-all and end-all of statesmanship. The pseudo-sciences of historical materialism and racialism are the precise analogues of that eighteenth-century rationalism which found itself in such strange, and yet inevitable, alliance with the blind irrationality of the French masses.

Thus the French Revolution—in so far as we mean by that the insurrection culminating in the Jacobin dictatorship and Terror—was truly the nemesis of a corrupt society; and once it had taken place there could be no going back upon it. But neither could it endure. Inasmuch as it was a manifestation of envy and revenge alone, the Revolution was bound to "devour its children": for envy cannot abide an equal. A struggle for power between the leaders of such a movement is inevitable. We have seen the classic struggle between the Jacobins, ending in the brief dictatorship of Robespierre—"incorruptible Robespierre, most consistent, incorruptible of thin acrid men"—re-enacted in our own day among the Bolshevik and Nazi leaders. It was useless for Lenin to warn his followers against the example of the Jacobins; a movement that has risen to power by out-hating the haters must, sooner or later, destroy itself. Stalin's "purges" and Hitler's are expressions of the innermost nature of Bolshevism and Nazism.

No enduring order of society can be founded upon the principle of self-interest, whether that principle be hidden or avowed: that is the first lesson of the Revolution. And the second is like unto it: that an enduring order can only be based upon justice, if not upon love itself. Even the satisfaction of the material desires of a people depends, in the long run, upon the satisfaction of its spiritual desires. There was but one way forward for France in 1795: it lay through the proclamation of a new principle altogether, transcending self-interest, and its embodiment in a new social order. That was the work of Napoleon, the third Hero of the Revolution. Napoleon united behind him all the disinterested elements of the French nation, all those who, when they had cried "Liberty!" had meant liberty for others as well as for themselves. The very detachment that had enabled him to see as they actually were the forces at work in the Revolution, and so to handle them, compelled him also to fashion society in the interest of detachment—the source of all the virtues. Hence the profound truth of Carlyle's conclusion, given in *Heroes and Hero-Worship*, that "What Napoleon *did* will in the long run amount to what he did *justly*; what Nature with her laws will sanction. To what of reality was in him; to that and nothing more". Truly, there is a God's-truth in the business of God-created men.

II

The Russian poet Tiutchev said of Napoleon that he carried the French Revolution within himself. The same is true of Carlyle. Carlyle was conscious in his own nature of all the passions that had gone to make up the phases of the Revolution. He knew from experience both the blind rebellion and antithetical rationalism of the Jacobins; he knew also the imagination that could comprehend and overcome them. *The French Revolution* is a product of this imagination, as the *Code Napoleon* had been. Both are manifestations of "post-revolutionary activity."[2]

Carlyle's victory over the Jacobin in himself was not, however, final—any more than Napoleon's had been. Just as battle and ambition betrayed Napoleon at the last, so, in Carlyle, the insurrectionary fervour of the rebel wages a constant guerilla warfare with the controlling imagination. It bursts forth in odd places in his work; in his dithyrambs to Cromwell, for example, upon the massacres in Ireland.

And again and again, in *The French Revolution*, we hear this volcanic voice of instinct challenging the supremacy of imagination—"where Force is not yet distinguished into Bidden and Forbidden, but Crime and Virtue welter unseparated,—in that domain of what is called the Passions."

It reminds us of Milton's unconscious identification with Satan; still more of Shelley's sympathy with the rebellious Titan of the *Prometheus Solutus*, whom he compared to Satan, and whom he resurrected, as Blake did the hero of *Paradise Lost*, in order that he should repent of his rebellion, forgive the God of Reason, and be reborn in the imagination. That rebirth is implicit in *The French Revolution*, as it is in *Prometheus Unbound*—but it is also precarious. So precarious that many a reader, from Wordsworth onwards, has gone away with the impression that the author was "of the Devil's party"—an advocate of insurrection—notwithstanding that the whole moral of his work is directed against it. For *The French Revolution* has a moral. It is stated at the end: "That there be no second Sansculottism in our Earth for a thousand years, let us understand well what the first was; and let Rich and Poor of us go and do *otherwise*."

It is not for nothing that Carlyle is charged with proclaiming Might as Right, although his real contention was that Right is Might. Nevertheless, his instinctive sympathy with the destructive forces of the Revolution was as much a strength as a weakness, in him: since no man knows better the flimsiness of the barrier dividing humanity from bestiality than he who is conscious of it in himself. Carlyle was fearfully conscious of it. In *himself* was the origin of iconoclasm and Terror: he bore his part in the general guilt. Of all the Romantics he was the most deeply convinced of the reality of Original Sin. Humanity, in his eyes, was forever playing on the brink of an abyss, into which it might at any moment be plunged—and the spectacle terrified him. That premonition of impending disaster which is so characteristic of the great Victorians reaches a crescendo in Carlyle. His whole life was devoted to averting it.

The French Revolution was one effort directed to that end. *Past and Present* was another. *Past and Present* is an elaboration of the moral of *The French Revolution*. It is a strange, repetitive, phantasmagoric indictment of the Shams and Semblances of nineteenth century England: in which Formula and Reality had again parted company—the Formulæ of Progress and *Laissez-faire*; the Reality of "over-production" and a destitute army of unemployed. Remarkable indeed that Carlyle should, more than a hundred years ago, have seized on the phenomenon of mass-unemployment as the outward, most visible sign of the falsity of capitalist society, and the instrument by which that society would destroy itself!

For such a society, history had taught him, could not endure. Founded upon self-interest openly proclaimed, either it would be revolutionised consciously and peacefully, or it would revolutionise itself, unconsciously and catastrophically. "Our England, our world cannot live as it is. It will connect itself with God again, or go down with nameless throes and fire-consummation to the Devils." He had no patience with the cant of "prosperity." Prosperity there would be, with the abolition of Corn Laws and the expansion of commerce—but it would be a respite only; a precious respite, to be used for the peaceable, or else to end still in the violent, revolution of society. "With our present system of individual Mammonism and Government by *Laissez-faire*, this Nation cannot live. And if, in the priceless interim, some new life and healing be not found, there is no second respite to be counted on."

But new life and healing depended upon the creation of a new Aristocracy; and that, in its turn, upon the general acceptance of a new morality, vitally different from the morality of capitalist democracy. A new Aristocracy, Carlyle said, would be "a real Priesthood." It would need to know that "Judgment for an evil thing is many times delayed some day or two, some century or two, but it is sure as life, it is sure as death! In the centre of the world-whirlwind, verily now as in the oldest days, dwells and speaks a God. The great soul of the world is *just*." It would need to know that only a just society can endure, and dedicate itself to the securing of justice. And not only would the Aristocracy have to adopt a morality other than self-interest; the people would have to do so also: otherwise such an Aristocracy would never get itself appointed. It needs a kind of heroism even to recognise the Hero.

Without this new morality, neither democratic nor any other forms of appointment would avail men anything. Carlyle's judgment on democracy as he knew it was severe. He recognised a new assertion of the validity of the individual, upon which there could be no going back; but ninety per cent. of it seemed to him a mere negation—of the false aristocracies that had preceded it. It meant "despair of finding any Heroes to govern you, and contented putting up with the want of them." Yet if the French Revolution had proved anything it was this: "That False Aristocracies are insupportable; that No-Aristocracies, Liberty-and-Equalities are impossible; that true Aristocracies are at once indispensable and not easily attained." To the individualistic anarchy of England he preferred the ordered despotism of Prussia. But what he really desired, most deeply of all, was something analogous to the "organic society" of the Middle Ages, so wonderfully, and wistfully portrayed in *Past and Present*.

In the last resort, as he knew, that depended upon a re-birth of religion—and of this he had little enough hope. Between the individualistic Nonconformity of England and the hollow semblance of contemporary Catholicism he could make no choice. Both were incapable of saving society. And if society were not saved, it would inevitably be damned: there was no half-way house between Heaven and Hell. He passed his latter years in complete despair.

For Carlyle was more realistic than Marx; he never succumbed to Messianism. And it is utterly untrue to say that Marx's historical materialism has discredited or superseded the "Great Man theory of history." These do not contradict, but complement one another. More, as they are popularly understood, they are false without one another. Historical materialism is false, if it postulates creative revolution without creative revolutionaries; and the Great Man theory is false if it presupposes the Hero's independence of historical Fate. But Carlyle himself did not presuppose that. Indeed, he did not believe that convulsions could be avoided: history was never more than partially willed. At most they could be tempered, made creative as well as destructive, by the agency of a prophet bidding Repent!—

> "Imminent perdition is not usually driven away by words of warning. Didactic Destiny has other methods in store; or these would fail always. Such words should, nevertheless, be uttered, when they dwell truly in the soul of any man. Words are hard, importunate; but how much harder the importunate events they foreshadow! Here and there a human soul may listen to the words—who knows how many human souls?—whereby the importunate events, if not diverted and prevented, will be rendered *less* hard."

It is only destructive revolution that is inevitable, and it is not inevitable at all. It can be prevented, or mitigated—by creative revolution. Grasp the distinction, and many things become clear: not least the final incompatibility of Danton and Robespierre, Socialism and Communism, Pacifism and super-national Nazism.

Unhappily, not many human souls did listen to Carlyle, preaching the necessity of an organic society in the hey-day of competitive capitalism; of "loving the best men best," when individualistic democracy was triumphant; of a re-birth of communal religion, to an audience of vigorous Non-conformists. Superficial honours were heaped upon him; his message was forgotten or derided. In so far as it had any influence, it was upon the Christian Socialism of Keir Hardie (*Sartor Resartus* was among Hardie's earliest reading)—and that failed. Re-born in the Christian Pacifism of Canon Sheppard, it failed again: and now "the unemployed nation of Europe" has taken history into its own hands. Mirabeau dead, Robespierre enjoys his brief supremacy; the Continent waits for its Napoleon. And yet, the proclamation of a new principle transcending self-interest, that re-birth of religion for which Carlyle longed, seems as remote as ever. "On the one side is dreary Cant, with a *reminiscence* of things noble and divine; on the other is but acrid Candour, with a *prophecy* of things brutal, infernal."

"His boding prophecies," announces Mr. H. D. Traill in the introduction to a centenary edition of *Past and Present* lying beside me, "are marred for us to-day by an ever-present consciousness of their subsequent falsification."

"A God's-message," exclaims Carlyle himself, a few pages further on: "A God's-message never came to thicker-skinned people; never had a God's-message to pierce through thicker integuments, into heavier ears."

NOTES

[1] Wordsworth, it will be remembered, greeted Carlyle's History with the indignant sonnet beginning:

> "Portentous change when History can appear
> As the cool Advocate of foul device . . ."

[2] To the same order he himself ascribed the work of those German Romantics with whom he felt so close an affinity; in whose passage beyond the *Stürm und Drang* phase of their own development he had, in fact, "found himself": "A French Revolution is one phenomenon; as complement and spiritual exponent thereof, a poet Goethe and German literature is to me another" (*Past and Present*).

"Carlyle's Method of History in *The French Revolution*"

THE CARLYLE SOCIETY OCCASIONAL PAPERS

9 (1982-83).

DAVID R. SORENSEN

[Revised for its republication in this volume.]

My objective in this essay is to outline the development of Carlyle's theory of history prior to the composition of *The French Revolution*, and to illustrate his method in several extracts from the great "Epos."

In speaking of Carlyle's "theory" of history, I use the word with great caution. He never conceived a coherent, systematic or consistent conception of history. On the contrary, it became part of his credo that a man's tendency to theorize was a symptom of his intellectual self-delusion and enchantment.[1] As he pointed out in a letter to John Stuart Mill in 1833, "A man's theory is valuable simply as it facilitates his practice; neither is there any other way of correcting it where wrong but by practice alone; for indeed till we have *tried* and *done*, we can never know what power there lies in us to do" (*CL* 6:412).

Carlyle's method of history is a spontaneous, intuitive, and slightly ramshackle arrangement designed to accommodate irresolvable contradictions in his "theory" of the past. It is a strategy of reconciliation between two versions of history—the Calvinist and the German Transcendentalist.[2] It is a thorny problem trying to determine the extent of the Calvinist influence on Carlyle's view of history.[3] There is little firm evidence to show that his historical viewpoint was affected by the creed of his parents, and any attempt to establish a link between Calvinism and his method of history must take this fact into account.

However, from a reading of the 1832 section of the *Reminiscences* it is clear that Carlyle had absorbed a vaguely Calvinist sense of history in his youth, and that this sense had lingered on in his mind long after he had rejected the theology of the creed. James Carlyle possessed an acute Calvinist grasp of history. In his 1832 memoir, his son remembers his father being "arrested strongly" by the political upheaval at home and abroad:

> I have heard him say in late years with an impressiveness which all his perceptions carried with them, that the lot of the poor man was growing worse and worse; that the world would not and could not last as it was; that mighty changes of which none saw the end were on the way. (*Reminiscences* 1:48)

James Carlyle's apocalyptic anxieties were balanced with the conviction that he was heading, in spite of this chaos, towards "'a city that had foundations.'" In another passage vividly assesses his father's psychological state. "Man's face he did not fear;" he remarks, "God he always feared; his Reverence, I think, was considerably mixed with fear: Yet not slavish Fear, rather Awe, as of unutterable Depths of Silence through which flickered a trembling Hope" (*Reminiscences* 1:10).

Fear, awe, reverence, trembling hope, silence—these are the characteristic attitudes of the Calvinist to history, which is the unfolding of God's will. The paradox of the Calvinist sense of history is that man's fate rests in God's hands, but that man finds the divine plan quite opaque. To James Carlyle, history in one moment seems to be a steady process of deterioration and decay, full of discord and turmoil, made tolerable only by the promise of imminent intervention by God. In another moment he speaks of history as an analogue of his own spiritual progress, a gradual movement of mankind towards the heavenly kingdom.

This conflict between an apocalyptic and organic vision of the past is apparent in Calvin's own writing. He recognizes that all men are subject to periods of doubt and despair. As he asserts in his *Institutes of the Christian Religion* (1536), history in these periods resembles a "storm." Man is unable to penetrate the "dark mist" of his own doubt in order to gaze at the "same quiet serenity" (*Institutes* 1.7.1). But even in moments of spiritual peace, man discovers that a transcendent view of this "serenity" is unattainable. He is unable to gain anything more than a faint flicker of hope from the study of history.

Calvin counsels in his commentary on Matthew, "As the kingdom of God is continually growing and advancing to the end of the world, we must pray every day that it may come; for to whatever extent iniquity abounds in the world, to such an extent the kingdom of God, which brings along with it perfect righteousness, is not yet come" (*Comm. Matt.* 6:10). However, this prophecy of organic, gradual spiritual evolution is undercut by Calvin's harsh notion of "polluted" human nature. Men are incapable of overcoming evil by their own will. Furthermore, Calvin contradicts his own advice to them to perform their duty by admitting that individual exertion makes no difference to the outcome of history. In A. M. Hunter's words, Calvin is faced with the "insoluble antimony that all depends upon God and yet that much seems to depend on man" (135).

This "antimony" is apparent in Calvin's twofold representation of experience. In the organic scheme, history is shown to repeat itself. In the apocalyptic scheme, history is a process of deterioration, during which every moment is pregnant with the threat of the last fiery judgment. But, Calvin is not perturbed by the discrepancy between these two theories. "It tends greatly to lighten grief," he observed in his *Commentary on Psalms* (1557), "to consider that nothing befalls us at this day which the Church of God has not experienced in the days of old; yea, rather that we are just called to engage in the same conflicts with which David and the other holy patriarchs were engaged" (*Comm. Psalms* 9).

Calvin is especially drawn to the Old Testament because of its portrait of men acting in a specific historical setting. God can be understood through history. The Covenant imposes a dialectic shape and unity on the past, and gives it purpose and direction. But how can the Covenant cycle of belief and unbelief be resolved? Faced with such confusion, Calvin invariably replies, "To the great truths, what God is in himself, and what he is in relation to us, human reason makes not the least approach" (*Institutes* 2.2.18).

James Carlyle resorts to a similar explanation of God's inscrutability when he attempts to explain the dire events of his time. Is the social ferment in Scotland and England a repetition of the French Revolution, or is it a unique phenomenon, heralding the Apocalypse? Unable to read the divine purport of these signs, he lives in a state of nervous anticipation while he waits for the moment of release from the nightmare of history.

Thomas Carlyle could never accept this Calvinist paradox. Ironically, his father's frequent advice to him to seek for evidence of God's ways in experience led the young man to question the fundamental principles of Christianity. Carlyle was a voracious reader in all subjects, and he enjoyed challenging orthodox opinion. When he was fifteen he shocked his mother by asking, "Did God Almighty come down and make wheelbarrows in a shop?" (Allingham 253).

The Edinburgh student was disciplined by his early interest in mathematics to think logically and concisely, and was impatient with nebulous definition. When he measured Calvinist theology by empirical standards, it fragmented into contradictory pieces. He read Hume and Gibbon, who demonstrated to him that Christianity rested on false historical grounds. Miracles were contrary to the laws of nature. To counter their influence, Carlyle studied the arguments of Paley and Campbell, in the hope that he might find some firm proof that the Bible was, as his parents claimed, a narrative of true events.

He remained unconvinced and drifted gradually away from both the creed and the religious community to which his parents belonged. Empirical pursuits provided him with only a temporary haven from doubt. An abyss soon opened in his mind between the certainty of science and the uncertainty of experience. Carlyle's confidence in empiricism evaporated after he applied it to moral questions. By 1818 he found himself wandering in a spiritual and intellectual wilderness, where the cry of the "Everlasting No" resounded.

He still wanted to believe that the universe was a divine manifestation, but he rejected the fatalistic scheme of history implied in Calvinist theology. What he retained was a pale replica of the creed in his conviction that nature and history were divine emblems. Carlyle was searching for a philosophy that would recognize the symbolic nature of the universe, but give man a greater role in determining the shape and meaning of history. He found such a faith in the writings of the German Transcendentalists, and especially in the work of Goethe.

Carlyle told William Allingham in 1877 that it was Goethe who had rescued him from the wilderness, and taught him "'that the true things in Christianity survived and were eternally true'" (253). In Goethe's writings Carlyle discovered a philosophy that cleansed history of fatalism, recognized its spiritual essence and gave man a dynamic role in the shaping of his fate. Goethe rejected any rigid scheme of predestination, and saw the past as a wondrous poem, in which mankind progressed gradually over an Infinite period of time to a communion with its common progenitor. Goethe regarded history as a comprehensible mystery. Intuitively and emphatically, an individual could penetrate "'the open secret'" of the universe and learn to see the past and future weaving themselves in the present in what Carlyle calls a "'conflux of eternities'" ("Death of Goethe," *CW* 27:377; *French Revolution*, *CW* 2:9).

Faust's vision of the "whole" symbolizes Goethe's view of history:

> How it all lives and moves and weaves
> Into a whole! Each part gives and receives,
> Angelic powers ascend and redescend
> And each to each their golden vessels lend;
> Fragrant with blessing, as on wings
> From heaven through the earth and through all things
> Their movement thrusts, and all in harmony it sings!
> How great a spectacle! But that, I fear,
> Is all it is. Oh, endless Nature, where
> Shall I embrace you? (*Faust* 4:447-54)

Faust's question echoes in the hearts of all people, but Goethe assures them that history moves in the direction of collective enlightenment. The solution to the chaos and discord of experience lies in individual self-reform. Man is capable of advancing the moment of communion by cultivating higher forms of spiritual wisdom. The poet, as teacher and prophet, has an important role to play in firing men's hearts with faith in themselves and in the divine meaning of history.

Goethe's philosophy answered to Carlyle's deepest yearnings. The German sage united empirical and intuitive modes of perception in one comprehensive poetic vision. He sought to convey an impression of the glorious "Ideal" that was dormant in the "Actual" world. Goethe's poetic vision was based on the observation of fact, and to Carlyle, it threw fresh light on the confusing spectacle of history. Free of messianic anxiety, Goethe's view of the past encouraged veneration for the miracle of human endeavor.

In a review of *Faust* in 1822, Carlyle refers to the symbolic aspect of the drama and conceives it as a representation of world-history. Calvinist influences continue to dwell in Carlyle's mind, and are apparent in his condemnation of Faust's "criminality." He blames Goethe's protagonist for seeking to "reach beyond the boundaries wherewith nature had circumscribed them . . . until his mind doubted the existence of Providence" (*Collectanea* 89-90).

By 1827 the predominance of the Goethean philosophy is discernible in Carlyle's revised interpretation of Faust's quest. He praises the Doctor for his heroic initiative, emphasizes its world-historical dimension, and predicts that the journey will end not in a fiery inferno, but in a "better Knowledge" of experience ("Goethe's Helena," *CW* 26:162). Later he applies the Goethean prognosis in his essay "Signs of the Times" (1829). The progressive, organic pattern of experience is visible even in "the age of Machinery," and Carlyle is modestly confident that "a new and brighter spiritual era was evolving itself for all men" (*CW* 27:81).

In the same essay he refers to the French Revolution as one consequence of a transcendent movement that is not yet complete. The pursuit of political freedom is a transitory stage in human development. Carlyle believes that human beings can break the mechanic yoke, ascend to higher plateaus of vision and change the course of history. What they must realize are their latent "Dynamic" powers. The solution to the recurrent crises in history lies in individual rather than social or political reform.

"Signs of the Times" marks the apotheosis of the Goethean influence on Carlyle. During this period he turns his attention to the life and writings of Luther. In 1828 he even refers to Goethe as the natural successor to the great reformer. "Be it for good or evil," he notes, "there is certainly no German, since the days of Luther, whose life can occupy so large a space in the intellectual history of that people." ("Goethe," *CW* 26:203). Luther's character seems to Carlyle to be "the most worth discussing of all modern men's." He possesses "the soul at once of a Conqueror and a Poet" (*Two Note Books* 151).

Gradually, Carlyle's interest in Luther prompts him to re-evaluate Goethe. More significantly, Carlyle begins to question Goethe's devotion to poetry rather than history. The German sage reveres "facts" that are too nebulous and tentative. Carlyle prefers Luther's fierce, unshakeable faith in God's might to Goethe's aesthetic musings, but he is careful to avoid criticism of the Weimar prophet:

> What is Poetry? Do I really love Poetry? I sometimes fancy almost not. The jingle of maudlin persons, with their mere (even genuine) "sensibility" is unspeakably fatiguing to me. My greatly most delightful reading is, where some Goethe musically teaches me. Nay, any fact, relating especially to man, is still valuable and pleasing. (*Two Note Books* 151)

Luther awakened Carlyle's "Calvinist" sense of history, but other factors contributed to its revival in his mind. Popular agitations in England and Europe intrigued and frightened him. It seemed to him that corrupt rulers were being punished by a wrathful God. Froude noticed this line of interpretation in Carlyle's essay on Voltaire (1829). In the essay he regards the French Revolution "as an illustration of his conviction that untruthfulness and injustice were as surely followed by divine revelation as the idolatries and tyrannies of Biblical Egypt and Assyria; that the Power which men professed of Sundays to believe in was a living Power, the most real, the most tremendous of all facts" (*Life* 2:52).

Carlyle judged the French Revolution in the framework of the Old Testament Covenant pattern of history. Israel repeatedly disobeyed the laws of God and was caught in a cycle of rejection, renewal and restoration. The prophetic vision of the apocalypse brought this cycle to an end, and presented the prospect of a last judgment and eternal renewal. Carlyle's Hebraic interpretation of the French Revolution conflicted with the view he had advanced earlier, that the Revolution was a transitional phase in humanity's spiritual development. His apocalyptic viewpoint fitted awkwardly with his Goethean organic perspective.

Ironically, Carlyle was re-living the Calvinist paradox that had tormented his father, but he faced the additional burden of having to reconcile the old theology with a new philosophy. He wanted to believe with Goethe that people were responsible for directing the course of history, but his Calvinist instinct made him suspicious of their efforts to reform themselves. He rejected determinism in one instance, while he endorsed it in another. To the Calvinist the plan of history was murky, but to the Transcendentalist, mystical forms of cognition could reveal the "'open secret'" of the universe.

In 1830 Carlyle elaborated his philosophy of history in the essay "On History," perhaps in the hope that he might solve the riddle in his outlook. He did not achieve a reconciliation, but he did outline a method that served to accommodate the two conflicting versions of history. In the scheme that he advanced, history was both unique and recurrent, unknowable and knowable, predetermined and indeterminate, apocalyptic and organic, and linear and cyclical. This strategy enabled him to attack rival schools of historiography without having to clarify his own position. For example, he chided the Whigs and Benthamites for assuming that history was a record of material progress, and argued that the past was a mysterious, incomprehensible phenomenon.

But Carlyle was too confident that history was indeterminate. When he discusses the probable direction that history might take, he ignores the fact that his own theory precludes such certainty. At one point in the essay he seems to suggest that history is, strictly speaking, an impossible task:

> Every single event is the offspring not of one, but of all other events, prior or contemporaneous, and will in its turn combine with all others to give birth to new: it is an ever-living, ever-working Chaos of Being, wherein shape after shape bodies itself forth from innumerable elements. And this Chaos, boundless as the habitation and duration of man, unfathomable as the soul and destiny of man, is what the historian will depict, and scientifically gauge, we may say, by threading it with single lines of a few ells in length. ("On History,"*CW* 27:88)

There is what Carlyle calls "a fatal discrepancy" between the historian's mode of perceiving events, and the occurrence of the events themselves. The historian seizes the facts, tries to interpret them, but they unravel into an indefinite which eludes definition. Only God possesses the omniscience to see the order that lies concealed behind the mask of chaos. History is his creation, his "Prophetic Manuscript," the pages of which are beyond the sight of mortals.

Elsewhere, Carlyle implies that this "Manuscript" can be glimpsed at, if the historian is imbued with sufficient belief. The strength of his faith in God is of more importance than the accuracy of his research, because ultimately, all history is a divine fiction. Every fact is a symbol of the whole creation. History is a matter of arranging events into what Carlyle calls "fictions of belief," patterns that correspond to God's own "Prophetic Manuscript," the archetype of which is the Bible.

The *"truest* of all Books" (*Shooting Niagara, CW* 30:25) contains a symbolic plan of history, and this plan is rehearsed in pagan literature and re-enacted in the present. Mythology is elevated to the status of history in Carlyle's theory. As his fictitious philosopher Sauerteig exclaims in "Biography" (1832), "'All Mythologies were once Philosophies; were believed; the Epic poems of old time, so long as they continued epic, and had any complete impressiveness, were Histories, and understood to be narratives of facts" (*CW* 28:49). Therefore history itself is a debased form of epic. The original "musical" unity of epic poetry has been broken by the collapse of belief, and the result is a "mechanical" division of history into various categories—ecclesiastical, constitutional, economical, philosophical and literary.

In "On History" Carlyle points out the weaknesses of these artificial distinctions. His ideal is a "Whole" representation, that unites the disparate branches of investigation. He sketches a working plan for himself in his proposal for a "proper History of Poetry":

> He who should write a proper History of Poetry, would depict for us the successive Revelations which man had obtained of the Spirit of Nature; under what aspects he had caught and endeavoured to body forth some glimpse of that unspeakable Beauty, which in its highest clearness is Religion, is the inspiration of a Prophet, yet in one or the other degree must inspire every true Singer, were his theme never so humble. We should see by what steps men had ascended to the Temple; how near they had approached; by what ill hap they had, for long periods, turned away from it, and grovelled on . . . other heights. (*CW* 27:94)

Carlyle describes a model of his own future method of history. As a historican, he would assume a prophetic role. His aim would be to return the craft to its original state of song by persuading his readers to believe the divine nature of "Fact." To achieve this goal, he effects a compromise between an organic and apocalyptic version of history in the awkward equation, "successive Revelations." The word "successive" suggests, among other things, a progressive, recurrent, organic view of history. Conversely, "Revelation" implies sudden intervention. The Goethean quest for transcendence is evoked in the humanity ascending the steps to the "Temple." The Calvinist sense is suggested in the image of inferior mortals groveling on "other heights."

These strains in Carlyle's viewpoint were intensified as a consequence of personal tragedy—the death of his sister in 1830 and father in 1832. Gradually, the balance in his "theory" began to tilt in the direction of Calvinism. In 1832 he paid tribute to his father in the *Reminiscences*. With a mixture of sadness and regret, Carlyle compared the world of his father to his own. The simple, rugged philosophy of the Ecclefechan Seceders seemed morally and spiritually superior to the

Utilitarian "isms" of the modern world. The "grand old Theorem" (*Reminiscences* 1:6) of the Puritans was perhaps too narrow, Carlyle admitted, but it was a surer source of stability and truth than any "mythos" that replaced it.

A year after he wrote this tribute, he was engaged in two separate projects—histories of the French Revolution and the Scottish Reformation. The two episodes were closely linked in his imagination. In the early months of 1833, he reports to John Stuart Mill, "My Scotch Church History studies have also advanced a little; strangely blended with these French Antichurch ones; with which however they are not so incongruous as might seem" (*CL* 6:303).

Carlyle eventually chose the French Revolution, but his treatment of the subject was influenced partly by his reading of Scottish literature, particularly John Knox's *History of the Reformation* (1566). He was at once frightened and intrigued by the Revolution. Was this startling event merely a phase, or was it a sign of imminent catastrophe? He had ridiculed apocalyptic fantasies in "Signs of the Times" and distanced himself from Edward Irving's prophecies of doom. But during the eighteen-thirties, he began to express concern that another version of the French Revolution would occur on English soil.

Moved by Knox's conception of revolt in his *History*, Carlyle believed that the French Revolution was God's judgment against the irresponsible *ancien régime*, which had misgoverned and abused their privileges for three centuries.[4] The French people, like ordinary people everywhere, possessed a dim insight into the eternal laws of God. They knew that their governors had transgressed these laws and forsaken their duties. Their physical hunger aptly symbolized the spiritual starvation of France itself.

Courageously, the masses rose against their oppressors in the cause of truth. However, their lack of a positive religious creed—the legacy of their irresponsible governors—led them to replace one set of false formulas with another. Knox had insisted that the object of any revolt was to restore the reign of God on earth, but he remained vague about the precise political realization of this goal.[5] Carlyle was similarly indefinite. He sympathized with the French Revolutionaries until they achieved power. As governors, they repeated the sins of their predecessors and glorified themselves rather than God. They committed the primal sin of Adam and reaped the harvest of their pride.

Carlyle adroitly meshed this "Calvinist" reading of the Revolution with a Transcendentalist one. In the Goethean vision, the Revolution was judged in the context of a timeless organic process. It was a natural disaster—akin to a flood or earthquake—and was both necessary and constructive. From this perspective, there was nothing unprecedented about the event. It was a repetition of countless other attempts by mortals to ascend too quickly to the supreme "Temple" of wisdom.

Carlyle's method in *The French Revolution* accommodates the Calvinist-apocalyptic and Transcendentalist-organic schemes, but it does not reconcile them. His desire to play the role of Biblical prophet is contradicted by his frequent assertions that history is a mysterious, barely comprehensible process. Carlyle traps himself in his own contradictions, but refuses to acknowledge his predicament. Initially, he had rejected the Calvinist scheme of predestination because it was too schematic and inhumane. In Goethe he discovered a philosophy that gave human beings a primary role in forging their destiny. The individual was united to the historical process through the act of self-cultivation. Carlyle eventually grew impatient with this nebulous version of change, and he demanded a clearer and more definite knowledge of the plot of history. By the logic of his own "theory," he was obliged to assume a more active part in fathoming the mystery of God's ways.

Carlyle played the role of prophet partly because he was frightened by the "burden" of history.[6] By treating it as a series of "successive Revelations," he mitigated his own anxieties about the inscrutable, terrifying spectacle of human affairs. He was somewhat reluctant to admit the possibility of irreversible change, yet he was restless with a melioristic view of reality. The prophetic posture simultaneously allowed him to threaten others with the prospect of the end while it assured him that the end was not in sight. His method of history also enabled him to disguise his uncertainty about the "condition of England" question. He did not necessarily want a French Revolution in England, but he enjoyed threatening his audience with the prospect of violent confrontation.

His confusion is mirrored in his summary of the causes of the Revolution in Book VI of his epic. Carlyle begins by acknowledging the difficulty of arriving at a coherent assessment of the event. He coyly concedes that the ultimate meaning of it might "depend on definition more or less arbitrary." Several paragraphs later he provides an explanation that is anything but "arbitrary":

> ... French Revolution means ... the open violent Rebellion, and Victory, of disimprisoned Anarchy against corrupt worn-out Authority: how Anarchy breaks prison; bursts-up from the infinite Deep, and rages uncontrollable, immeasurable, enveloping a world; in phasis after phasis of fever-frenzy;—till the frenzy burning itself out, and what elements of new Order it held (since all Force holds such) developing themselves, the Uncontrollable be got, if not reimprisoned, yet harnessed, and its mad forces made to work towards their object as sane regulated ones. For as Hierarchies and Dynasties of all kinds, Theocracies, Aristocracies, Autocracies, Strumpetocracies, have ruled over the world; so it was appointed, in the decrees of Providence, that this same Victorious Anarchy, Jacobinism, Sansculottism, French Revolution, Horrors of the French Revolution, or what else mortals name it, should have its turn. The "destructive wrath" of Sansculottism: this is what we speak, having unhappily no voice for singing. (*CW* 1:211-12)

The passage at once defines and enacts Carlyle's confused philosophy of history. It is a reading from the "Prophetic Manuscript" of God, transmitted accurately by an inspired believer. The images of volcanic eruption, earthquake, whirlpool and whirlwind that are evoked in the rhythm and syntax serve a twin purpose: they give a very tactile impression of the chaos of history, and yet they suggest its continuity. These violent upheavals occur with regularity, "in phasis after phasis of fever-frenzy," and they belong to an eternal pattern of events. Carlyle can derive comfort from the realization that social and political upheaval imitates the cataclysms of nature.

Torn between giving human beings responsibility for history and attributing all change to God, Carlyle tries to steer a middle passage. Individuals are free in that they are given the choice of obeying or disobeying the will of the Creator. When they obey His laws, they live outside of history. But when they disobey, they fall back into the nightmare of chaos and disorder.

How can Carlyle prove that the French Revolution is simply another illustration of the Covenant cycle of belief and unbelief, or the organic unity of the world? His strategy is necessarily complex because his "search for authority" always yields elusive results.[7] In his epic every historical fact is treated as an efflorescence of a "whole," and corresponds to a Biblical archetype or a prefigurement of the archetype in pagan literature. Together with an assortment of scientific, naturalistic and musical analogues, these archetypes constitute the skeleton of Carlyle's representation.

He fleshes out the body of his narrative with material from his French sources that "coincides" in his imagination with the archetypal descriptions. Opaque facts are clarified to fit into the divine plan of history, so that the "whole" always remains partially visible. An "Epos" is built from the fragments of previous epics, the common theme of which is man's disobedience to God. Carlyle cannot "sing" this song because he lives in a doubting time. But he hopes that the poetic force of his epic will inspire his audience to re-create the conditions in which the first "songs" were believed.

One example from *The French Revolution* can be used to demonstrate Carlyle's method in practice. In the section on the "Insurrection of Women," Usher Maillard taps his drum to restore order among a group of frenzied "Menads," who are about to tear him apart. For Carlyle, his heroic behavior has a rich epic and prophetic lineage:

> O Maillard, when, since War first was, had General of Force such a task before him as thou this day? Walter the Penniless still touches the feeling heart: but then Walter had sanction; had space to turn in; and also his Crusaders were of the male sex. Thou, this day, disowned of heaven and earth, art General of the Menads. Their inarticulate frenzy thou must, on the spur of the instant, render into articulate words, into actions that are not frantic. Fail in it, this way or that! . . . Menads storm behind. If such hewed off the melodious head of Orpheus, and hurled it into the Peneus waters, what may they not make of thee,—thee rhythmic merely, with no music but a sheep-skin drum!— Maillard did not fail. Remarkable Maillard, if fame were not an accident, and History a distillation of Rumour, how remarkable wert thou! (*CW* 1:255-56)

Carlyle deviously defies the very tenets that are supposed to qualify Maillard's status as an epic hero, by praising the "Usher's" heroic feats and judging them in an epic context. If fame is an accident and history a "distillation of Rumour," then no fact can be believed. On the other hand, any fact can be used to represent historical truth and all facts are equally true. To paint Maillard as a descendant of Walter the

Penniless and Orpheus, Carlyle was obliged to twist his evidence and disregard conflicts of interpretation in his sources. Ironically, his text for the information about Maillard's life was the fiercely anti-republican *Dictionnaire . . . des hommes marquans* (1800). The author of the book Coiffier de Verseux refers to Maillard as "Cet homme sanguinaire" (2:466) and accuses him of cynically exploiting the women's rage for his own private gain. Carlyle found similar accounts in less biased sources, but he ignored them. That Maillard was a conniving murderer, or may have been, was irrelevant to his purpose here, which was an epic and prophetic one.

Carlyle ignores the conflicting evidence because it contradicts his own vision of the hero's divine function in history as the agent of order and authority. The power and beauty of his description of the event cannot be underestimated—for that matter, the power and beauty of *The French Revolution* should never be underestimated. But this beauty is a dangerous one—in Yeats's words, it has the potential to be "a terrible beauty."

NOTES

[1] In his haste to attribute a "Chaos" theory to Carlyle, Hayden White tends to underestimate the intellectual confusion inherent in Carlyle's approach. He could not give this "Chaos" a "comprehensible meaning" precisely because his own perspective was confused (White 148).

Citations to *The French Revolution* will be taken from the Centenary Edition, noted in the text as *CW*, followed by volume and page number. References to Carlyle's letters will be noted by *CL*, followed by volume and page number.

[2] Again, this strategy is more confusing and spontaneous than A. Abbott Ikeler suggests in his analysis of the "unresolved tension in Carlyle's view of the arts which is sustained, in public and private, throughout the whole of his life" (34). The heterogeneous method that Cumming explores in Carlyle's "multilayered writing" (12) is the product of this energetic confusion. Harbison's analysis of the Calvinist sense of history is especially pertinent to Carlyle's attitudes.

[3] Froude's piece on Calvinism in *Short Studies* is far more pertinent to an understanding of Carlyle's religion than his comments on the "Calvinist without the theology" in his biography. As he points out in the essay, "Illustrious natures do not form themselves upon narrow and cruel theories" (2:8). Campbell's discussion of Carlyle's Scottish background and Fielding's introduction to volume nineteen of the *Collected Letters* deserve careful consideration. As Fielding rightly notes, "though it is easy to construct intricate schemes of what Carlyle thought and meant, his letters often should force us to realize that he was a man of inconsistency, variety, and unexpectedness, an ironist consistent mainly in his challenging sincerity (*CL* 19:x).

[4] As John R. Gray has observed, Knox was not interested in politics apart from religion. He was "too completely intoxicated with God to pay attention to the values of monarchy, aristocracy, democracy of ecclesiocracy in themselves" (145). As I have pointed out in my own article on Carlyle and Knox, the Reformer as a historian "moulded every episode to fit his plan of the cosmic battle between light and darkness, belief and unbelief" (5).

[5] Knox's political uncertainty, like that of so many of Carlyle's heroes, benefits him as an activist. Philip Rosenberg's argument that Carlylean heroes are defined by their ability to stay "in touch with 'reality'" (191) needs to be qualified in this respect.

[6] John Rosenberg (25-31) underestimates the degree to which Carlyle relieves himself of this "burden" by inventing a method to conceal his confusion.

[7] Chris Vanden Bossche analyzes these elusive possibilities with great patience and insight (62-71), but, like John Rosenberg, he is reluctant to admit that confusion lies at the heart of Carlyle's historical mission.

WORKS CITED

Allingham, William. *A Diary*. Ed. H. Allingham and D. Radford. Intro. John Julius Norwich. 1907; rpt. Harmondsworth, Eng.: Penguin, 1985.

Calvin, John. *Commentary on a Harmony of the Evangelists, Matthew, Mark and Luke*. Ed. William Pringle. 3 vols. Edinburgh: Calvin Translation Society, 1845-46.

___. *Commentary on the Book of Psalms*. Ed. James Anderson, James Maclean and George MacCrie. 5 vols. Edinburgh: Calvin Translation Society, 1846-49.

___. *Institutes of the Christian Religion*. Trans. Henry Beveridge. 3 vols. Edinburgh: Calvin Translation Society, 1845-46.

Campbell, Ian. "Carlyle's Religion: The Scottish Background." *Carlyle and His Contemporaries*. Ed. John Clubbe. Durham, NC: Duke UP, 1976: 1-20.

Carlyle, Thomas. *Collectanea*. Ed. S. A. Jones. Canton, PA: Kirkgate P, 1903.

___. *Reminiscences*. Ed. Charles Eliot Norton. 2 vols. London: Macmillan, 1887.

___. *Two Note Books. From 23rd March 1822 to 16 May 1832*. Ed. Charles Eliot Norton. New York: Grolier, 1898.

___. *Collected Works*. Ed. H. D. Traill. 30 vols. London: Chapman and Hall, 1896-99.

___, and Jane Welsh Carlyle. *Collected Letters of Thomas Carlyle and Jane Welsh Carlyle*. Ed. Charles R. Sanders, K. J. Fielding, Clyde de L. Ryals, et al. 24 vols. Durham, NC: Duke UP, 1970-.

Coiffier, de Verseux, Henri Louis. *Dictionnaire biographique et historique des hommes marquans*. 3 tom. Londres, 1800.

Cumming, Mark. *A Disimprisoned Epic: Form and Vision in Carlyle's* French Revolution. Philadelphia, PA: U of Pennsylvania P, 1988.

Froude, J. A. *Life of Carlyle*. 4 vols. London: Longmans and Green, 1882, 1884.

___. "Calvinism." *Short Studies on Great Subjects*. New ed. 5 vols. London: Longmans, 1893: 1:1-59.

Goethe, Johann Wolfgang von. *Faust. Part One*. Trans. David Luke. Princeton, NJ: Princeton UP, 1964.

Gray, John. "The Political Theory of John Knox." *Church History* 7 (1939): 132-47.

Harbison, E. H. "The Calvinist Sense of History." *Christianity and History*. Princeton, NJ: Princeton UP, 1964. 270-88.

Hunter, A. M. *The Teaching of Calvin: A Modern Interpretation*. 2nd ed., rev. London: Clarke, 1950.

Ikeler, A. Abbott. *Puritan Temper and Transcendental Faith: Carlyle's Literary Vision*. Columbus, OH: Ohio State UP, 1972.

Rosenberg, John. *Carlyle and the Burden of History*. Cambridge, MA: Harvard UP, 1985.

Rosenberg, Philip. *The Seventh Hero: Thomas Carlyle and the Theory of Radical Activism*. Cambridge, MA: Harvard UP, 1974.

Sorensen, David. "Carlyle's Scottish French Revolution." *The Carlyle Society Papers* n.s. 2 (1988-89): 1-8.

Vanden Bossche, Chris. *Carlyle and the Search for Authority*. Columbus, OH: Ohio State UP, 1991.

White, Hayden. *Metahistory: The Historical Imagination in Nineteenth-Century Europe*. Baltimore, MD: Johns Hopkins UP, 1973.

CRITICAL RESPONSE
TO *ON HEROES, HERO-WORSHIP, AND THE HEROIC IN HISTORY*

MONTHLY REVIEW

155 (May 1841): 1-21.

[JOSEPH H. BARRETT]

During the month of May, last year, Mr. Carlyle delivered these six lectures to admiring and enlightened audiences; and now that they are published, thousands will read and re-read them with ever-increasing delight and profit; for there is more thought, strength, and strangeness in the *duodecimo* than in all the books put together that have come under our notice for months.

"On Heroes, Hero-Worship, and the Heroic in History!"—It is tantamount to a redundancy of speech to say that it is impossible for any one to predict how an original thinker will treat of any subject, even after the title of it be given out, and with some degree of particularity too. Certainly, at least, no one, or very few, will form any distinct notion of the meaning which Mr. Carlyle attaches to the words which appear in the title-page of his volume, much less of the sort of detailed handling of them in the course of the work. It will therefore be our endeavour, by a general account of the purpose and plan of the Lectures, and by extract or abstract, to convey an impression of the scope of our author's views, of the matter of them as doctrines, of the manner of them, and also of some of the things suggested rather than expressed; reserving certain critical remarks to the conclusion of our paper, upon the merits of this extraordinary thinker and writer, as displayed in one of his most extraordinary productions.

A "Hero," according to Mr. Carlyle, is a great man; the history of what man has accomplished in this world, being "at bottom, the history of the great men who have worked here;" in other words, the lives and characters of a few great men embody universal history, some one representing its spirit and essence at every distinct stage and epoch, both by being modified and the modifier in respect of prevailing influences and impressions. Every such distinct and decidedly great man has obtained the worship of all other men in his particular epoch, although frivolity, selfishness, and scepticism may have been the characteristics of that epoch, as when the French worshipped or unlimitedly admired and copied Voltaire. "They were the leaders of men, these great ones; the modelers, patterns, and in a wide sense creators, of whatsoever the general mass of men contrived to do or to attain; all things that we see standing accomplished in the world are properly the outer material result, the practical realization and embodiment of thought that dwelt in the great men sent into the world. The soul, the marrow of the whole world's history, were the history of these." A divine relation, he calls it, in all times unites a great man to other men; and Heroism is the term which he uses to express *the* greatness, the grand elements of which are sincerity, practical earnestness, and unceasing efforts to carry mankind to a higher sphere of light and action than any one man ever before contemplated. Such a one "is the living light-fountain;" his is "the light which enlightens, which has enlightened the darkness of the world; and this not as a kindled lamp only, but rather as a natural luminary, shining by the gift of Heaven; a glowing light-fountain, as I say, of native original insight, of manhood and heroic nobleness."

The chief fact in the history of such a man in his religion, just as it is of a nation's history. Not that by the term *religion* is meant the church-creed professed by the man, "but the thing a man does practically believe (and this is often enough *without* asserting it to himself, much less to others); the thing a man does practically lay to heart, and know for certain, concerning his vital relations to this mysterious universe, and his duty and destiny there; that is in all cases the primary thing for him, and creatively determines all the rest." His religion, therefore, may be mere scepticism and *no-religion*: the manner it is in which he feels himself spiritually related to the unseen world or no-world."

. . . From the examples we have given, any one, however unacquainted previously with the writing of Mr. Carlyle, will be competent to form an opinion of his manner; and probably will remark upon that manner before passing judgment upon his matter, the cast of his philosophy, or the accuracy of his theory of what constitutes a man-hero, and concerning the universality of hero-worship.

It is very likely that such a reader will pronounce our author's style to be exceedingly affected, and assert that there is a constant effort to appear singular, not merely by uttering paradoxes, but by expressing ideas which are often original only in form. The system of word and epithet coining, the profusion and cloud of figurative speech, and the torrent of eloquence when the language is as homely as the notions are extravagant, are points which in all likelihood will call forth the observation of the reader. And then, when the reasoning and philosophy of our author come to be more immediately regarded, it is probable that nine out of ten will declare that exaggeration, mysticism, and wild Germanism are his characteristics.

A longer and proper study, however, of Mr. Carlyle, as beheld in his writings, will modify the reader's opinion of him, and result in a strong conviction, that affectation and commonplace, in respect of mental powers or cherished ideas, belong not either to his manner or matter. The truth unquestionably is, that he is an originalist of a very high order; that while naturally his mind runs in peculiar channels, its grasp is large and potent, the whole frame of the man having been still further individualized by long and profound study of German authors. True, a more dangerous model than Mr. Carlyle, as regards style of composition, could not be chosen. Were the majority of our writers to ape him, our language would soon be *un*-Englished; while simplicity and soundness of thought would be lost amid a chaos of things and a confusion of sounds. But while no one ought to be more sedulously avoided as a pattern, no person capable of judging for himself will deny, that for independence as well as comprehension of thought, boldness of speculation, and, taken as a whole, completeness and clearness of views, perhaps there has hardly ever been a philosophical work more distinguished than the present volume. The earnestness, the heart-felt energy of the author, is of itself a grand feature in its pages; while the humanity which it breathes, and the sympathy which it cherishes and communicates, are notable and deeply attractive. Affectation would be incompatible with these excellences. Mr. C. is too eager, too full of his subject, too conscious of power, and too firmly persuaded of the importance of the views which he inculcates for that; so that whether pleasingly discursive, or masterfully abrupt, the mind of the reader never fails to accompany him, very seldom feeling inclined to dissent from the course adopted.

With regard to the choice of heroic characters by our author, we are inclined to think that the classification is good, and the number sufficiently complete, provided his theory be just. There does not appear to us to be partiality in the selection; and the soul of history is very clearly indicated by the men. But we must observe, that although every one of these heroes may be made legitimately to stand as the representative of an epoch, and although the novel estimate which is frequently formed of their characters, both in respect of sentiment and of conduct, may be as just as it is striking, yet that panegyric and overlaying are general faults in the book; Mr. Carlyle's admiration of the heroes, and enthusiasm in support of his theory, finding terms that are extravagant and unmeasured. Very often during the perusal of the work, and after having been carried away captive by the spell thrown over us by the author's genius and singular eloquence, the questions have after a pause forcibly suggested themselves,—what might not such a writer have made Mahomet or Cromwell, had he taken up another theory?—What, if he had happened to look at first upon his hero in a different light?—What, above all, is or will be the Eternal's judgment?—So that however gratifying, purifying, and ennobling, are the spirit and the matter of these Lectures, something not short of distrust has accompanied our reading of them.

After all, and whatever may be the merits of our author's theory, and of many of the details, we cannot sufficiently admire the lesson and example taught by him, of weighing men and historical phases, not according to any hacknied current of opinion, but by boldly and philosophically speculating for himself, and as guided by the lights of each particular age, and inspired by generous sympathies. The science of historical and biographical writing can never by any other manner of spirit or of procedure be satisfactorily obeyed; nor can the practical teachings afforded by any epoch or any hero be otherwise correctly and usefully apprehended.

THE DIAL

2 (July 1841): 131-33.

[MARGARET FULLER]

Although the name of Thomas Carlyle is rarely mentioned in the critical journals of this country, there is no living writer who is more sure of immediate attention from the large circle of readers, or who exercises a greater influence than he in these United States. Since the publication of his article on the characteristics of our time in the Edinburgh Review, and afterwards of the Sartor, this influence has been deepening and extending year by year, till now thousands turn an eager ear to the most distant note of his clarion. To *be* and not to *seem*; to know that nothing can become a man which is not manlike; that no silken trappings can dignify measures of mere expediency; and no hootings of a mob, albeit of critics and courtiers can shame the truth, or keep Heaven's dews from falling in the right place; that all conventions not founded on eternal law are valueless, and that the life of man, will he or no, must tally with the life of nature;—this creed indeed is none of the newest! No! but as old and as new as truth itself, and ever needing to be reenforced. It is so by Carlyle with that depth of "truthful earnestness" he appreciates so fully in his chosen heroes, as also with a sarcastic keenness, an overflow of genial wit, and a picturesque skill in the delineation of examples, rarely equalled in any age of English literature.

How many among ourselves are his debtors for the first assurance that the native disdain of a youthful breast for the shams and charlatanries that so easily overgrow even our free society was not without an echo. They listened for the voice of the soul and heard on every wind only words, words. But when this man spoke every word stood for a thing. They had been taught that man belonged to society, the body to the clothes. They thought the reverse, and this was the man to give distinct expression to his thought, which alone made life desirable.

Already he has done so much, that he becomes of less importance to us. The rising generation can scarcely conceive how important Wordsworth, Coleridge, and afterwards Carlyle were to those whose culture dates farther back. A numerous band of pupils already, each in his degree, dispense bread of their leaven to the children, instead of the stones which careful guardians had sent to the mill for their repast.

But, if the substance of his thought be now known to us, where shall we find another who appeals so forcibly, so variously to the common heart of his contemporaries. Even his Miscellanies, though the thoughts contained in them have now been often reproduced, are still read on every side. The French Revolution stands alone as a specimen of the modern epic. And the present volume will probably prove quite as attractive to most readers.

Though full of his faults of endless repetition, hammering on a thought till every sense of the reader aches, and an arrogant bitterness of tone which seems growing upon him (as alas! it is too apt to grow upon Reformers; the odious fungus that deforms the richest soil), though, as we have heard it expressed, he shows as usual "too little respect for respectable people," and like all character-hunters, attaches an undue value to his own discoveries in opposition to the verdict of the Ages, the large residuum of truth we find after making every possible deduction, the eloquence, the wit, the pathos, the dramatic power of representation, leave the faults to be regarded as dust on the balance.

Among the sketches, Odin is much admired, and is certainly of great picturesque beauty. The passages taken from the Scandinavian Mythology are admirably told. Mahomet is altogether fine. Dante not inaccurate, but of little depth. Apparently Mr. Carlyle speaks in his instance from a slighter acquaintance than is his wont. With his view of Johnson and Burns we were already familiar; both are excellent, as is that of Rousseau, though less impressive than are the few touches given him somewhere in the Miscellanies. Cromwell is not one of his best, though apparently much labored. He does not adequately sustain his positions by the facts he brings forward.

This book is somewhat less objectionable than the French Revolution to those not absolutely unjust critics, who said they would sooner "dine for a week on pepper, than read through the two volumes." Yet it is too highly seasoned, tediously emphatic, and the mind as well as the style is obviously in want of the verdure of repose. An acute observer said that the best criticism on his works would be his own remark, that a man in convulsions is not proved to be strong because six healthy men cannot hold him. We are not consoled by his brilliancy and the room he has obtained for an infinity of quips and cranks and witty turns for the corruption of his style, and the more important loss of chasteness, temperance, and harmony in his mind observable since he first was made known to the public.

Yet let thanks, manifold thanks, close this and all chapters that begin with his name.

THE BIBLICAL REVIEW, AND CONGREGATIONAL MAGAZINE

3 (March 1847): 183-86.

PROFESSOR THOLUCK

[Originally published in the *Literarischer Anzeiger für Christliche Theologie und Wissenchaft Überhaupt*. Translator not named.]

In this production we have an instance of that so-called poetical pantheism. . . . With this celebrated author it has almost still less of philosophical basis than with his American kindred spirit. It is, as with Emerson, a pantheistic intellectual intoxication, which neither rests upon philosophical clearness, nor even knows how to regard history philosophically. In this embryo form of pantheism, produced only by the excitement of feeling, the question of the personality of God and of man is left, as is by the mystic both of the East and the West, in a half-mist.*

The immediate and only effect of the perusal of such writings upon many is to dissolve the positive forms of traditional piety and dogmatic theology. Where there is religious experience, the necessity for an ideal representation of the blessings of faith thereby gained is at once felt; where that religious earnestness is wanting, then will men's minds, set free from their earlier traditions, become a prey to the rigid scientific form of Strauss's pantheism, so soon as this becomes better known; especially as there is no doubt that his system of belief will shortly be transferred into the English language. Schleiermacher is still to Englishmen an unknown great man. Who can fail to perceive that his writings are destined to clear the way, at this particular crisis, for a new form of faith in England, as they have done in Germany?

We allow the author, first of all, to give his idea of "*Hero*"— which designation he has (though very unsuitably) made to occupy the position of Strauss's "*Genius*." For the first time in the course of the work, on page 244 [251, first edition] a definition occurs: "The hero is he who lives in the inward sphere of things, in the True, the Divine, and Eternal, which exists always, unseen to most, under the Temporary, Trivial: his being is in that; he declares that abroad, by act or speech as it may be, in declaring himself abroad. His life is a part of eternal nature herself:" and presently he says that "Fichte has declared that under all Appearance lies as the essence of the things —'the Divine Idea of the World.'" Here already is betrayed the want of keen insight, since according to this, every religious man has a claim to the title Hero; yet by "Hero" he actually understands what we should call "the Genius"— the beginner and discloser of new stages of advance in mind, and new epochs in the world's history. In the introduction he says that "Heroes were the leaders of men, the modellers, patterns, and in a wide sense creators, of whatsoever the general mass of men has contrived to do or to attain." He marks out the following classes of Heroes. 1. The Hero as Divinity—Odin; Paganism; the Scandinavian Mythology. 2. The Hero as Prophet—Mahomet; Islam. 3. The Hero as Poet—Dante; Shakespeare. 4. The Hero as Priest—Luther; Reformation: Knox; Puritanism. 5. The Hero as Man of Letters—Johnson; Rousseau; Burns. 6. The Hero as King—Cromwell; Napoleon; Modern Revolutionism. This classification, as well as the instances chosen to represent it, will appear to the reader a strangely arbitrary grouping, and the working out in no respect removes this first impression. Certainly, the author indicates that he intends making the progressions of humanity depend upon the veneration of the Divine in man; but he retains this intention by no means firmly. Thus he begins the section "The Hero as Poet," with the words, "The Hero as Divinity, the Hero as Prophet, are productions of old ages, not to be repeated in the new. They pre-suppose a certain rudeness of conception which the progress of mere scientific knowledge puts an end to." In the following section, "The Hero as Priest," it is said on the contrary "The Priest too is a kind of Prophet: in him too, there is required to be a light of inspiration." "I do not make much," says he, "of the Progress of the Species"— and yet the *fact* itself seems certain enough, and now he intimates that reformers are indispensable. Mere mistiness! In what way is the priest distinguished from the prophet? Why is the *reformer* forthwith placed in the position of the *priest*? If the advance of the species is a fact, why does he make it of no account? Was there with the reformation such an advance made on the heroism of the poet? At least it is then as *advance*, that the positions of the scholar and the king are to be justified. The author should not have aimed from beginning to end, at the indication of a chronological progress in hero-worship. In his view there have always been heroes in the various spheres of mind; but a transfer of the worship which mankind have paid them, from one sphere to another, is incapable of being marked out; only that mankind within the religious sphere have advanced from paganism to the incarnate Deity of Christianity; from this to the worship of Genius they are still capable, according to his view, of being led onwards.

As for his choice of illustrations, it is arbitrary in the extreme. Why take Odin as an historical personage, when, as he himself mentions, the very historical existence of this Odin is, according to Grimm and other inquirers, doubtful? Why not, for example, rather take the fact of the deification of a Romulus? And when speaking of men of letters, what could induce the author to bring forward as examples, Rousseau and Johnson, and even the Scottish poet Burns, instead of such men as Aristotle, Leibnitz, and others—men who really did create new epochs in knowledge? And he actually makes Mahomet representative of the prophets, when upon this weak and empty man (giving him all due merit,) there rested at most but a very moderate amount, if any, of prophetic spirit, while on the contrary, an Isaiah, Ezekiel, Habakkuk, Jeremiah—the most noble examples of the prophetic office, even in the author's estimation, were ready to his hand. But a secret inclination to glorify Mahomet appears to have induced the author to make this selection. It is easy to see that he should rather have taken Christ as an instance. He says, "We have chosen Mahomet, not as the most eminent prophet, but as the one we are freest to speak of."

Would that for these minds, which, at least mystically, are touched with religion, a Schleiermacher might arise, who would teach them at least that peculiar *Christian* mystery which they know not; then alone will the day dawn upon them, when they shall be able to reconcile themselves with the doctrines of Christianity in their more concrete form, ("dem konkreteren christlichen Dogma.")

---

*In an interesting Scotch periodical, "Lowe's Edinburgh Magazine," for February, 1846, which is likewise pervaded with the *conservative* German spirit, is to be found a critique upon Emerson, in the christian sense, which quite accords with us in its judgment on his semi-obscurity and downright contradictions.

"The Hero and the Führer"

ABERDEEN UNIVERSITY REVIEW

27 (March 1940): 99-105.

SIR HERBERT GRIERSON

There has been of late a remarkable revival of interest in Carlyle, inspired in part, we fear, by the suspicion that Hitlerism, Fascism, etc., represent a final development of the revolt against reason which was latent, at least as a potentiality, in the Romantic revolt against the spirit of the *aufklärung*, the rationalism of the eighteenth century. This is obviously the motive of M. Seilière's book.[1] Professor Cazamian's[2] had no reference to later developments, though he had to consider the relation of Carlyle to Nietzsche; and Nietzsche has much relevance for the student of all that we are suffering from. Miss Young's thesis[3] makes only a passing reference to these later developments. "The disintegration of modern governmental authority," she writes, ". . . Carlyle would probably regard less as a vindication of his theories of authority (though they are that) than as a fulfillment of his prophetic warning regarding the shortcomings of democracy." The present writer came to much the same conclusion in a short pamphlet, "Carlyle and Hitler." Miss Young's subject is the art of Carlyle in its relation to his philosophy of history, her aim to vindicate Carlyle against critics who accuse him of being a subjective, dramatic and lyrical historian, interested solely in individuals, heroes, picturesque personalities.

Carlyle is the great historian produced by the Romantic Movement. His attitude towards history is that of Wordsworth towards Nature in "The Prelude" and other poems. In his rejection of the rationalist history of Gibbon and Hume and Robertson, Carlyle resembles Blake rejecting Sir Joshua Reynolds and all painting which could be taught, and could be judged by rules. The rationalist historian conceived, or seemed to conceive, of the events of human history as explicable on rational grounds. When dealing with ancient history containing a miraculous element they fell, Leslie Stephen indicates, into the error of conceiving the ancients to be "men of the modern type under the action of a totally different set of laws, instead of being regarded as men in a different mental stage under the action of precisely the same law." A rationalist, sceptical historian like Gibbon was well aware that forces of unreason had operated in history, the fanaticism of mobs, the superstition of hermits and monks, etc. But these were definitely forces of unreason. All progress had been by and towards reason, all retrogression a falling away from reason.

The discovery of the Romantics, Herder and Schiller, Blake and Wordsworth, was the importance of the irrational, the subconscious, of the reason that is at work in unreason. "Carlyle's theory of society," writes Miss Young, "is posited on the psychological assumption of irrationalism. In his view the springs of human action lie in the primitive subconscious whereby we partake of the essence of the Infinite. The primary principle of life . . . is mysterious, anti-rational and anti-mechanistic." Its inner sanctuaries lie in the "domain of the unconscious, by nature infinite and inexhaustible," an "abyss of mystery and miracle." From that region alone "all wonders, all poesies and religions and social systems have proceeded."

Miss Young's quotations from Carlyle are enough to show the element of emotional writing, of poetry, which invested his philosophy of history. One may agree that reason is at work in apparently irrational instincts and impulses, but when we go on to speak of these as partaking "of the essence of the Infinite," the "abyss of mystery and miracle," we are using the language of poetry, as Wordsworth does when he speaks of "Nature and her overflowing soul," or writes:

> I saw one life and felt that it was joy,
> One song they sang, and it was audible,
> Most audible then when the fleshy ear,
> O'ercome by grosser prelude of that strain
> Forgot its functions, and slept undisturbed.

Carlyle himself speaks at times, especially in *Sartor*, of Nature in the same strain; but for him as for Herder it is the universal history of mankind which is at once "the sublimest revelation and most indubitable proof of a purposeful Deity working with the plastic force of the collective destiny of Man" (Miss Young).

What the purpose of the Deity is Carlyle knows no more than the rest of us. Miss Young describes his view of the process of history as a conflict, "a ceaseless process of action and reaction, through phase after phase spiralling upwards towards a better realization of man's latent capacities." So she tells us at one place, but in another admits that his conception is of a "vague goal of spiritual realization with which in the final analysis Carlyle has little interest." That the process is spiralling upwards is a matter of faith, and Carlyle's faith grew ever dimmer as his trust in the people failed him. Like Milton he had started with a too high estimate of his fellow men and, like him, came to think that most men are fools and many of them knaves.

Moreover, when Carlyle speaks of man partaking of the essence of the Infinite, of man as an embodied, visualized Idea in the Eternal mind, a divine apparition, he combines two ideas of the Deity which are not quite the same,—the deity of the German transcendentalists, a being beyond good and evil, working out his purposes through what we call good and evil alike; and quite another idea,—a God who, in Pascal's words, is *not* the God of the philosophers but of Abraham and the patriarchs, the God of the Old Testament, ever intent on punishing the sins of men. The result is that an historical event is not only an episode in the upward spiralling of the history of mankind. It may be also a proof of God's anger with men. In the Revolution the French, like the Jews when carried off by the Assyrians, were being punished for their sins. A history by Carlyle is also a sermon, a warning to others, especially the English people; and while writing of Cromwell and the Puritan Revolution he tells Emerson: "My heart is sick and sore on behalf of my own generation . . . thus do the two centuries stand related to me, the seventeenth *worthless* except in so far as it can be made the nineteenth."

Carlyle's art of history follows from his philosophy, his belief in the important part played by the irrational element in men's minds. It is not enough with such rationalist historians as Gibbon and Hume to relate the events and indicate the general forces at work. The historian must, by an effort of imagination and a study of details and characters, get back, as it were, inside the period and see the events as they actually unrolled themselves before the eyes, affected the feelings, of contemporaries. Carlyle's aim was to combine the art of the historical novelist, of Sir Walter Scott, whose importance for the writer of history Carlyle had early recognized, with the laborious research of the historian. Hence his interest in individuals, in heroes, Mirabeau, Napoleon, Cromwell, Frederick, and hence his vivid, dramatic, moving pictures of events. For to Carlyle these were not dramatic and decorative embroideries but were a third dimension added to the two-dimensional picture of Gibbon and Hume. How far such imaginative reproductions can be trusted remains a question. Bainville's more sober narrative of incidents in the Revolution supplies many corrections of Carlyle's dramatic presentations and interpretations.

Carlyle's great heroes are not just Nietzsche's supermen. Both Miss Young and Cazamian differentiate them. "With Nietzsche," says Cazamian, "the individual is the centre and the summit; he acquires knowledge and power in order fully to realize his possibilities; his egoism spurs him to an activity of which he is the beginning and the end, the cause and the effect. Carlyle . . . begins by proclaiming the essential inequality of men, so that he may more surely compel all men to bear a common yoke, the yoke of what one might call a moral collectivism." His interest is in the hero in relation to the community. He is the voice of the community, or rather he has the seeing eye which divines the end which the community is feeling after, and the means to achieve it.

But Carlyle's thought underwent changes under the pressure of the time and of his own impatient temperament. It was, to begin with, a democratic feeling, an interest in the poor, *die Sache der Armen*, that set Carlyle out on his quest for good government, a leader or leaders, a true aristocracy, a Führer. That is clear in *Sartor Resartus*, and still more clear in *Past and Present* (1843), which Mr. Trevelyan has insisted marked the culmination of Carlyle's early thought. With *Latter Day Pamphlets* (1850) a change of tone and temper became obvious, an increasing impatience with democracy, due mainly to the glaring results of the industrial revolution and the doctrine of *laissez faire* and free trade, which last is just *laissez faire* in the relation between countries. Carlyle had, as I have said, become convinced that most men are fools and many knaves, neither fit to vote. "The fact is, slaves are in a tremendous majority everywhere; and the voting of them (not to be got rid of just yet) is a nuisance in proportion, a nuisance of proportionally tremendous magnitude, properly indeed the great fountain-head of all the nuisances whatsoever." And so Carlyle is on his way to the Führer, the leader who has become his own policy, who, however he may have begun with the help of promises and popular or influential support, retains that leadership by dint of secret police, concentration camps, and the murder of inconvenient individuals, whether opponents (who must all be reckoned enemies) or his early friends and colleagues. The career of Hitler and Stalin (so far as we can follow them), a study of Caulaincourt's account of the Russian venture of Napoleon, and of Mr. Raymond Moley's *After Seven Years* (1939), suggest that there is a common tendency in all such dictators' histories. The dictator is at first the embodiment of a policy, the leader of a party or, it may be, of many parties with, for the time, some common measure of agreement, it may be merely a negative one. As his power grows and his position becomes secure, he is himself the policy. "You seem to be interested in personalities," Mr. Moley represents Mr. Roosevelt as saying.

"I am not interested in personalities. It's not what you say or think about an individual in the administration or about a specific issue. There's one issue in this campaign, it's myself, and people must be either for or against me."

"That really was all I needed to know."

It was on just such grounds that Talleyrand and Fouché deserted Napoleon. He had subordinated the interests of France to his personal ambitions. Mr. Moley's may or may *not* be a fair presentation of Roosevelt.

Whatever his philosophy or art as an historian, the final question is what value attaches to Carlyle's histories of the French Revolution, the Puritan Revolution in the seventeenth century, the growth of Prussian power? Carlyle, Sir Charles Firth said, was a poet and prophet by nature, an historian by accident. Miss Young says in like manner that in history Carlyle found the best subject for the poet. Homer was the greatest of historians. Is Carlyle's poetical imaginative history justified as history? Is, for example, Carlyle's account of Cromwell and the Puritan Movement, which Mr. Trevelyan accounts his most solid contribution to history, to be relied on? Miss Young has hardly faced up to Sir Charles Firth's criticism (his name is not included in her index) of Carlyle's treatment of his sources, his ignorance of English history generally, his too Scottish view of the events in England. But Firth's chief criticism is that Carlyle's history is subjective. This is indeed the word with which Miss Young herself describes it, but she seems to mean by "subjective" imaginative. For the word suggests something more, a history coloured by the writer's prejudices, and this is Firth's charge against Carlyle. His view of the seventeenth century was coloured by his feelings about the nineteenth. "He had no scientific interest in the past, no interest in the seventeenth century for its own sake . . . he looked at the seventeenth century through the spectacles of the nineteenth, and brought to his study of it preconceptions which warped his views of many things." But the most passionate of Carlyle's prejudices was his hatred of, and contempt for, democratic, representative government. "According to Mr. Froude the lesson which Carlyle drew from his study of Cromwell's times was a general inference of the incapacity of a popular assembly to guide successfully and permanently the destinies of this or any other countries. It would be truer to say that he began his Cromwellian researches with this belief in his mind, and that it moulded all the conclusions that he drew from the facts."[4] Prejudice led him to a complete misapprehension of Cromwell's own policy, for Cromwell did not share Carlyle's preference of military to parliamentary government. His strenuous effort was to restore the government of parliament and secure the freedom to vindicate which he had taken up the sword. The same prejudice closed Carlyle's eyes to the significance of a conflict in his own day which should have had a very material bearing on his speculations or prophecies, a conflict in which a democracy vindicated its ability to govern itself, to find and to follow a hero who, leading not forcing his people, brought them through the perils of a civil war with no help from suppression of criticism, lying propaganda, secret police, and concentration camps, a hero perhaps equal in ability and certainly superior in character to any of Carlyle's choice, whose peers are, if any, Alfred the Great and William the Silent. When, in the middle of the Civil War, Abraham Lincoln was re-elected President, despite the efforts of those who sought an inconclusive end to the war, he wrote: "It has long been a grave question whether any government, not too strong for the liberties of the people, can be strong enough to maintain its existence in great emergencies. On this point the present rebellion brought our republic to a severe test, and a presidential election during the rebellion added not a little to the strain. The election has demonstrated that a people's government can sustain a national election in the midst of a great civil war. Until now it has not been known to the world that this was a possibility." Carlyle remained blind to the significance of what was happening, could see nothing in it but "merely the efflorescence of the Nigger Emancipation agitation," which he always despised. "No War ever raging in my time to me more profoundly foolish-looking. . . . Neutral I am to a degree for me." To Carlyle the great event of European history in the nineteenth century was the emergence of Prussia and military power. His hero is well on the way to become a Hitler or a Stalin.

NOTES

[1] Ernest Seilière, *Un Precurseur du National Socialisme: L'Actualite de Carlyle*. Paris, 1939.

[2] Louis Cazamian, *Carlyle*, trans. E. K. Brown. 1913; rpt London and New York: Macmillan, 1932.

[3] Louise Merwin Young, *Thomas Carlyle and the Art of History*. Oxford UP and Philadelphia: U of Pennsylvania P, 1939.

[4] Sir Charles H. Firth, "Introduction" to *The Letters and Speeches of Oliver Cromwell with Elucidations by Thomas Carlyle*. Ed. S. C. Lomas. 3 vols. London: Methuen, 1904.

"Pattern and Paradox in *Heroes and Hero-Worship*"

STUDIES IN SCOTTISH LITERATURE

6.3 (January 1969): 146-55.

ROBERT W. KUSCH

Not Carlyle's most ambitious work nor his favorite, *Heroes and Hero-Worship* still prefigures the shape his imagination will take in later works, especially *Past and Present*, *Cromwell*, and *Frederick*. Most scholarship has concentrated on the philosophic refinement of the work—the definition of the hero, the exposure of certain inconsistencies, the placement of the hero theory inside a continuing tradition.[1] By the late eighteen thirties, however, Carlyle was more prophet than philosopher, well aware that he must create "not the ideas and the sentiments, but the symbols and mood of mind."[2] Certainly *Heroes* is not a construct of ideas alone; it evokes a much wider experience. The "symbols and mood of mind," the patterns of choice, the structure and especially the metaphor of the Tree Igdrasil tell us as much about *Heroes* as the isolation of the theory. And one major artistic problem that Carlyle fails to solve—the artistic dislocation of the "eighteenth century" from the "heroes" it supposedly restrains—intimates that he has not fully grown into the maturity of his later works; he still has fragments of himself to integrate.

After *The French Revolution*, where he recorded the destruction of an entire way of life, and *Chartism*, where he saw certain incipient stages of the French Revolution repeating themselves in England, his readers might well have thought he would predict inevitable ruin for his time and country. His solution of unquestioning trust in the hero did not, of itself, engender heroes and none others had offered themselves. Like the German Romantics, he saw the eighteenth century and the early part of his own age as feckless and formula-ridden, dominated by a scepticism that influenced its most promising representatives toward irony, despair, or misconceived sentiment. Though he was able to create a viable hero in *Sartor*, he could not, when he faced the French Revolution, find a man who could master its serpentine and divisive courses. Mirabeau died too soon and Danton did not have the right chemistry to transmute chaos into order. Not even Napoleon, whose actions near the close of the book form a "small visible" where we can see the emperor in the lieutenant, represents the ultimate in heroism. Though Carlyle once contemplated writing Napoleon's life instead of *The French Revolution*, he saw from the first a certain unbounded arrogance that predicted a fall.[3] Among Carlyle's contemporaries, only Robert Peel appeared to have the makings of a hero—"the one statesman we had"[4] Carlyle said of him on his death in 1850—but when Carlyle wrote *Heroes*, he knew little of Peel or his work.

He was still an optimist, however, the fires rising deep from reflections of the last five years. That change would occur seemed inevitable since he interpreted three commentators—Goethe, St. Simon, and Novalis—as saying that history flows in cycles, a "critical" or unbelieving age followed by an "organic" or believing one. Furthermore, at the close of the second book of *Sartor*, he recorded his faith in the "Everlasting Yea," a faith that, as Carlisle Moore has pointed out, quickly became a social gospel.[5] His conviction that the call for heroism still sounded, that all men were united in a mystical bond, and that truth is pyramidal because no truth ever dies, led him to hope a new society might be forming. He was now persuaded that the phoenix metaphorically interpreted the turns of history and that the French Revolution prefigured a birth as well as a death. Moreover, he saw himself as a prophet— one whose generic *raison d'etre* is hope, even if he must ground himself in the absolute to look beyond the dregs of the present. Thus, in the spring of 1840, when Carlyle wrote *Heroes*, he buoyed himself up with a view of the future, believed in the necessity of the hero, and projected a model of heroism from eleven chosen lives of the past.

He possessed the one necessary filament for creation. He usually fashioned a book, or a book fashioned itself in him, when he could edge his thought along the contours of an intricate metaphor. Certainly the clothes and phoenix metaphors guide the design of *Sartor*, and the "spontaneous combustion" of the eighteenth century is one of the controlling perspectives of *The French Revolution*. In *Heroes*, the metaphor emerges early:

> I like, too, the representation they have of the Tree Igdrasil. All Life is figured by them as a Tree. Igdrasil, the Ash-Tree of Existence, has its roots deep down in the kingdoms of Hela or Death; its trunk reaches up heaven-high, spreads its boughs over the whole Universe: it is the Tree of Existence. At the foot of it, in the Death Kingdom, sit Three *Nornas*, Fates,—the Past, Present, Future; watering its roots from the Sacred Well. Its "boughs" with their buddings and dis-leafings,—events, things suffered, things done, catastrophes,—stretch through all lands and times. Is not every leaf of it a biography, every fibre there an act or word? Its boughs are Histories of Nations. The rustle of it is the noise of Human Existence, onwards from of old. It grows there, the breath of Human Passion rustling through it. . . .[6]

If the "Life-Tree" appeared only once in *Heroes*, it might simply have the force of an epic simile, but its influence is so pervasive that it deserves to be explored further. In one sense, it is the triple image of existence itself, since it spatially embraces all mankind, temporally brings together past, present, and future; and metaphysically involves life and death. In another sense, its interrelatedness specifically suggests the organic bond of contraries: one nation with another; the future and present as inheritors of the past; and death as the other half of life. For Carlyle, however, the "Tree" has other meanings consistent with his own way of seeing, but probably foreign to the Norse Sagas. He has already applied the rhythms of life and death to the growth and decay of spiritual response in various ages, and the "Tree" now becomes a natural image for his view of history. In the following quotations, the

"Tree" retains few suggestions of the "Tree of Existence." It is the primordial rhythmic force of life and death in history, mysterious in its specific workings, but sure in its turns. The first quotation is from "The Hero as Poet," the second from "The Hero as Man-of-Letters":

> Curious enough how, as it were by mere accident, this man came to us. I think always, so great, quiet, complete and self-sufficing is this Shakspeare, had the Warwickshire Squire not prosecuted him for deer-stealing, we had perhaps never heard of him as a Poet! The woods and skies, the rustic Life of Man in Stratford there, had been enough for this man! But indeed that strange outbudding of our whole English Existence, which we call the Elizabethan Era, did not it too come as of its own accord? The "Tree Igdrasil" buds and withers by its own laws,—too deep for our scanning. Yet it does bud and wither, and every bough and leaf of it is there, by fixed eternal laws; not a Sir Thomas Lucy but comes at the hour fit for him. (*CW* 5:329)

> How mean, dwarfish are their ways of thinking, in this time,—compared not with the Christian Shakspeares and Miltons, but with the old Pagan Skalds, with any species of believing men! The living TREE Igdrasil, with the melodious prophetic waving of its world-wide boughs, deep-rooted as Hela, has died out into the clanking of a World-MACHINE. "Tree" and "Machine:" contrast these two things. I, for my share, declare the world to be no machine! I say that it does not go by wheel-and-pinion "motives," self-interests, checks, balances; that there is something far other in it than the clank of spinning-jennies, and parliamentary majorities; and, on the whole, that it is not a machine at all!—The old Norse Heathen had a truer notion of God's world than these poor Machine-Sceptics: the old Heathen Norse were sincere men. (*CW* 5:393)

There is one other sense in which the "Tree" suggests a series of meanings and even an essential structure for *Heroes and Hero-Worship*. In the first paragraph of his opening lecture, Carlyle says, "all things that we see standing accomplished in the world are properly the outer material result, the practical realization and embodiment, of thoughts that dwelt in the Great Men sent into the world" (*CW* 5:393). The principle of growth in the "Tree" may very well suggest a principle of growth in this world,[7] and, for Carlyle, the germ of that earthly principle is in the achievements of the great man. In its particular aspect of development, then, the "Tree Igdrasil" is also a natural image for the historical vitality of heroes, and in charting the nature of that vitality, Carlyle is simultaneously recording much of what he sees as the world's significant history.

One of the artistic complexities of *Heroes* lies in the occurrence of several structural patterns, and ultimately in the union of image and theme. Of course Carlyle ostensibly divides his heroes by class ("Prophet" from "Poet" and "Divinity" from "King"), but every class of hero has fundamental analogies with others, so that one emerging pattern is cyclical. What is the generic difference between the "Hero as Poet" and the "Hero as Man of Letters," between Shakespeare and Burns? Or between Mahomet and Luther, "Prophet" and "Priest"? Carlyle says that the soul of the hero is the same in every age, "the Hero can be Poet, Prophet, King, Priest, or what you will" (*CW* 5:307), but, apparently, the subtle connections between circumstance, character, and vocation force certain heroes to be more like others.

Cromwell is more like Odin than he is like Napoleon, with whom he is so dissimilarly yoked. Knox and Mahomet are of a piece. By repetition of analogous classes, Carlyle seems to be saying that certain ages call for a special kind of hero (and certainly Carlyle sees his own age calling for the "Hero as King," which he treats as a contemporary problem).

A chronological pattern informs the book also. Excepting Cromwell, who is treated in the last lecture, and Shakespeare, who is only slightly out of the series, the personalities are ordered here as they appear in time. Even Jesus and Goethe, whom Carlyle mentions but does not portray, are in sequence: the "one whom we do not name here" (*CW* 5:307) is first noted in "The Hero as Divinity" and Goethe is used as a preface to "The Hero as Man of Letters." As an informal structural device, Carlyle also suggests that human consciousness, through continual exploration of its surroundings, evolves towards a more intelligent conception of psychological "reality." Each lecture may be read as a chapter in the history of man's mind. Though he disparages "the progress of the species," by which he means the Encyclopedists' suggestion that mankind is traveling on a straight and simple path towards the perfection of wisdom, he recognizes also that there may have been some ancient subliminal chicanery in elevating the hero to divinity or prophet. "The Hero as Divinity, the Hero as Prophet, are productions of old ages; not to be repeated in the new," he says at the opening of his third lecture, "They presuppose a certain rudeness of conception, which the progress of mere scientific knowledge put an end to. . . . We are now to see our Hero in the less ambitious, but also less questionable, character of Poet" (*CW* 5:307). And, at the beginning of the fifth lecture, he suggests further that, in their pure form, the recurrence of several previous classes of heroism is unlikely because of an irreversible change in the human mind. "Hero-Gods, Prophets, Poets, Priests are forms of Heroism that belong to the old ages, make their appearance in the remotest times; some of them have ceased to be possible long since, and cannot show themselves in the world" (*CW* 5:377). The implicit conclusion here is that, if the hero is to appear in the nineteenth century, he will probably appear as man-of-letters or king, classes an evolving humanity has prepared itself to honor.

No contradiction exists in reading *Heroes* in all of these ways. There may be no generic differences between "Divinity" and "King" (both charismatic leaders), "Prophet" and "Priest" (both religious revolutionaries), or "Poet" and "Man-of-Letters" (both verbal dramatists), but there are enough differences in degree— differences, that is, between the scope and intensity of the individual's vision, the ultimate response he awakens in humanity and the reception given by his contemporaries—to justify a significant titular variation. Thus, Carlyle sees the "Hero as Man-of-Letters" as the "Poet" in modern dress, a "Singer and Speaker" (*CW* 5:400) but with all of the possibilities for broad and instant communication through the device of printing. "The Priest, too, as I understand it, is a kind of Prophet. . . . He is the spiritual Captain of the people . . . [but] He is the Prophet shorn of his more awful splendor" (*CW* 5:341-42). Humanity's change does not preclude recurrence of types, then, and Carlyle brings a very complex perspective to the movement of *Heroes*.

No one of these patterns holds the essential design of the book, however, for Carlyle is not primarily concerned with chronology, evolution, or recurrence. His title is *On Heroes, Hero-Worship, and the Heroic in History* and his intent is to write both of heroes and of "their reception and performance" (*CW* 5:235)—the man and his acts, namely, in concert with the response of his contemporaries, his reciprocal response to them, and, ultimately, on those human qualities that will stand in critical times. Much more than a personal sketch is involved. Very often, Carlyle has to detail the *milieu* if he is to justify the hero's sources of action, and, just as often, he has to portray the hero's reception by the people if he is to show how first acts generate others. Since the hero's life encircles other lives and interrupts many cultural economies, these too must be delineated. Through all the mire of circumstance, heroism itself emerges as no simple thing. Whether in poetry or religion or war, all of Carlyle's heroes are distinguished by some concrete achievement—there are no mute inglorious Miltons among them—and most bring to their time some spiritual quality it would have lacked otherwise. Carlyle variously names this quality "intensity" or "breadth," but his recurrent term is "sincerity" and every one of his examples possesses it in some form. The most complete definition of sincerity occurs in "The Hero as Prophet":

> No, the Great Man does not boast himself sincere, far from that; perhaps does not ask himself if he is: I would say rather, his sincerity does not depend on himself; he cannot help being sincere.

> The great Fact of Existence is great to him. Fly as he will, he cannot get out of the awful presence of this Reality. His mind is so made; he is great by that, first of all. Fearful and wonderful, real as Life, real as Death in this Universe to him. Though all men should forget its truth, and walk in a vain show, he cannot. At all moments the flame image glares in upon him; undeniable, there, there!—I wish you to take this as my primary definition of a Great Man. A little man may have this, it is competent to all men God has made: but a Great Man cannot be without it. (*CW* 5:276)

The definition seems vague, but it does describe with fidelity what sustains Carlyle's heroes. The "Fact of Existence" is before them, and in a dual sense. Spiritually, they are possessed by a view of the awful immediacy of the universe and, simultaneously, by a desire to express their deepest response to it. Odin's glorification of nature, Mahomet's "Allah Akhbar" (*CW* 5:286), Dante's Catholic vision, Shakespeare's cohesive dramatic expression, Luther's theme of salvation by faith, Cromwell's commitment to purity, even Napoleon's humility before the unknown—all, for Carlyle, are sculpted from the same profound reverence for spiritual fact. Practically, they are overwhelmed by the "Fact of Existence" also. Excepting the specifically literary heroes (where production for necessity is not always a virtue), Carlyle's great men are decisive and sure, with a developed sensitivity to the needs of a situation. Carlyle does not dissect Knox's meetings with Queen Mary or Napoleon's maneuvers through his scores of battles, but, in every sketch, he gives enough of the pragmatic man through anecdote and dialogue to show that greatness is not simply visionary. The high moments in *Heroes*—Mahomet's refusal to stop preaching "even if the sun stood on his right hand and the moon on his left, ordering him to hold his peace"; Luther's "Here stand I; I can do no other" at the Diet of Worms; Cromwell's "God be the judge between you and me" before the second Parliament—are charged with spiritual energy, but just as well with the concrete polemic rightness that elevates them above the common to priests and prophets and kings (*CW* 5:289, 360, 452). *Heroes and Hero-Worship*, then, is about the substance and unqualified importance of heroism in this world; for Carlyle is implicitly saying that history turns a corner only when the unique individual directs its course. In at least one of its senses, then, the "Tree" is a natural metaphor for the book itself, because, as the "Tree" develops, so Carlyle sees the significant life of man developing, with direction and point, from the center of great men.

Carlyle's lecture on the hero in the eighteenth century, "The Hero as Man-of-Letters," is the least successful of the series, because it is caught in logical and aesthetic difficulties. Until this lecture, Carlyle has presented his heroes as figures who have mastered their time, replacing doubt with faith, or blindness with vision, and he has added, at the beginning of the first lecture, that "no Time need have gone to ruin, could it have *found* a man great enough, a man wise and good enough: wisdom to discern truly what the Time wanted, valor to lead it on the right road thither" (*CW* 5:246) In this lecture, however, Johnson, Rousseau, and Burns are not "heroic bringers of light," but merely "heroic seekers of it" (*CW* 5:381), men who "could not unfold themselves into clearness, or victorious interpretation of that 'Divine Idea'" (*CW* 5:381). The reasons for their failure are close at hand. As in so many of his previous lectures (Mahomet, Luther, Shakespeare, and Cromwell particularly), Carlyle prepares the way of the hero by unfolding the spirit of the time, and he does it in this lecture also, but with a difference. Previously, he conceived the time as either life-giving or destructive, but if destructive, he selected those details that showed the hero's indomitable "sincerity" in conquering his element. And his heroes achieved. Here, however, the destructive element of the eighteenth century is grounded so completely in the natural cycle of events that its magic cannot be broken—or, conversely, the hero's strength is not great enough to conquer, which, according to the thematic logic of the book, makes him less than a hero. The design of the lecture shows how the dilemma arises. Using the "Tree Igdrasil" as a metaphor for the rhythms of life and death. Carlyle begins by evoking the turn of history and the immaleable constraints of the eighteenth century. To repeat a few lines quoted:

> How mean, dwarfish are their ways of thinking, in this time—compared not with the Christian Shakspeares and Miltons, but with the old Pagan Skalds, with any species of believing men! The living TREE Igdrasil, with the melodious prophetic waving of its world-wide boughs, deep-rooted as Hela, has died out into the clanking of a World-MACHINE." (*CW* 5:393)

That our Hero as Man-of-Letters had to travel without highway, companion-less, through an inorganic chaos,—and to leave his own life and faculty lying there, as a partial contribution toward *pushing* some highway through it: this, had not his faculty itself been so perverted and paralyzed, he might have put up with, might have considered to be the common lot of Heroes. His fatal misery was the *spiritual paralysis*, so we may name it, of the Age in which his life lay; whereby his life too, do what he might, was half paralyzed. (*CW* 5:392)

The time reduces the universe to its own measure. The three representative heroes struggle, by "originality," "sincerity," and "genius" to express their vision; but they do not succeed, for Carlyle's concluding image of each man (Johnson standing with his single worshiper, "Bozzy"; Rousseau in the chains of his own delirium; Burns, like a firefly, carried on a spit to serve as a tiny public light) leave the impression that the skeptical temper of the century is the real victor. Something has happened along the way, as it has not happened to Luther or Napoleon or Cromwell.

The difficulty lies in locating the point of failure. If the highest doctrine Johnson can preach is only a kind of moral prudence, and if the cause of his failure is in the mechanical extravagance of the age, then where are those subtle interconnections, those responses in nerves and will, that show how Johnson is shaped by the age? With Rousseau, the problem is only slightly different. If the final cause of Rousseau's failure is the spiritual paralysis of the time, and if Carlyle details only Rousseau's egoism and operatic talent, then what are the bonds that show how an age bodies forth into a Rousseau? The relation between man and age is more convincing with Burns because the age is focused through the image of Edinburgh society; but even here, the sources of Burns' failure and their relation to Edinburgh are so little detailed that the two hemispheres of man and society seem to be separate worlds. Professor Frederic E. Faverty has said that one of the faults of *Heroes* is the lack of criteria by which we can recognize a hero,[8] and another is the lack of an articulate analysis showing how a potential hero falls before the opinion in his time. Both of these *lacunae* are failures in "pragmatic imagination," and the second is particularly grave, because, in failing to trace the internal relations of his statements, Carlyle implicitly raises the larger question: Is the hero as man of letters a hero at all?

Carlyle's use of the eighteenth century in *Heroes* is that of scapegoat. Without evidence or study of the reciprocal relations between man and time, he transfers the century into the receptacle for all the confusions that prevent his men of promise from being fathers of change. Simply the reappearance of terms—"sceptical," "insincere,' "doubtful," "sick"—shows how one insistently narrow perspective is stressed. And the ultimate difficulty of *Heroes* is centered here: what begins as the disarray of one lecture becomes the problem of the book. If the three representative men do not succeed in replacing blindness with vision, or doubt with faith (either through the victory of the time or the lack of personal effort—the causes are not artistically distinguished) and if the theme is the importance and unambiguous necessity of individual heroism in this world, then their heroism is questionable and their contribution to the heroic in history negligible. The theme of the book is severely deflected from its course. One of the mysteries of *Heroes* is Carlyle's choice of Johnson, Rousseau, and Burns as subjects for this lecture. Originally, Goethe was very seriously considered. "Our chosen specimen of the Hero as Literary Man would be this Goethe," he writes at the beginning, "but at present such is the general state of knowledge about Goethe, it were worse than useless to attempt speaking of him in this case" (*CW* 5:381). Paradoxically, it is Goethe who would have been Carlyle's ideal subject, for in providing the details that would have clarified his life, Carlyle would probably have avoided the gross generalizations on the eighteenth century and the critical vacuum between consciousness and circumstance.

NOTES

[1] Cf. Louis Cazamian, *Carlyle*, trans. E. K. Brown, (New York, 1932); rpt (Hamden, CT: Archon, 1966): 167-81; C. F. Harrold, *Carlyle and German Thought: 1819-1834* (New Haven: Yale UP, 1934): 184-96; Benjamin H. Lehman, *Carlyle's Theory of the Hero* (Durham: Duke UP, 1928); Emery Neff, *Carlyle* (New York: Norton, 1932): 193-95; René Wellek, *Confrontations* (Princeton UP, 1965): 82-113; and Louise M. Young, *Carlyle and the Art of History* (Philadelphia: U of Pennsylvania P, 1939): 82-86.

[2] Carlyle, *Two Note Books*, ed. C. E. Norton (New York: Grolier, 1898): 215.

[3] *Collected Letters of Thomas Carlyle and Jane Welsh Carlyle*, 24 vols. Charles R. Sanders, K. J. Fielding, Clyde de L. Ryals, et al., eds. (Durham: Duke UP, 1970): 1:6-9.

[4] J. A. Froude, *Thomas Carlyle, A History of His Life in London: 1834-1881* (London: Longmans, 1884): 48.

[5] Carlisle Moore, "The Persistence of Carlyle's 'Everlasting Yea,'" *Modern Philology* 54 (February 1957): 189.

[6] *On Heroes, Hero-Worship and the Heroic in History*, Centenary Edition, ed. H. D. Traill, (London: Chapman and Hall, 1899): 24:253. Hereafter cited in text by volume and page.

[7] The ceaseless activity of the "Tree Igdrasil" is expressed in Carlyle's first description of it: "It is Igdrasil, the Tree of Existence. It is the past, the present, and the future; what was done, what is doing, what will be done; 'the infinite conjugation of the verb *To do*'" (*CW* 5:254).

[8] *Your Literary Heritage* (Philadelphia: Lippincott, 1959): 102.

"Ishmael as Prophet: *Heroes and Hero-Worship* and the Self-Expressive Basis of Carlyle's Art"

TEXAS STUDIES IN LANGUAGE AND LITERATURE

11 (Spring 1969): 705-32.

DAVID J. DELAURA

No reader of Thomas Carlyle's lectures *On Heroes, Hero-Worship and the Heroic in History*, delivered in May 1840, has missed the crucial unifying theme of the possibility of "Prophecy" in the nineteenth century. Carlyle is guardedly optimistic as he glances at the achievement of Goethe, about whom he had written for two decades. If the prime quality of the prophet is his "vision of the inward divine mystery," then Goethe eminently qualifies; for under Goethe's "guise of a most modern, high-bred, high-cultivated Man of Letters," Carlyle discerns that his works are "really a Prophecy in these most unprophetic times."[1] Writing to Mill the following February, Carlyle notes that the message of *Heroes*—"a stranger kind of Book than I thought it would [be]"—already lay, for the perceptive reader, "mostly legible in what I had long since written" (*CL* 13:47). And indeed, the theme of prophecy, especially in its relation to modern times, was a chief concern of Carlyle's early essays, above all in "Characteristics," where he had suggestively invoked the metaphysics and "higher Literature" of modern Germany to support his view that "This age also is not wholly without its Prophets" (*CW* 28:41).

The present paper explores the implications of the idea that the unity of *Heroes*, and with it much of Carlyle's early thought, is to be found in the deeply personal character of his painstaking attempt to define the characteristics, the message, and the social role of the prophet, especially in the nineteenth century. The pervasiveness of this theme, and the intensity of personal involvement with which it is pursued, suggest that in it we touch a central and vital source of Carlyle's literary dynamism, a key to the intentions of his career as well as to its substantive content. The mingled literary and biographical problems which this theme brings up are nearly unique; rarely has a developed literary art occupied so large a tract of the frontier between personal experience and objective artistry. Carlyle's favorite heroes and prophets are presented as figures who struggle for insight and for public recognition. His own parallel struggle is twofold: at the personal level, the search for a public and for literary distinction; in a larger context, the search for a "message" and the question of whether he could really affect the mind and sensibility of his times. As we shall see, the problem of "voice"—already recognized as crucial in a work like *Sartor Resartus*—is at issue here. For it seems clear that the youthful generation of the 1840's which was so strongly attracted to Carlyle—the generation of Matthew Arnold and Arthur Hugh Clough[2]—was responding not only to the prophetic strain in Carlyle (a point long recognized) but also to the uniquely authentic and authoritative presence of Carlyle in his own prophecy. Through the variety of roles and attitudes he assumes in a work, Carlyle convinces us of the integrity of his own embodied personality, sensed as a single energizing force behind all particular statements. This constantly expanding and controlling "virtual" personality is the basis of the integrity of the work as a whole. The theme of prophecy thus goes some distance toward clarifying the precise power and effect of Carlyle's complex art.

I

The familiar story of Carlyle's intense struggle and bitter frustration of the 1820's, reflected in the unfinished *Wotton Reinfred* and in *Sartor Resartus*, is the backdrop for Carlyle's early concern for prophecy. Though *Sartor* finally represented a style and literary form adequate to Carlyle's slowly maturing philosophy of dynamic idealism,[3] the work on its appearance in *Fraser's* in 1833-1834 was greeted with almost universal disapproval. Only with the publication of *The French Revolution* in 1837 can Carlyle be said to have begun to find the public he sought. But even in the first essay in which Carlyle discovered his authentic tone and manner, "Signs of the Times" (1829), he had fulfilled three traditional functions of the inspired prophet: the analysis and denunciation of the present as somehow falling below a divine standard; the announcement of a direct "message" from, or "insight" into, truth; and a literal prophecy or prediction of man's future or at least of his potentialities. "Characteristics" (1831), however, was to prove even more important in the humanist struggles of the nineteenth century, in its definition of "the region of meditation" as superior to "the region of argument and conscious discourse" (*CW* 28:4-5). A generation of younger readers responded to the assertion that, in the contemporary rupture of the natural tie between religion and this meditative mode, "the Thinker must, in all senses, wander homeless, too often aimless, looking up to a Heaven which is dead for him, round to an Earth which is deaf" (*CW* 28:29-30). Carlyle must have seemed close to the surface as he announced that the noblest now are those who do not fall back on a "worn-out" creed or end in scepticism or hedonism, but who "have dared to say No and cannot yet say Yea, but feel that in the No they dwell as in a Golgotha, where life enters not, where peace is not appointed them" (*CW* 28:31). The nobler such men, the harder their fate:

> In dim forecastings, wrestles within them the "Divine Idea of the World," yet will nowhere visibly reveal itself. They have to realise a Worship for themselves, or live unworshipping. The Godlike has vanished from the world; and they, by the strong cry of their soul's agony, like true wonder-workers, must again evoke its presence. (*CW* 28:31)

The struggle of the nobly prophetic spirit, seeking in vain the revelation of the divine but compelled nevertheless to evoke its presence, is plainly a program for Carlyle's career, now that through *Sartor* and the essays of this period he had found his special voice and métier. The sketch Carlyle provides of the approved prophet—alone and wandering, detached from institutions and lacking a sympathetic audience, but always struggling both for insight into the divine and for means adequate to express it—is very much the pattern he was to find for the most sympathetic of his great men in *Heroes*. The personal force suffusing his elaborate discussion of the possibilities of prophecy in the nineteenth century becomes even clearer near the end of "Characteristics" when he announces, as we have seen, "This age also is not wholly without its Prophets"; the reader is thoroughly prepared, even if not wholly conscious of the effect, to apply the remark—made in the first place with reference to German philosophy and literature—to Carlyle himself. Evidently the Carlyle who ended by predicting that "The genius of Mechanism . . . will not always sit like a choking incubus on our soul; but at length, when by a new magic Word the old spell is broken, become our slave, and as familiar spirit do all our bidding" (*CW* 28:42-43), felt, increasingly, that *he*, above all others of his generation in England, was in possession of that "new magic Word."

Carlyle's discovery of himself and of his role through his definition of the prophet in *Sartor* and the essays of 1829-1831 is the prelude to a larger cluster of concerns in the thirties which reveal his growing insight into the relationship of artistry to self-knowledge—though generally overlooked, this is one of the richest bodies of reflection on the creative process in the nineteenth century. Froude, praising the *French Revolution* as Carlyle's "most perfect" work, speaks of his defective sense of form in the others: "He throws out brilliant and detached pictures, and large masses of thought. . . . There is everywhere unity of purpose. . . . But events are left to tell their own story. He appears continually in his own person, instructing, commenting, informing the reader at every step of his own opinion. His method of composition is so original that it cannot be tried by common rules."[4] What has not been studied is how Carlyle's "unity of purpose" is largely secured precisely by his various modes of self-presentation.

As early as 1827, in his first two essays on Jean Paul, Carlyle had added to the familiar Romantic view that Jean Paul's works are "emblems . . . of the singular mind where they originated" (*CW* 22:127), the more fruitful perception that in his works, whether fictional or not, the author "generally becomes a person in the drama himself (*CW* 26:12).[5] But only in 1833, with the writing of the "Diamond Necklace," had Carlyle achieved considerable freedom in handling his own "presence" in his writing. As Carlisle Moore has showed, Carlyle in this work not only indulges in his familiar didactic "tendency to moralize, to philosophize, to judge the significance of things," but he also steps into the narrative "as a person of as many moods as ideas." Though Carlyle continually reveals his ignorance of the reader's personality, he becomes a kind of stage director who also repeatedly addresses the reader, warning, commanding, conversing, and persuading.[6] But this same year, 1833, is also important because it was then that Carlyle seems first to have seen the convergence in himself of the various burdens of the nineteenth-century prophet. Two remarkable journal entries reveal that Carlyle's still unresolved religious crisis is at the center. He writes on March 31: "Wonderful, and alas! most pitiful alternations of belief and unbelief in me. . . . Meanwhile, continue to believe in *thyself*. . . . Neither fear though that this thy great message of the Natural *being* the Supernatural will wholly perish unuttered."[7] The message is even less secure in an entry dated August 24, where his acknowledgment that "For the last year my faith has lain under a most sad eclipse" preludes his plaintive insistence: "In *all* times there is a word which, spoken to men, to the actual generation of men, would thrill their inmost soul. But the way to find that word? The way to speak it when found?" (*FF* 2:354). Obviously, "faith" or "belief," in startlingly traditional senses of those terms, precedes belief in oneself, the external "word" or message of the Natural Supernatural, the style of its expression, and the hoped-for soul-shaking effect on the present generation.

The only element lacking in this self-analysis, the cultural crisis of the age, was supplied in one of Carlyle's most penetrating letters to Emerson, dated August 12, 1834. Far from defending himself against Emerson's "saucy" objection that his idiosyncratic style results from his not knowing his public, Carlyle agrees and calls it "questionable, tentative, and only the best that I in these mad times could conveniently hit upon." For he has a strikingly modern sense "that now at least we have lived to see all manner of Poetics and Rhetorics and Sermonics, and one may say generally all manner of *Pulpits* for addressing mankind from, as good as broken and abolished." He sees the modern prophet's problem as the fact that, though "pasteboard coulisses, and three unities, and Blair's lectures" are now gone, even perennially sacred "inspired utterance" will remain "inconceivable, misconceivable to the million; questionable (not of *ascertained* significance) even to the few." He pictures himself as trying new methods, and getting "nearer the truth, as I honestly strive for it." But he ends, more guardedly than in his journal, with a weak and bleakly voluntaristic version of his contentless religious "faith": "Meanwhile I know no method of much consequence, except that of *believing*, of being sincere . . ." (*CL* 7:265-66). This line of thought is renewed a year later, in June 1835, when he argues against Sterling that "Purism of Style" cannot be his concern: "With whole ragged battalions of Scott's-Novel Scotch, with Irish, German, French and even Newspaper Cockney (when 'Literature' is little other than a Newspaper) storming in on us, and the whole structure of our Johnsonian English breaking up from its foundations,—revolution *there* is visible as anywhere else!" (*CL* 8:135).

These concerns are refocused and clarified in a later stage of self-awareness, during and after the writing of the *French Revolution*. As early as June 1831, Carlyle had told Goethe that in *Sartor* "It is . . . not a Picture that I am painting . . . but a half-reckless casting of the brush, with its many frustrated colours, against the canvas" (*CL* 5:289). In July 1836, near to finishing the *French Revolution*, he repeats the image, saying that he will "splash down what I know, in large masses of colour; that it may look like a smoke-and-flame conflagration in the distance, which it is" (*CL* 9:22). And Carlyle is aware that even his relatively objective history reflects his special temperament and situation. He is excessively self-depreciating to Emerson in November 1836—"it is a wild savage ruleless very bad Book; which even you will not be able to like"; but revealingly, he insists that these qualities are the very sign of its authenticity: "Yet it contains strange things; sincerities drawn out of the heart of a man very strangely situated" (*CL* 9:82). This is amplified in a letter to his brother John the following February: "It is a Book written by a *wild man*, a man disunited from the fellowship of the world he lives in, looking King and beggar in the face with an indifference of brotherhood and an indifference of contempt" (*CL* 9:145).

Carlyle, then, shows a developing consciousness of his complex, perhaps unique, artistry, a development which draws on his experience and on his insight into his experience as *both* (in Eliot's phrase) the man who suffers and the mind which creates. His scattered formulation by 1837 of the personal basis of his style, for which there can be no premeditated "Art," involves the convergence of his insights into the profound cultural crisis of the age; the consequent breakdown of traditional categories of truth; a corresponding disablement of traditional modes of utterance; the difficulty which even divine truth has in finding a fit audience; and most important, the fact that he is one of a special class of individuals with an historic mission, marked to suffer in the self-annihilating task of apprehending essential moral and social truth. These, then, are the awarenesses and burdens of what we may call the "pilgrim" prophet, the only adequate prophet for the nineteenth century. His oracles are emphatic enough, but they inevitably reflect, and are the product of, his own vanguard position, pushing on into truth a few steps ahead of his fellows. He will proclaim a new truth, at least to the extent that Natural Supernaturalism has never before been preached in England; his is a new mode of discovery, drawing on the prophet's own personal quest, suffering, and sincerity; his is a uniquely "personal" mode of disjointed utterance, a hectic "splashing" down; and finally, his discovery of his unknown audience, even his creation of that audience, is part of the truth-seeking process. The splashing-down images suggest that truth is not objective, pre-existent, waiting for its recorder; instead, it is found as part of the act or process of artistic creation itself: prophecy discovers and perhaps even creates truth.

Here is the complex heart of the usual simplicity attributed to Carlyle, that the great artist is simply the great-souled man.[8] To employ his tentative and heuristic method, to "speak" sincerely, is to educe "strange," even frightening, aspects of truth. This is Carlyle's central, and modern, insight that truth is, in a fundamental sense, correlative to personal quest, very nearly a function of personality and moral disposition. We are not far here from some of the later insights into the "personal" quality of truth in Newman, especially in the *Grammar of Assent*. Thus Carlyle in effect sees that his not easily described method develops certain premises of Romantic egoism—above all, the efficacy of the suffering self—for their "expressive" power. In *Heroes and Hero-Worship*, as we shall see, it even becomes a quasi-structural principle and a source of "meaning" as the narrative pattern of the hero's struggles emerges as representative of the experience of the age. It predicts a Victorian mode, too, in being a kind of extended monologue or a series of interlocking monologues.

II

By the time he came to compose *Chartism* in the second half of 1839, Carlyle was far more confidently the prophet than he had been when he composed *Sartor* in obscurity. The peculiar personal pressure discernible in his early discussion of the prophet's mission had by 1839 become the fully developed manner of the assured sage. To attempt to describe the prophet's message and manner was indeed increasingly to *act* the prophet, to *adopt* his message and manner.[9] Though Carlyle could depreciate his lectures of 1838 as "a mixture of prophecy and play-acting" (*LL* 1:136), the phrase is suggestive in clarifying the nature of Carlyle's art in this period. For the four series of lectures (1837-1840) not only mark the culmination of his fame and influence, the reward of his years of suffering; they also bring out a new and intensified awareness of the basis of his art in a special apprehension of "self." In *Chartism*, and in some of the most striking passages of *Heroes* and *Past and Present*, Carlyle is able to present *himself* far more directly as teacher and seer—and for the most part without the disguise of a Teufelsdröckh or even a Sauerteig—than he had in *Sartor* or the early essays. The question of "voice" becomes crucial here.

I point especially to a mechanism at work in a passage quoted at length for its special and elaborate use of the first-person pronoun. Carlyle retorts against "the British reader" who would limit the function of society to that of protecting property:

> And now what is thy property? That parchment title-deed, that purse thou buttonest in thy breeches-pocket? Is that thy valuable property? Unhappy brother, most poor insolvent brother, I without parchment at all, with purse oftenest in the flaccid state, imponderous, which will not fling against the wind, have quite other property than that! I have the miraculous breath of life in me, breathed into my nostrils by Almighty God. I have affections, thoughts, a god-given *capability* to be and do; rights, therefore,—the right for instance to thy love if I love thee, to thy guidance if I obey thee: the strangest rights, whereof in church-pulpits one still hears something, though almost unintelligible now; rights stretching high into Immensity, far into Eternity! Fifteen-pence a-day; three-and-sixpence a-day; eight hundred pounds and odd a-day, dost thou call that my property? I value that little; little all I could purchase with that. For truly, as is said, what matters it? In torn boots, in soft-hung carriages-and-four, a man gets always to his journey's end. Socrates walked barefoot, or in wooden shoes, and yet arrived happily. They never asked him, *What* shoes of conveyance? never What wages hadst thou? but simply, What work didst thou?—Property, O brother? "Of my very body I have but a life-rent." As for this flaccid purse of mine, 'tis something, nothing; has been the slave of pickpockets, cutthroats, Jew-brokers, gold-dust robbers; 'twas his, 'tis mine;—'tis thin, if thou care much to steal it. But my soul, breathed into me by God, my *Me* and what capability is there; that is mine, and I will resist the stealing of it. I call that mine and not thine; I will keep that, and do what work I can with it: God has given it me, the Devil shall not take

it away: Alas, my friends, Society exists and has existed for a great many purposes, not so easy to specify! (*CW* 29:163-64)

The "I" here rises to an altogether more elevated and intense note of personal involvement than in the rather conventional "we" and "us" which is the sustained usage of "Chartism." Carlyle presents himself, first, as directly testifying to the special quality of his own prophetic mission. This openly "stagy" performance (the Shakespearean echoes would not be missed by an educated reader) becomes a dramatized authentication of that mission, working by the true prophet's heightening, repetition, and intensity. Second, the "I" is representative: Carlyle presents himself as a divinely commissioned, archetypal human being. "Brother" and "friends" are not the usual lecturer's amenities here, for Carlyle is acting out a higher, quasi-religious sense of community, his very topic being "Society" in a transcendent sense. In both of these uses of the first-person pronoun, Carlyle speaks directly, without the most usual mask, and with the special accent of one "inspired" and the bearer of a divine message.

The evidence so far presented goes to support the contention that Carlyle's continuing concern with prophecy in his writings through "Chartism" is a function of his personal quest to define his own prophetic mission and message, to achieve an adequate style, and to find an audience. The letters of the period of "Chartism" and *Heroes* are even more explicit on Carlyle's conception of himself as prophet. For Carlyle's own struggles of these years, especially as he is vindicated in his emergence from obscurity, strikingly parallel the full pattern of experience which he discovers in his favorite prophets of the *Heroes* lectures. In the spring of 1839 Carlyle delivered a lecture series called "On Modern Revolutions." He writes Emerson on April 13, concerned quite literally with prophetic inspiration: "How true that is of the Old Prophets, 'The *word of the Lord* came unto' such and such a one! When it does not come, both Prophet and Prosaist ought to be thankful (after a sort), and rigorously hold their tongue" (*CL* 11:81). Four days later, he writes of the agony of composition: "My Lectures come on, this day two weeks: O Heaven! *I* cannot 'speak'; I can only gasp and writhe and stutter, a spectacle to gods and fashionables,—being forced to it by want of money" (*CL* 11:92). But on May 29, the lectures now over, he is eager to master the art of public speaking: "I found . . . that extempore Speaking . . . is an *art* or craft, and requires an apprenticeship, which I have neve[r] served. Repeatedly it has come into my head that I should go to America, [this] very Fall, and belecture you from North to South till I learn it!" (*CL* 11:120). Obviously, Carlyle does in some sense conceive of himself as a prophet, and "inspired," and he wishes to conquer a broad public on both sides of the Atlantic. Even his complaint about finding the proper mode in which to "speak" is, we perceive, part of the prophet's role; for, as *Heroes* was to make clear, a gasping, writhing, stuttering speech is a common sign of the divinely given power whelming up in the authentic prophet. Carlyle again and again suggests that *smoothness* of speech and of mental process indicates superficiality; the "open secret" of Nature is essentially simple, but it can be captured only by intuition, which resists easy formulation.

Although Carlyle regularly speaks of lecturing as "intensely disagreeable" (*CL* 11:180, 12:16, 117, 141), he is much concerned about his influence upon the British public. A letter to his brother, June 20, 1839, indicates his satisfaction that his opinions, "pretty well uttered now," are "making their way with unexpected undeserved rapidity in my generation" (*CL* 11:136). This was not, it is important to note, a conventional search for "fame," about which Carlyle could be impressively scornful. But a crucial letter to his mother of October 24, 1839, makes clear that this year of marvels—signalized by the publication of the *Critical and Miscellaneous Essays* and Sterling's laudatory article in the *Westminster*—marked the end of his period of obscurity and heroic struggle.

> What reason have I to thank a kind Providence that has led me so mercifully thus far! It is a changed time with me from what it was but a few years back; from what it had been all my life. My sore sufferings, poverty, sickness, obstruction, dispiritment were sent me in kindness; angrily as I rebelled against them, they were all kind and good. My poor painful existence was not altogether in vain. (*CL* 11:208-9)[10]

This sentiment is to be distinguished from self-pity by the fact that Carlyle's personal vindication after his years of struggle exactly parallels his heroes' path of suffering, poverty, and obstruction leading to triumph. This new conviction did not, of course, imply that the newly recognized prophet had been exempted from the struggle of *expressing* his vision, any more than the writing of *Sartor* eight years before had meant the achievement of perfect clarity of vision.[11] He wrote Emerson on December 8, 1839, distressed that he can find no publisher for "Chartism": "nevertheless I had to persist writing; writing and burning, and cursing my destiny, and then again writing." Moreover, though the "thoughts were familiar to me, old, many years old," the problem remained that of "the utterance of them, in what spoken dialect to utter them!" (*CL* 11:226-27). By "dialect," a favorite word of Carlyle's, he seems to mean something more than "style," almost what we would today call "dramatic voice" or rhetorical posture.

Certainly the tone and content of *Chartism* in no sense represent a conscious attempt to meet the tastes or the expectations of the English public. The great essay he had written "cursing" was done in obedience to some higher impulse: "I do not care very much," he writes on December 30, 1839, "*what* the world say or forbear to say or do in regard to the thing: it was a thing I *had* to write." At the same time, he is a mixture of pride and self-depreciation about the favorable reception of the *Essays*: "It rather seems the people like them in spite of all their crabbedness." Perhaps it is this matter of "crabbedness" which makes him reflect wistfully that "ten years of my life lie strangely written there; it is I, and it is not I, that wrote all that!" (*CL* 11:236). Carlyle was concerned, then, about his perhaps forbidding style (along with the problem of what "I" it could be said to represent), about the essential integrity of his witness before his generation, and, in a complex way, about his effect upon the public consciousness. He shows some apprehension concerning what *public* he was in fact addressing. His references to the "fashionables" and the "beautiful people" who attended his lectures are a mixture of scorn and flattered vanity. At times he seemed to imagine—perhaps sentimentally and, surprisingly, in the vein of Matthew Arnold—that he had access to a body of "rational and just" readers freed from class and party thinking. In January 1840 he has no hope of affecting "the present Radical Members and Agitators": "for the cause of the Poor, one must leave them [the Radicals] and their battles out of view, and address rather the great solid *heart* of England, the rational and just men of England, and avoiding all outposts and their inconclusive tumult, go right to the heart of the matter" (*CL* 12:23).

The intermingled concerns with style, "audience," and prophetic message were intensified during the months of the composition, delivery, and revision of the lectures on *Heroes*. Carlyle was pleased with his increasing audience during the lecture series in May, and in mid-June he describes his intention in rewriting: "I am endeavouring to write down my Lectures somewhat in the style of *speech*" (*CL* 12:169-70). This new emphasis on *speech* marks what is very likely the high point of Carlyle's personal enthusiasm for the prophetic office; for impassioned speech, as an indicator of sincerity and authenticity, was, he evidently felt, the appropriate mode for what he explicitly called his "preaching," a preaching done "in the name of God." As he explained in May, *Heroes* occupied a special position among his lecture series, since "I am telling the people matters that belong much more to *myself* this year, which is far more interesting to me" (*LL* 182; emphasis added). Some of this relation to himself is revealed in an extraordinary letter to Emerson of July 2, where Carlyle is found, in a mood of mingled exuberance and conviction, bursting forth in the high-prophetic tone in which he would *like* to preach the otherwise familiar message of *Heroes*:

> The misery of it was hardly equal to that of former years, yet still was very hateful. I had got to a certain feeling of superiority over my audience; as if I had something to tell them, and would tell it them. At times I felt as if I could, in the end, learn to speak. The beautiful people listened with boundless tolerance, eager attention. I meant to tell them, among other things, that man was still alive, Nature not dead or like to die; that all true men continue true to this hour. . . . On the whole, I fear I did little but confuse my esteemed audience: I was amazed, after all their reading of me, to be understood so ill;—gratified nevertheless to see how the rudest *speech* of a man's heart goes into men's hearts, and is the welcomest thing there. Withal I regretted that I had not six months of preaching, whereby to learn to preach, and explain things fully! In the fire of the moment I had all but decided on setting out for America this autumn, and preaching far and wide like a very lion there. Quit your paper formulas, my brethren,—equivalent to old wooden idols, *un*divine as they: in the name of God, understand that you are alive, and that God is alive! Did the Upholsterer make this Universe? Were you created by the Tailor? I tell you, and conjure you to believe me literally, No, a thousand times No! Thus did I mean to preach, on "Heroes, Hero-worship and the Heroic," in America too. (*CL* 12:183-84)

The fire dwindled, the mood of the lion passed; still, he resolves to publish the lectures, "and in *some* way promulgate them farther." The urgency persists: he writes his brother on July 15 that the message, "in some way or other, must not be lost. It is not a new story to *me*; but the world seemed greatly astonished at it; the world cannot too soon get acquainted with it" (*CL* 12:192). But by August 1 the lectures looked to Carlyle "absolutely worth nothing at all," precisely because, "wanting all the unction of personal sincerity expressed by voice and face, they look entirely dull and tame on paper" (*CL* 12:210). "Nothing which I have ever written pleases me so ill," he continues later in the same month, as he strives to make the lectures "low-pitched, as like talk as possible" (*LL* 195).

The printed lectures also evoked in Carlyle a familiar but suggestively intense ambivalence. On the one hand, fretting over proofsheets, he sees the completed book with a kind of wondering incomprehension: "This thing on Heroes [he writes Mill on February 24, 1841] proves to be a stranger kind of Book than I thought it would. Since men do read without reflexion, this too was worth writing" (*CL* 13:47). It was even "a *goustrous* [strong, boisterous] determined speaking out of the truth about several things. The people will be no worse for it at present" (*LL* 207). And yet within a month he writes Mill again, in an almost suspicious fit of revulsion: "now that it all lies there, little is visible but triviality, contemptibility,—and the happy prospect of washing one's hands of it forever and a day. No Book of mine ever looked more insignificant to me" (*CL* 13:63). But the prophet in Carlyle, however much dismayed by his own most "prophetic" book, was not to be put down. Less than two months later—on May 13—we find him struggling over Cromwell's life, fearful, as he tells Sterling, that "the man to write it will probably never be born." But he all at once changes subject and exclaims: "Or leaving History altogether, what do you say of Prophecy? Is not *Prophecy* the grand thing? The volcanic *terra da lavoro* of Yorkshire and Lancashire: within that too lies a prophecy gran[der] than Ezekiel's...!" (*CL* 13:131). To the end the Carlyle who doubted whether it was "the duty of a citizen to be silent, to paint mere Heroisms, Cromwells, &c." (*LL* 222) admitted only one "secret of *Kunst*" in his method, that of the chosen sufferer for truth who must yet struggle heroically to express it, part sublime prophet and part impromptu play actor. The "*intelligence* of the *fact*," as he writes Sterling early in 1842, "once blazing within me, if it will ever get to blaze, and bursting to be out, one has to take the whole dexterity of adaptation one is master of, or has ever gathered from the four winds, and with tremendous struggling, really frightful struggling, contrive to exhibit it, one way or the other" (*CL* 14:24).

III

"Is not *Prophecy* the grand thing?" The evidence of the letters, along with an internal analysis of *Heroes*, suggests that much of the "strange" quality of the lectures was due precisely to its "prophetic" character, as an intense focusing of Carlyle's deepest desire to be recognized in his own generation as seer and sage and, to a degree difficult to gauge, as a leader. The subject chosen for the lectures, the lecture form itself, as well as the precise moment of Carlyle's critical engagement with the English public—all these conjoined to evoke from him his profoundest exploration of the prophet's mission: the prophet's credentials, his message, and his special mode of utterance. In doing so he rather wonderfully revealed his fundamental conception of himself, of his own role, and of the titanic stance he had adopted in this most "unheroic" and "unprophetic" time. The ultimate hero of the *Heroes* lectures, as well as the source of its unity, is Thomas Carlyle: he is implicitly the chief character, and the work is nearly as autobiographical as Book II of *Sartor*.

Heroes is so staged as to throw Carlyle's own role in his generation into the strongest light, and to give it the greatest significance. The series of historic figures brought forward for description and moralizing are so many cases which bear upon the regularly recurring theme of the Prophetic Office in the nineteenth century. Implicitly, the man with special insight into Heroes and Heroism is inevitably a hero himself: this impression is conveyed both in Carlyle's own prophetic assertions, which simply duplicate the rather restricted range of his heroes' perceptions, and his own special style or mode of utterance, which exhibits their "rude" and "rugged" character. Moreover, Carlyle's conception of himself, as well as his personal and literary problems, which we have seen revealed in the correspondence of this period, are worked into the pattern which he more or less arbitrarily imposes upon his most congenial heroes—Mahomet, Dante, Luther, Knox, Johnson, Cromwell. The final evidence of the autobiographical pressure in *Heroes* is the frequent approximation to the pattern of experience elaborated much more fully in *Sartor*, a book which has long been recognized to be autobiographical in important respects. Without great exaggeration, then, *Heroes* can be read as an extended essay, in the artistic guise of a series of biographical studies, on Carlyle's talent and vocation.

Carlyle is continually at pains, first of all, to point out the contemporary relevance of his reflections on heroism. Again and again—through the repeated use of expressions like "still," "yet," "to this hour"—he insists that the Poet, the Prophet, or the Priest, even in "such a time as ours," is "a voice from the unseen Heaven": "So in old times; so in these, and in all times" (*CW* 5:9, 11-12, 28, 24, 80, 115). The climax of this constant pointing forward to the nineteenth century comes in Lecture V, on The Hero as Man of Letters, who, though "altogether a product of these new ages," speaks forth his inspiration as did the Gods, Prophets, and Priests of past times. In "uttering-forth . . . the inspired soul of him," the Man of Letters becomes "our most important modern person," "the soul of all." His exalted function—to proclaim Carlyle's familiar message that "the True, Divine and Eternal . . . exists always, unseen to most, under the Temporary, Trivial"—is exactly what all heroes "are sent into the world to do" (*CW* 5:154-56). Carlyle repeats an idea of Fichte's he had first approved in the 1820's, that the Man of Letters, preaching the "Divine Idea of the World," in fact *guides* the world, "like a sacred Pillar of Fire, in its dark pilgrimage through the waste of Time" (*CW* 5:157). This attempt to enhance the importance of the modern Man of Letters is bolstered by a recurrent theme: that "at bottom the Great Man, as he comes from the hand of Nature, is ever the same kind of thing: Odin, Luther, Johnson, Burns; . . . these are all originally of one stuff" (*CW* 5:43). Differentiated only by "the different *sphere*" in which he works and by "the kind of world he finds himself born into" (*CW* 5:78; see 115), the hero, even of modern times, retains an amazing omnicompetence: "A Hero is a Hero at all points" (*CW* 5:28).

The climactic ordering of the lectures toward the apotheosis of the Man of Letters is aided by Carlyle's frequently reiterated definition of the Hero as essentially a *Prophet*, the *speaker* of the "revelation" of the open secret of the universe: the "word" is his province. The prophet is of course "inspired," and he is everywhere marked by *insight* and *sincerity*: as Seer and Thinker he *sees* the truth, and as Prophet he *utters* it, with whatever difficulty. The great man's "word is the wise healing word which all can believe in" (*CW* 5:13). The "shaped spoken Thought" of "the great Thinker, . . . the *original* man, the Seer," articulates what "all men were not far from saying, were longing to say" (*CW* 5:21). The image Carlyle presents of the prophet is that of the "earnest man, speaking to his brother men" (*CW* 5:26). As a "messenger . . . sent from the Infinite Unknown with tidings to us," we all feel of the Prophet that "the words he utters are as no other man's words." If the Prophet is always "a voice from the unseen Heaven" (*CW* 5:115), the Man of Letters is the key modern figure "endeavouring to speak forth the inspiration" in him through printed books (*CW* 5:154). For such men are above all "Prophets" and "speakers . . . of the everlasting truth" (*CW* 5:178).

But the peculiarly personal concern which unifies Carlyle's reflections is most evident in the pattern of experience he assigns to his heroes, and in their special qualities of style. The personal qualities of the hero are fairly uniform: these are rendered by recurrent epithets like "rude," "rugged," "earnest," "fervent." Some— for example Shakespeare and Johnson—are presented as "unconscious," apparently as a consequence of the very inexpressibility of their intuitive apprehension of the divine. Frequently, too, these favorite heroes are melancholic by temperament; certainly they are compelled to accept a full share of sorrow and sadness in life. These "rude" figures are almost always presented as titanic, struggling, even "wild" and "savage" ("there is something of the savage in all great men" [*CW* 5:193]). Above all, they are uniformly men of *sincerity* ("rude sincerity," "Wild sincere heart") and *insight* ("the clear, deep-seeing eye," "depth of vision"). The fundamental double image of *Heroes*, in fact, is one of *depth* and *penetration*, repeated in literally dozens of forms. The hero is thus a man of what we might call down-and-in-sight, suggested by what is in effect a series of highly kinetic images of plunging and piercing.[12] Of course the man who can penetrate to the depth in each of these heroes is himself a man of insight and depth. But the effect is incalculably strengthened by a seemingly innocent device, Carlyle's constant repetition of "at bottom," a simple adverbial expression which becomes part both of the prophetic message and of Carlyle's credentials as a prophet in his own right.

Coming even closer to Carlyle himself, his rugged, earnest hero is presented as undergoing a special pattern of experience. Hampered usually by disadvantageous origins, he is literally or figuratively at some time outcast, wandering, solitary, in exile; but he valiantly struggles forward under the burden of suffering, sorrow, and darkness and eventually wins through to clarity, triumph, vindication. One is frequently struck by the similarity of this heroic course to that undergone by the autobiographical figure of Teufelsdröckh in *Sartor*.[13] Even more pertinent, only six months before he composed *Heroes* we saw Carlyle speaking of the "changed time" a merciful Providence had suddenly brought him: "My sore sufferings, poverty, sickness, obstruction, dispiritment were sent me in kindness; angrily as I rebelled against them, they were all kind and good. My poor painful existence was not altogether in vain." (*CL* 11: 208-209). At this period, it seems clear, Carlyle saw himself and his struggles in the lives of his chief heroes, and this fact was conveyed to his audience, including even the residue of self-pity latent in "my poor painful existence." He, like them, had run the full harrowing gauntlet of the heroes' course and had at length emerged into the daylight of recognition and full articulateness.

The plausibility of this view of the autobiographical basis of *Heroes* is strengthened by Carlyle's open avowal of personal affinity with several of his struggling heroes. Mahomet, for example, is displayed as an exile, "driven foully out of his native country, since unjust men had not only given no ear to his earnest Heaven's-message, the deep cry of his heart, but would not even let him live if he kept speaking it" (*CW* 5:60). Later, Carlyle's tone regarding the portrait of Dante takes on a very personal urgency: "To me it is a most touching face; perhaps of all faces that I know, the most so"; "lonely," bespeaking "deathless sorry and pain" as well as "the known victory which is also deathless," this "mournfulest face" is "altogether tragic, heart-affecting." Clearly Carlyle felt a special affinity with the Dantean temperament, its mature softness and tenderness "congealed into sharp contradiction, into abnegation, isolation, proud hopeless pain." Of special interest is the fact that Carlyle—whom R. H. Hutton once described as spending "all his energies in a sort of vivid passion of scorn"[14]—is deeply affected by Dante's "silent scornful" pain, his "godlike disdain," his "implacable indignation" against the world (*CW* 5:86). But Dante had a "nobler destiny" appointed him "and he, struggling like a man led towards death and crucifixion, could not help fulfilling it." For Dante, "poor and banished," "there was now no home in this world. He wandered from patron to patron, from place to place" (*CW* 5:88). He realized "that he had no longer any resting-place, or hope of benefit, in this earth. The earthly world had cast him forth, to wander, wander; no living heart to love him now" (*CW* 5:89).

These two literal wanderers provide the pattern of more metaphorical struggle, exile, and triumph for Carlyle's latter-day heroes. We hear of Luther, "born poor, and brought-up poor," plagued by "all manner of black scruples, dubitations": "He fell into the blackest wretchedness: had to wander staggering as on the verge of bottomless Despair" (*CW* 5:128-30). The pattern is found in Knox, too, with an added fillip of personal concern: "This Prophet of the Scotch is to me no hateful man!—He had a sore fight of an existence: wrestling with Popes and Principalities; in defeat, contention, life-long struggle; rowing as a galley-slave, wandering as an exile. A sore fight: but he won it" (*CW* 5:151). The climax and clarification of the pattern comes with Carlyle's prediction that "Men of Letters will not always wander like unrecognised unregulated Ishmaelites among us!" (*CW* 5:165). For we must be brought to see that even a Burns fits the titanic role: "He must pass through the ordeal, and prove himself. *This* ordeal; this wild welter of a chaos which is called Literary Life; this too is a kind of ordeal!" (*CW* 5:167). Carlyle's intention becomes explicit finally in the assertion that the literary man must accept "the common lot of Heroes": "our Hero as Man of Letters had to travel without highway, companionless, through an inorganic chaos,—and to leave his own life and faculty lying there, as a partial contribution towards *pushing* some highway through it." We suddenly realize that Carlyle's ultimate hero is the literary man after the pattern earlier presented in *Sartor*. If Luther's "blackest wretchedness," as he wandered "staggering as on the verge of bottomless Despair," sounded remarkably like the struggles of Teufelsdröckh in his Baphometic Fire-Baptism, our suspicions are confirmed by the fact that Carlyle's modern literary hero has the "fatal misery" of "the *spiritual paralysis*" of the sceptical eighteenth century, involving both intellectual and moral doubt. Indeed, rarely in history has a life of heroism been more difficult than in modern times, for the last age was "a godless world," without wonder or greatness (*CW* 5:170-71). Thus Carlyle's supreme heroes, especially the men of letters, undergo struggles very similar to those of the earnest nineteenth-century agnostic, struggling for intellectual clarification and moral certitudes; these were the struggles also embodied, semifictionally, in *Sartor*; they are, finally, the struggles of Carlyle's career.

If the hero is fundamentally a prophet, or *speaker* of truth, the quality of his utterance will be unique, especially since the truth he expresses, though simple, resists rational formulation. The struggle for expression, indeed, becomes a chief mark of the prophet's authenticity, the chief arena of the titanic hero's agony. The pattern is established in Carlyle's discussion of the Koran as a "wearisome confused jumble, crude, incondite; endless iterations, long-windedness, entanglement" (*CW* 5:64-66):

It is the confused ferment of a great rude human soul; rude, untutored, that cannot even read; but fervent, earnest, struggling vehemently to utter itself in words. With a kind of breathless intensity he strives to utter himself; the thoughts crowd on him pellmell: for very multitude of things to say, he can get nothing said. The meaning that is in him shapes itself into no form of composition, is stated in no sequence, method, or coherence;—they are not *shaped* at all, these thoughts of his; flung-out unshaped, as they struggle and tumble there, in their chaotic inarticulate state. . . . The panting breathless haste and vehemence of a man struggling in the thick of battle for life and salvation; this is the mood he is in! A headlong haste; for very magnitude of meaning, he cannot get himself articulated into words. (*CW* 5:66)

Now, this elaborate passage (which partially imitates what it is describing) far exceeds any possible knowledge Carlyle might have had of Mahomet's habits of composition. What this discussion of the "prophetic" manner, which in varying proportions he attributes to all his heroes, seems above all to embody is Carlyle's sense of his own creative habits. We recall his description of the *Heroes* lectures as "the rudest *speech* of a man's heart" going direct to other men's hearts. Where Mahomet's thoughts were "flung-out unshaped as they struggle and tumble there," we found Carlyle writing: "I there *splash* down (literally as fast as my pen will go) some kind of paragraph on some point or other. . . . I shall be the better able to *speak* of the things written of even in this way." And in revising he tries to write "in the style of *speech*."

This struggle is repeated throughout the book. We sense a personal note behind Carlyle's description of Dante's *Comedy*: "His Book, as indeed most good Books are, has been written, in many senses, with his heart's blood. It is his whole history, this Book" (*CW* 5:90)—and we inevitably think of *Sartor*. We are not surprised that Luther, with his personal "rugged honesty" and "rugged sterling sense and strength," "flashes-out illumination" in his "smiting idiomatic phrases," that his common speech "has a rugged nobleness, dramatic, expressive, genuine" (*CW* 5:139, 141). But it is in his extended discussion of Cromwell's "inarticulate" eloquence that Carlyle reveals the intensity of his personal concern. For in it, I would argue, we have something like a rationale of Carlyle's struggle to create a "dialect" of his own (what Sterling called "Carlylism" and Matthew Arnold, less sympathetically, "Carlylese"), the struggle which in the years before *Sartor* meant the rejection of the eighteenth-century style-of-all-work in which his earliest essays were written.[15] Carlyle heaps scorn on that "respectable" style of speech and conduct "which can plead for itself in a handsome articulate manner" (*CW* 5:208). The eighteenth century could not recognize the greatness of Cromwell, a "King coming to them in the rugged *un*formulistic state": "their measured euphemisms, philosophies, parliamentary eloquences" leave the heart cold (*CW* 5:208-09). Thus "Poor Cromwell,— great Cromwell! The inarticulate Prophet; Prophet who could not *speak*. Rude, confused, struggling to utter himself, with his savage depth, with his wild sincerity"—Cromwell is made, in Carlyle's theory of inspired utterance, the archetypal prophet. Such struggling for speech, like his and Samuel Johnson's, under the weight of misery, sorrow, and hypochondria, "is the character of a prophetic man; a man with his whole soul *seeing* and struggling to see" (*CW* 5:217-18). Significantly, though Cromwell could not speak, he could *preach*: his "rhapsodic preaching" relied on no method, simply "warmth, depth, sincerity" (*CW* 5:218). "He disregarded eloquence, nay despised and disliked it; spoke always without premeditation" (*CW* 5:219). We recall Carlyle's attempt, in revising *Heroes*, to retain the spontaneous quality of *speech*, "all the unction of personal sincerity expressed by voice and face."

But Carlyle himself makes almost explicit the apologetic relevance of his discussion of Cromwell's "rugged bursts of earnestness," his "helplessness of utterance, in such bursting fulness of meaning" (*CW* 5:226, 233-34). He had discerned in Cromwell "a real *speech* lying imprisoned in these broken rude tortuous utterances; a meaning in the great heart of this inarticulate man!" (*CW* 5:235). Now, when he comes to end his own final lecture, Carlyle turns directly to his auditors:

> . . . there was pleasure for me in this business, if also much pain. It is a great subject. . . . It enters deeply, as I think, into the secret of Mankind's ways and vitalest interests in this world, and is well worth explaining at present. . . . I have had to tear it up in the rudest manner in order to get into it at all. Often enough, with these abrupt utterances thrown-out isolated, unexplored, has your tolerance been put to the trial. . . . The accomplished and distinguished, the beautiful, the wise, something of what is best in England, have listened patiently to my words. (*CW* 5:243-44)

In the very act of ostensibly asking for indulgence, Carlyle is, first, attributing to himself the rude, abrupt, ejaculatory mode proper to his highest heroes; second, acknowledging that he has at last gained the ear of the "accomplished" audience he had sought; and third, claiming to have special access to "the secret" of Mankind's most vital interests—the very sphere of the prophet.

The theme of hero worship, as it recurs throughout the lectures, suggests the complexity of Carlyle's relation to his "audience." The letters reveal Carlyle to have been quite extraordinarily indifferent to easy popular success, with its attendant celebrity and money. On the other hand, we have noted his insistence that "the world cannot too soon get acquainted" with the "story" he had to tell it. The explanation evidently is that, though by no means unflattered by the tolerance and attention of the "beautiful people," Carlyle conceived himself as standing in a relationship to his age unlike that of the literary man to his "public." The theme of the reception of heroes in their own time provides a clue; and again, it is developed with noticeable personal intensity, and with almost unvarying attention to the contemporary situation. Carlyle announces in his first lecture, "To me there is something very touching" in primitive Scandinavian hero-worship, "in such artless, helpless, but hearty entire reception of a Hero by his fellow-men. . . . If I could show in any measure, what I feel deeply for a long time now, That it is the vital element of mankind, the soul of man's history here in our world,—it would be the chief use of this discoursing at present" (*CW* 5:29). We sense the nineteenth-century relevance in the assertion, "The most significant feature in the history of an epoch is the manner it has of welcoming a Great Man" (*CW* 5:42), as well as in the rather nervous exhortation concerning the Poet and Prophet: "we must listen before all to him" (*CW* 5:46). As usual, the status of the man of letters and the needs of the present age are uniquely intertwined: "the world knows not well at any time what to do with him, so foreign is his aspect in the world," says Carlyle of the man of letters, observing, perhaps with a trace of self-pity, that he rules "from his grave, after death, whole nations and generations who would, or would not, give him bread while living" (*CW* 5:154-55). Carlyle's own perplexities appear when he says of the Hero-King: "That we knew in some tolerable measure how to find him, and that all men were ready to acknowledge his divine right when found: this is precisely the healing which a sick world is everywhere, in these ages, seeking after!" (*CW* 5:199). But Carlyle's perhaps more realistic, if pathetic, assessment of the relation between the hero and the age is evident in the remark, "Not a Hero only is needed, but a world fit for him; a world not of *Valets*;—the Hero comes almost in vain to it otherwise!" (*CW* 5:216). The tragedy of Carlyle's life can be measured in the distance between this scornful judgment of his age and the figure he employed to express what heroes, implicitly including Carlyle, should be able to expect: "the Great Man was always as lightning out of Heaven; the rest of men waited for him like fuel, and then they too would flame" (*CW* 5:77). Instead, the beautiful people applauded and bought his books, and young men wrote letters in playful mock-Carlylese.[16]

Perhaps most important of all, Carlyle himself repeatedly acts the prophet in the course of the lectures. The prophetic message is simple enough, so simple and so often repeated with little variation, that one suspects that therein lies at least part of the cause for the intense revulsion Carlyle later felt for the book. The Goethean "open secret of the Universe" is almost totally exhausted in the announcement that both the world and man's life are miraculous, mysterious, living, and divine—the revelation of the workings of God, an awful Fact and Reality, full of Divine Significance. But there is also a considerable amount of literal "prediction" in *Heroes*; despite the gloomy fate of prophets and the traces of his own temperamental melancholy, Carlyle exerts himself almost galvanically to a series of optimistic statements regarding the future of modern society. His imagination has a natural affinity for crisis and violent incendiary disaster; for him, the Prophet becomes the sponsor of a new Revolution and a new Reformation. The Great Man, we saw, is "the lightning out of Heaven" who will kindle the dry dead fuel. That fuel is "common languid Times, with their unbelief, distress, perplexity, with their languid doubting characters and embarrassed circumstances, impotently crumbling-down into ever worse distress towards final ruin" (*CW* 5:13): the reference is clearly to his own age. But scepticism itself has a hopeful prognostic: it is "not an end but a beginning." "Let us have the crisis; we shall either have death or the cure"; Utilitarianism is only "an approach towards new Faith" (*CW* 5:172). Protestantism likewise is but the first of a series of honest demolitions, for beyond even the present confusion we look "afar off to a new thing, which shall be true, and authentically divine!" (*CW* 5:123). This world in preparation will be a "world all sincere, a believing world: the like has been;

the like will again be,—cannot help being" (*CW* 5:127). The tone rises ringingly once or twice: "I prophesy that the world will once more become *sincere*; a believing world: with *many* Heroes in it, a heroic world!" (*CW* 5:176). But of course he does not spell out the details of this new "union," beyond stating that it will be a "Theocracy," making "a God's Kingdom of this Earth" (*CW* 5:153). These hopes that "Dilettantism, Scepticism, Triviality" will be cast out—"as, by God's blessing, they shall one day be" (*CW* 5:85)—are at once distantly visionary and no doubt somehow futile and peevish, a product of wish fulfillment; though sometimes Carlyle more cautiously reminds us that in times of inevitable revolution "there are long troublous periods before matters come to a settlement again," and that this is a time of "*transition* from false to true" (*CW* 5:119, 203).

Carlyle's prophecies are not convincingly managed for the twentieth-century reader and very likely were not always fully satisfying even to the Victorian public, who sought and sometimes found in him an ethical and metaphysical assurance he himself did not firmly possess. But we are concerned here with the manner and tone which Carlyle adopts in *Heroes*, and the inferences his auditors and readers would draw from them. As the weight of the evidence presented here suggests, Carlyle (perhaps with less than the fullest self-consciousness) was presenting himself as the prophet and leader to his times; in the England of 1840, there was scarcely any other candidate for the role as Carlyle had defined it. It should not be impossible for the modern reader to imagine that a nineteenth-century reader of *Heroes*, and much more an auditor of the lectures, would have been able to *believe*, even if only for the moment, that here was indeed the great man whose "wise healing word" would enkindle the dry fuel of contemporary unbelief and perplexity. Convinced that men of letters were "incalculably influential," Carlyle seems in 1840 to have believed that his own prediction concerning them—that they "will not always wander like unrecognised unregulated Ishmaelites among us!"—had been fulfilled in himself. The exuberance of the letter of July 2 to Emerson, in which in "the fire of the moment" he planned to preach "like a very lion" throughout America, and the immediately following collapse of his plans; the "strange" quality he musingly detected in the completed work, and the almost immediate extreme depreciation of the book: these oscillations suggest that Carlyle himself may have detected there more of one side of himself, unprotected by irony and masks, than he was customarily willing to reveal.

An important device helps indicate finally the extent of Carlyle's unique omnipresence in *Heroes*. It is that of "voice," of the assumed stance and authority of the first-person speaker. Perhaps three or four modes of self-presentation can be distinguished. There is, pervasively, the "I" of the reasonable, ingratiating nine-teenth-century lecturer. The opening pages of the first lecture are thickly strewn with phrases like "as I say," "as I take it," "what I call Hero-worship," "could I . . . make manifest to you," "I must make the attempt," "it seems to me," "I find," "I cannot yet call." These are intermingled with a tissue of plurals designed conventionally to draw in his benevolently disposed audience: "We cannot look, however," "we see men of all kinds," "a thing that fills us," "we may pause," "We shall not see," "if we do not reject," "Let us consider," "we may say," "Let us try," etc. But a second, more authoritative tone is detectable in the accumulation of slightly more emphatic versions of the same terms. We sense the personal authority assumed in the following phrases, rather reminiscent of John Henry Newman's manner, all from two successive paragraphs: "I do say," "I will not," "I say," "I define," "truly" (*CW* 5:173-74). Even more emphatic, if hard to classify, are those memorable moments when Carlyle steps forward to evince special interest in his favorite heroes. "This Prophet of the Scotch," he says of Knox, "is to me no hateful man!" (*CW* 5:151). "To me," he says of Dante, "it is a most touching face; perhaps of all faces that I know, the most so" (*CW* 5:86). Perhaps most remarkable, however, is a passage in which Carlyle shifts, without benefit of quotation marks, from his own intensely personal mode to the putative words of Luther:

> I, for one, pardon Luther for now altogether revolting against the Pope. The elegant Pagan, by this fire-decree of his, had kindled into noble just wrath the bravest heart then living in this world. The bravest, if also one of the humblest, peaceablest; it was now kindled. These words of mine, words of truth and soberness aiming faithfully, as human inability would allow, to promote God's truth on earth, and save men's souls, you God's vicegerent on earth, answer them by the hangman and fire. You will burn me and them. . . . (*CW* 5:133)

And so on: the result being that the final assertion of the paragraph—"that Life was a truth a not a lie!"—though actually the words of Carlyle, hovers suggestively between the two dramatic voices, and adds to Carlyle's personal sincerity the thundering authority of Luther. The effect is comparable, in its heightened prophetic tone and its note of intense personal conviction, to the long passage cited above from *Chartism*.

IV

I have argued that the fundamental unity of *Heroes* derives from Carlyle's varied but continuous forms of self-presentation, the totality conveying the impression that Carlyle is indeed a prophet, at times *the* prophet whose wise and healing word the age looked for.[17] This is not to deny that he does not always speak in his own person; John Holloway has authoritatively studied Carlyle's "dramatization of discussions."[18] Nevertheless, *Heroes* is admittedly freer of dramatization, of mask and irony, than *Sartor* and even than the relatively more "objective" early essays. Nor is this to fall, in any simple way, into the intentional fallacy, though Carlyle's works defy many of our usual and valid canons of critical separation between the art work and its biographical and historical origins. For if *Heroes* is a peculiarly personal statement of Carlyle's, the letters of the period only corroborate and clarify what is evident in the work itself.[19] Nor would I deny, finally, that the prophet's role assumed in *Heroes* is *itself* a "mask," a necessary pose. Carlyle's "sincerity" and personal conviction are evident, but the letters, as well as a frequent uncertainty of tone in the lectures, reveal that the prophetic afflatus was at best intermittent with him and that the manner had to be wilfully maintained and at times forced. Moreover, at bottom Carlyle very likely harbored a contempt for—or at least a strong reservation regarding—the "mere" man of letters: his instinctive sympathies always (and increasingly as he grew older) lay with the man of decisive *action*.[20]

There was, indeed, one further cause of Carlyle's special willingness in the spring of 1840 to adopt the prophet's tone, a cause which throws light on the intentions of the lectures. For *Heroes* represents a decided heightening of the style of the *Lectures on the History of Literature*, delivered two years earlier, in which Carlyle dealt with four of the major figures of *Heroes* (Dante, Shakespeare, Knox, Johnson) and some of its major themes (sincerity, earnestness, unconsciousness, humor) in an altogether flatter manner. If there is any single major cause for the newfound confidence which is evident in the adoption of the prophet's tone, it is to be found in John Sterling's long, adulatory review of "Carlyle's Work" in the *Westminster* of the preceding autumn. Sterling, though he had known Carlyle well since 1835, did not blush to refer to him as "among . . . the immortals of history," "the most resolute and mighty preacher in our day," the man of "the most fervid, sincere, far-reaching genius" to have arisen in England in twenty years.[21] Sterling, who had a capacity for hero-worship, had found a hero:

> . . . clear, swift, far-sounding as a torrent his words spread forth, and will stream into many hearts. The heavy lamentation will come as a voice of hope. . . . Amid the clamorous snarl and gossip of literature, and the dead formulas of superficial science, here sounds a true prophetic voice. . . . Nor will it be without fit audience among us. . . . (38)

Sterling's review was a decisive event in Carlyle's career, because he had at last found an adequate disciple. He saw the review late in September and wrote Sterling: "there has no man in these Islands been so reviewed in my time; it is the most magnanimous eulogy I ever knew one man utter of another man whom he knew face to face"; "incredible to all men, incrediblest of all to me; yet sweet in the highest degree, for very obvious reasons, notwithstanding" (*CL* 11:192). That this was a turning point in Carlyle's life is evident when we note that the letter in which he told his mother of the "changed time" in his fortunes was dated October 24. In fact, a reading of Sterling's review suggests that it provided the germinal conception of the *Heroes* lectures—not simply the "doctrine" of heroes, which had been adumbrated much earlier, but the peculiarly personal intensity of its presentation. For Sterling saw not only that Carlyle was a hero-worshiper, prophet, and hero himself, but that Carlyle's art had a specially autobiographical basis. Sterling spoke of Carlyle's "fervid worship of many a ragged, outcast heroism" (22): "to Mr. Carlyle the objects of chief interest are memorable persons—men who have fought strongly the good fight. . . . especially . . . those living nearest to our own time and circumstances, in whom we may find monumental examples of the mode in which our difficulties are to be conquered" (12-13). Carlyle studied the "hindrances such a man had to overcome, the energies by which he vanquished them, and the work, whatever it may have been, which he thus accomplished for mankind" (13).

More important, Sterling again and again detected in Carlyle the qualities of Carlyle's heroes. He speaks of Carlyle's "apparent rudeness, harshness, lawless capriciousness of style; full of meanings and images, but these looking incoherent, or at least as yet unreconciled" (9-10). Carlyle is like Jean Paul in being one of the "inspired painters of symbols for the fundamental realities of our existence" (10-11); but he goes beyond him in that "he lives to fight, breathes war-flames of disdain and zeal, and moves only to wrestle and trample forward." The requirements of the hero are one by one applied to Carlyle as we hear that his "tumultuous abruptness" and "gloomy spectral fervour," his "rugged" sentences and his "short, sharp, instantaneous mode of expression," are explained by the fact that "he is not naturally fluent" and is unable "to use with smooth dexterity a conventional mechanism of discourse" (21-22). He paints Carlyle as "large of bone, . . . sturdy, and with a look of combat, and of high crusader-enthusiasm," "resembling, perhaps, a great Christianized giant of romance, a legendary Christopher" (24). Even more suggestive, perhaps, is Sterling's elaborate comparison with Luther, whom Carlyle most resembles "in the essentials of his character." There is a likeness "in the type and scale of their tendencies and faculties" (64); in both there is "sincerity, largeness, fervour, . . . sudden and robust eloquence, and broad and unshackled views of all things; a flowing cordiality based on deep and severe, often almost dismal and sepulchral conscientiousness" (64-65). In each man there is "fierce and scornful prejudice" and great exaggeration: "Their fundamental unity of conception lives in a religious awe of the Divine" (65).

These reflections had been adumbrated in Sterling's well-known letter of May 29, 1835, which was in effect the first serious literary criticism Carlyle had received. In discussing the "form" of *Sartor*, Sterling had aligned Carlyle with the "subjective" masters of modern literature—and put him in the company of Rabelais and Montaigne, Sterne and Swift, Cervantes and Jeremy Taylor. Most important, he noted that the "multitude of peculiar associations and relations" in such writers, which open them to charges of lawlessness and capriciousness, cannot be defended aesthetically by "any one *external* principle" but are in fact "connected by the bond of our own personality" (*CW* 11:109-10). This line of thought, culminating in the review of 1839, must have had an important influence on Carlyle as his own reflections on the personal basis of his art gathered to a focus. That the review in the *Westminster* marked an epoch in Carlyle's conception of himself is evident, not only in the letter of October 24 to his mother, but in a passage in the *Life of John Sterling*, published more than a decade later. Carlyle remembers

> . . . the deep silent joy, not of a weak or ignoble nature, which it gave to myself in my then mood and situation; as it well might. The first generous human recognition, expressed with heroic emphasis, and clear conviction visible amid its fiery exaggeration, that one's poor battle in this

world is not quite a mad and futile, that it is perhaps a worthy and manful one, which will come to something yet. . . . The thought burnt in me like a lamp, for several days; lighting-up into a kind of heroic splendour and sad volcanic wrecks, abysses, and convulsions of said poor battle, and secretly I was very grateful to my daring friend, and am still, and ought to be. (*CW* 11:191-92)

The role of "heroic splendour" in which Sterling had cast his friend carried Carlyle through the composition of *Heroes and Hero-Worship*, and contributed to the temporary identity—some would say confusion—of Carlyle with his own heroes.

I submit that in the page of Sterling's review we find the germs, not merely of the substance of *Heroes*, but of that peculiar implicit presentation of himself which unifies and vivifies Carlyle's lectures, a unique and not easily formulated unity in Carlyle's writings, resting on the deepest ground of his experience and personality. Sterling's review conjoined with the other favoring circumstances of Carlyle's life to produce the euphoria of 1839 and 1840; it also, by suggesting the unstated personal basis of the hero doctrine, goes some distance in explaining the unique tone and rhetorical stance of *Heroes*. In the review, no doubt to some extent unconsciously, Carlyle had discovered a series of formulas which led him to the precise point where his fundamental doctrine and his personal quest for self-definition met, enabling him to write what is perhaps the most openly "prophetic" book of the nineteenth century in England and a masterpiece of Romantic art.

NOTES

[1] For purposes of this reprint, references will be to the Centenary Edition of Carlyle's *Works*, H. D. Traill, ed. (London: Chapman and Hall, 1896-99), and to the Duke-Edinburgh edition of the *Collected Letters*, 24 vols. Charles R. Sanders, Clyde de L. Ryals, Kenneth J. Fielding, et al., eds. (Durham: Duke UP, 1970-). *CW* will prefix references to Carlyle's *Works*; *CL* his letters.

Also *Sartor Resartus*, Charles Frederick Harrold, ed. (New York: Odyssey, 1937).

[2] On Carlyle's strong and widespread influence on the youthful generation of the 1840's, see Kathleen Tillotson, "Matthew Arnold and Carlyle" (Warton Lecture on English Poetry), *Proceedings of the British Academy* 42 (1956): 135-38. I have further discussed Carlyle's continuing influence in "Carlyle and Arnold: The Religious Issue," in *Carlyle Past and Present*, K. J. Fielding and Rodger L. Tarr, eds. (London: Vision P, 1976): 127-54.

[3] The two best studies of "form" in *Sartor* are Leonard Deen's "Irrational Form in *Sartor Resartus*," *Texas Studies in Literature and Language* 5 (Autumn 1963): 438-51, and chapter four, "The Structure of *Sartor Resartus*," in G. B Tennyson's, *"Sartor" Called "Resartus"* (Princeton UP, 1965). See also Daniel P. Deneau, "Relationship of Style and Device in *Sartor Resartus*," *Victorian Newsletter* 17 (Spring 1960): 17-20; and John Lindberg, "The Artistic Unity of *Sartor Resartus*," *ibid.*: 20-23.

[4] James Anthony Froude, *Thomas Carlyle: A History of His Life in London 1834-1881*, 4th ed., 2 vols. (London: Longmans, 1885): 1:87. Hereafter cited in text with the abbreviation *LL*.

[5] Equally important is the fact that, in both essays, Jean Paul becomes one of the major prototypes, not only of Teufelsdröckh and his style, but of the "vehement" and "rugged" heroes of the *Heroes* lectures.

[6] Carlisle Moore, "Carlyle's 'Diamond Necklace' and Poetic History," *PMLA* 58 (June 1943): 537-57, esp. 544ff.

[7] Qtd. in James Anthony Froude, *Thomas Carlyle: A History of the First Forty Years of His Life, 1795-1835*. 2 vols. (London: Longmans, 1882): 2:345. Hereafter cited in text as *FF*.

[8] See F. W. Roe, *Thomas Carlyle as a Critic of Literature* (New York: Columbia UP, 1910): 148-49, for the principles of Carlyle's historical and biographical method of criticism.

[9] The discussion in John Holloway's *The Victorian Sage* (London: Macmillan, 1953): 21-85, is easily the best we have of the identity of "expression" and "confirmation" in Carlyle's work, of his "modifying the reader's perceptiveness" as opposed to "persuasion" in the classical sense. Holloway's concern, however, is largely atomic, and he does not, except for the histories, apply his insights to the unity of a whole work.

[10] Carlyle had told his brother in May 1837 that his "new profession" was his way to "get delivered out of this awful quagmire of difficulties in which you have so long seen me struggle and wriggle," since his three years in London have been "sore and stern, almost frightful" (*CL* 9:215-16). Even with the success of the *French Revolution*, Carlyle pictured himself, late in 1837, as "a half-dead enchanted spectre-haunted nondescript," disgusted with the literary profession (*LL* 120; and see 130, February 19, 1838). Only in early 1838 does he first admit that "these long years of martyrdom and misery . . . were not utterly in vain" (*LL* 128), though his "remorse" over his "conceit" and "ambition" in his new success—not to speak of his evident inability to allow any feeling of "happiness"—continue through the delivery of the *Heroes* lectures to fill the letters and journals.

[11] See Carlisle Moore, "The Persistence of Carlyle's 'Everlasting Yea,'" *Modern Philology* 54 (February 1957): 187-96.

[12] The continuous use of "deep," "deep-hearted," "deep-feeling," "deep-seeing," "the perennial Deeps," "depth," etc., is supported by a multitude of suggestive phrases using words like "kernel," "heart," "inner," "inmost," "unfathomable," "central essence," "roots," "underground"—not to speak of numerous sea images.

[13] Teufelsdröckh is presented as "our young Ishmael," "'the Wanderer,'" and is twice compared to the Wandering Jew (113-14, 78, 17, 156). Carlyle even once referred to himself as "a Bedouin, . . . a rough child of the desert" (*LL* 1:288).

[14] *Essays on Some of the Modern Guides to English Thought in Matters of Faith* (London, 1888): 138.

[15] See F. X. Roellinger, Jr., "The Early Development of Carlyle's Style," *PMLA* 72 (December 1957): 936-51.

[16] See letter of March 1845, in *Letters of Matthew Arnold to Arthur Hugh Clough*. Ed. Howard Foster Lowry (London and New York: Oxford UP, 1932): 55-57; and one of May 1848 in *The Correspondence of Arthur Hugh Clough*. Ed. Frederick L. Mulhauser (Oxford UP, 1957): 1:207.

[17] John Lindberg, in "The Decadence of Style: Symbolic Structure in Carlyle's Later Prose," *Studies in Scottish Literature* 1 (January 1964): 183-95, makes several comments on Carlyle as prophet and as "sympathetic suffering hero," but from a point of view somewhat different from my own.

Albert J. LaValley, in *Carlyle and the Idea of the Modern* (New Haven: Yale UP, 1968), which appeared after the present essay was completed, declares (248) that the heroes Carlyle "really admires are images of himself or a wish-fulfilled self." LaValley fascinatingly presents *Heroes* (236-52) as an example of retreat, confusion, distortion, failure, and rationalization; still, in my opinion he fails to see the positive importance of the book in Carlyle's personal development up to 1840.

[18] *Victorian Sage*, 27.

[19] B. H. Lehman, in *Carlyle's Theory of the Hero* (Durham: Duke UP, 1928): 196ff., reverses the process and looks for the ways in which Carlyle the man attempted to conduct himself in accordance with the hero theory. George Levine, in "*Sartor Resartus* and the Balance of Fiction," *Victorian Studies* 8 (December 1964): 131-60, using what I believe is a method somewhat similar to my own, explains that the "form" of *Sartor*, as well as the hitherto unsolved problem of the relation of the Editor to Teufelsdröckh, can only be understood as Carlyle's "deeply personal affirmation and discovery of his identity" and as the expression of his "self-awareness" of his complex relation to his audience (154, 146). I agree that *Sartor*, through its fictional devices, represents the high point of Carlyle's "flexibility and openness to experience"; but I would argue that as late as 1840 Carlyle still maintained a considerable complexity and "uncertainty" and a quasi-fictional set of "masks."

[20] Froude comments that Carlyle "was conscious of possessing considerable powers, but he would have preferred at all times to have found a use for them in action" (*LL* 1:48). For Froude's own startling comments on literature as "but the shadow of action; the action the reality, the poetry the echo," see *LL* 1:130-31.

[21] *London and Westminster Review* 33 (October 1839): 10, 37, 52. Hereafter cited parenthetically by page number alone.

CRITICAL RESPONSE
TO *PAST AND PRESENT*

MAGAZINE OF DOMESTIC ECONOMY AND FAMILY REVIEW

N.S. 1 (January 1843): 561-64.

ANON.

The present is, indeed, a most momentous era in the history of Great Britain. Legislation, no longer based upon the experience of the past, and compelled to deal with a condition of society hitherto unexampled, pauses: and when, urged on by new necessities, it makes a forward step, it does so with hesitation, standing prepared meanwhile to draw back, as well knowing that it is indeed venturing into unknown paths obscured by a fearful gloom.

The motion of Mr. Charles Buller on systematic emigration, made in the House of Commons on the 6th April, may be regarded as one of those hesitating steps with which legislation feels its way in uncertain paths; and very great has been its effect in awakening public interest on that important subject.

Mr. Carlyle, also, has used that pen which he wields with a vigour not readily to be equalled, in the consideration of the same condition of things which prompted Mr. Buller's motion; and with that wide-grasping boldness which is his characteristic, he contrasts the condition of society during the middle ages with that of our own days.

Perhaps it may not be unjust to say that Mr. Carlyle's power lies rather in throwing striking lights on the salient points of his subject, than in thoroughly exploring the profoundest depths; but his happy tact and native acuteness frequently lead him to sound conclusions, without the pains of proving every intermediate step. Thus, like all who would laud antiquity at the expense of our own times, he forgets or disregards evils and faults in the structure of the society of those days that more than counterbalance the errors of our own; but there is justice in the contrast which he draws between the more trusting and religious spirit of the past, and the sceptical indifference and mammon worship which induces a neglect and even a contempt for all things morally great in human nature, which is an evil of modern growth.

The capitalist employs more or fewer "hands" according to the exigencies of his trade; but there is no sympathy between him and his men; no bearing of each other's burthens; no mutual reliance, as in a more primitive state of society; and, except when strikes and "*émeutes*" bring them into closer contact, the capitalist looks, and can only look, on his "hands" as expensive machinery, not to be made use of a moment longer than is absolutely needful; while the men are dissatisfied at a state of things which renders their condition so precarious, and thousands upon thousands—able and willing to work—are compelled to remain involuntarily idle. . . .

But whilst Mr. Carlyle expends all his force and ingenuity in proving that this state of things is to be attributed solely to the want of a right spirit in the breasts of the capitalists, the more practical statesman dwells upon the fact that not only labour but capital lies idle at home, and by a very different train of reasoning arrives at the same conclusion with the philosopher, both agreeing that a partial remedy, at least, may be found in a well-conducted scheme of emigration, for such is the object of Mr. Carlyle's book, as of Mr. Buller's speech and motion.

We should much like to see a Return of the actual number of able-bodied men supported by the Unions of the United Kingdom on any given day of this present month of May, a period when trade of every description once more presents a firm and prosperous aspect, distinguishing those receiving out-door relief from those in the houses, and specifying by classification their ages, trades, or *occupations*, and number and ages of their families: for we think that such an accurate return would prevent a good deal of misapprehension which is likely to arise in discussions on emigration schemes when not considered with a due knowledge of the actual capability of our surplus population for an emigrant's life—a condition fitted, with very few exceptions, to the agricultural class only. Much advantage might also be derived from such a statistical Table in forming a judgment on the actual causes which have filled our workhouses, and of the real extent of the improvidence with which their inmates have been so indiscriminately charged.

Neither Mr. Buller nor Mr. Carlyle has presented us with any detailed scheme of emigration: nor, had they done so, would these pages be the fitting arena for its discussion; but we may notice incidentally two letters lately inserted in the *Ipswich Journal*, and transferred to the columns of the *Poor Law Guide* for the 20th May last, in which the writer, the secretary to the East Suffolk Agricultural Association, submits a plan of parochial emigration, proposing that a government grant of 10,000 acres of land in Canada should be made to each of the 538 unions in England, Wales, and Ireland, "for the benefit of such union, and the employment of their surplus population. That upon each allotment of 10,000 acres there should be an establishment, or union-house, for the receptions and support of all persons sent out by the parent union, and as near upon their own regulations as well may be—that is, food, clothing, and lodging in cases of need—employment, when to be obtained with advantage,—and that, which is most needed by this description of emigrant, a house, food, clothing, and rest, upon their arrival." He proposes that one moiety of the expense of emigration should be borne by government, and calculates that the cost to the parish sending out the emigrant would not exceed nine months' maintenance in the union workhouse; and that, upon arrival at the Canada location, the emigrant would find immediate profitable employment either to himself or the union. So far from contemplating anything like compulsory emigration, the writer would make it a boon to be granted only to able-bodied men of good character, with wives and small families, to whom allotments of ten acres or more, either on lease, or to be paid for by small annual payments should be made, which "would enable him in ten years to work out his independence, and to become a man of substance; to such only the boon should be offered—they would unquestionably do well, and soon become valuable members of the new colony."

There is so much plausibility, to say the least of it, in this scheme, that we have been induced to bring it under the notice of our readers, although in doing so we have keen led away from our immediate subject—Mr. Carlyle's work.

Truly does he observe, that the most successful scheme of emigration can only after all be a temporary expedient, and that repetition of the same causes must lead to the same effects. The spirit of the age, he contends, must be changed; and he appears convinced that the spirit can be changed by education. Into this very speculative position we cannot enter, but would refer the reader to Mr. Carlyle's own exposition of his belief, contenting ourselves with remarking, that to our unenlightened understanding it appears too evident that the spirit of the age is the result of that struggle upwards which leads us forward so rapidly in our investigations into the Arcana of Nature, and the application of our discoveries to the benefit of mankind; and that any alteration of this spirit would, by taking away the only impulses that have been hitherto found strong enough to prevent human nature from retrograding—necessity and selfishness—throw us back in the scale of intellectual beings, and have simply the effect of once more engendering the ancient spirit in, perhaps, a worse form, and forcing us to retread our former course under greater disadvantages than before; and that, unless we shall ever so far conquer Nature as to render want impossible, we can scarcely desire that the spirit of the age should be entirely changed, although it may admit of much modification.

We have not spoken of the merits of this work in a merely literary point of view, since Mr. Carlyle's reputation is so well established, and the originality and vigour of his remarkable style is so well appreciated, that any critical examination is needless. Write what he will, Mr. Carlyle *cannot* write what is not well worth reading. . . .

Yet, out of this mournful reality Mr. Carlyle draws hope, and argues, that since it is found possible to organise such a sufficing reality for evil, it may equally be effected for good. We are afraid that philosophers, as well as statesmen, are too apt to leave out the elements of human nature from the very calculation on which they ground their effort for its improvement; and that the establishment of an army of philanthropists can never be rendered so effective as that one "universal complete thing" which is based upon the passions of mankind.

THE EXAMINER

1839 (April 1843): 259-61.

[JOHN FORSTER]

The Chronicle of Jocelin of Brakelond, lately printed by the Camden Society, is here Mr Carlyle's text for a discourse on the Condition of England. Little dreamed good Jocelin of Brakelond of seven centuries since, that his light-hearted, cheerful gossip would find itself neighboured in a nineteenth century, with so much heavy-hearted zeal and indignation, with so many thoughtful, fiery, austere denunciations! But truth to say, the connection between them is of the slightest after all. . . .

What sacristan is uppermost, what cellarer in disgrace; how about the cooks and scullions; whether the almonds were boiled; what was done to outwit royal commissions of inquiry; how the brothers prayed for a new abbot, and would not have prayed so devoutly had they known who he was to be; what scandals were talked when the general (anti-apoplectic) bleeding of the monks went on; and, all and sundry, the sayings and doings of officers and sub-officers, novices, monks, priors, and abbots, drunken sacrists and exorbitant Jews, touching and respecting the debts and credits of the abbey, the rebuilding of its churches or the mending of its barns, the concealment of its poverty or the resuscitation of its wealth, the auditing its accounts, the collecting its rents and tithes, the granting or renewing its leases, and all its endless disputes with great folks, clerical or lay, who envied its prosperity and would have sapped its power:—these are the darling themes of good Jocelin of Brakelond. A strange text, it would seem, for thoughtful and earnest Discourse on the Eternal relations of Past and Present, but in Mr Carlyle's view, very strictly applicable. For there were two abbots in Jocelin's time, and in the midst of all his cheerful chit-chat it is clear, that whereas under The One the convent decayed, and the Jews throve upon it, and the good worshippers declined, and the whole affair had set out upon a rapid journey to the dogs; under The Other the convent revived, and the Jews had their fangs drawn, and the faithful prospered, and the shrine of the good and great St Edmund resumed its ancient lustre. Whereupon Mr Carlyle's lesson is, that we of the nineteenth century, like those worthy monks of the twelfth, have been living much too long under Abbot Hugo, and have now a most vital need of Abbot Samson.

Utterly drear and dark is the picture which Mr Carlyle's book would exhibit to us, of the *"Present"* of England. No mirthful gossip, no cheery, smiling talk, as in the *"Past"* of Jocelin of Brakelond. According to our modern chronicler, there is nothing but wretchedness and falsehood on the earth, none but fierce and gloomy portents in the sky. We have closed our eyes, universally, to the eternal substance of things, and opened them to their shews and shams. The truth of the Universe has become everywhere supplanted by the mere profit and loss of it, the pudding and praise. We are without union, without faith, without heroism. We are a godless, and mechanical generation. Our moral conscience is gone clean out of us. We protect property, and never think of protecting what makes property; mere symbols being sacred with us, and things signified cast to the dogs. Our Land Aristocracy is turned to Land Auctioneership, and the owners of the soil, doing nothing in return for the soil, are running fast to the end of ownership. Our work, and our no-work, are alike wrong. Joe Manton Captains of Idleness are drones to be extinguished, Steam Engine Captains of Industry are buccaneers to be reformed. Our Abbot Hugo is QUACK, whose work and governance is Plausibility, Falsity, Fatuity. Our Abbot Samson—alas! no Abbot Samson is yet in sight. There is much to be done, more to be undone, before we get view of our Abbot Samson.

There is little in all this to startle those who have read *and understood* the former writings of Mr Carlyle. There is much in it all, we think, not only to startle but do good to those who have admired without understanding them. Pleasant in the days of Whig-Radical Ministries and reforming majorities, were denunciations of a sham government and a godless people, but what is now to be said? Will *Quarterly Reviews* make fresh attempt to fit their well loved shovel hat on the head of Mr Carlyle? Will the men and women of "Longacre cabs and carriages" still perseveringly fancy the philosopher their own? "The accomplished and distinguished," said Mr Carlyle very truly, at the close of his striking "Lectures on Heroes," "the accomplished and distinguished, the beautiful, the wise, something of what is best in England, have listened patiently to my rude words." To *Past and Present*, what will Accomplished and Distinguished have to say?—*O Heavens!* as Mr Carlyle is apt to exclaim, when, incapable of farther speech in a crisis of energetic argument, he resorts to the unspeakable.

It will not be assumed that we agree in all the statements of this book, when we say that we honour the writer of it, and rejoice that it has been written. It is a tolerably safe venture of abuse, we know, to abuse all sides; but distinctions of a certain kind, unpalatable as they are brave, are without difficulty to be noted here. Frankly we will say, that not a few passages have been unintelligible to us; but with equal frankness may add, that this fault is most probably our own, and that a little time, and more reflection, might have made matters plain enough. The style is wilder, more lawless, more outrageous than ever, but yet enriched with passages more stamped with rugged energy, strong original feeling, exquisite gentleness, surpassing beauty and tenderness—passages more graphic and picturesque, and at the same time substantial, significant, and of the good old Saxon homeliness and purity—than any other living man could have written. In estimates of *great* and *small*, we find ourselves often opposed to Mr Carlyle; his perpetual settings forth of class against class, and not a few of his doctrines of property, and yearnings for a new feudal system, we strongly condemn; and if, as some hints would have us suppose, his idea of a modern governor can get no farther than the Oliver Cromwell of two centuries back, we would rather take our place among the Dead Sea Apes, where Mr Carlyle would in that case infallibly place us, than in the file of such an Abbot Samson's worshippers. But all deductions and drawbacks made, we repeat that this is a most remarkable book, and imperatively claims the attention of all thinking people. It is the book of a sincere man, of a man terribly in earnest. It is no indifferent sign of the times, no unmeaning type of the matter they are laden with, that such a book should be deliberately published for the class among whom Mr. Carlyle's readers are found. Full as they may think it of anomalies and discords, disfigured by hyperbolical and exaggerated phrase, weakened by its oracular tone of vehemence and self-reliance—there is not one of them that will fail to discover something of the rare and pure truth that is in it, the broad unshackled views, the freedom of mind and heart, the genuine faith and enthusiasm. No listener can be wholly indifferent when a man of genius speaks. . . .

Mr Carlyle has no specific remedy to offer for this deplorable condition of things. He sees no hope but in a kind of radical universal alteration of our ways of life and regimen, whereby we shall begin to know ourselves healthier, he tells us, when in the work of self-reform the veil drops off from quackery, and we find ourselves suddenly ashamed of the worship of sham heroes. . . .

But though the philosopher has no Morison's pill for us, he is not without his special decoctions of senna, of rhubarb, of purgative drug, to aid us in the cure. There is Free Trade for the first. To him most prominent of all doomed things is the Corn Law, which, if only to make room for other things' beginning, must itself end and be abolished straightway. . . .

Mr. Carlyle's general opinion of the main matter in issue we gather to be this: that whereas in the present state of the world, the progress of Democracy is inevitable, to every state of government the influence of Sovereignty is indispensable, and the two can only be safely reconciled by an effective Governing and an effective Teaching class. As things stand we have neither, and what substitutes we have cannot much longer endure. The Christianity which cannot get on without a minimum of four thousand five hundred a year, must give place to a better Christianity which can; and the Aristocracy which does nothing but eat and drink, and kill cotton manufactures with partridge corn laws, is hurrying headlong to its doom. . . .

So would Mr Carlyle have Emigration United Services, Teaching United Services, and, sundry and divers, other United Services than those of the red coats and fighting swords. We will wish him all success in such, and at any rate join him in a hearty prayer for the speedy substitution of a *Past* Abbot Samson Government in place of our *Present* Government of Quack.

"Thomas Carlyle's Past and Present"

TAIT'S EDINBURGH MAGAZINE

10 (June 1843): 341-48.

ANON.

What are we to make of Thomas Carlyle?—how often have we been asked this question! and yet we wish we had been asked it somewhat oftener; for there are many persons in the world—in the limbo of the literary world more perhaps than anywhere else—who never think of asking any questions at all, but carry all their judgments ready-made with them in their pockets, prepared, packeted, and labelled, according to the exact recipe of some traditionary pharmacopæia of classicality; these men have made of Thomas Carlyle what they make of everybody whose name does not appear upon the superscription of their stamped papers;—he is not classical, he is not orthodox, according to their neat articles: therefore he is naught. But we have had too many turnings and overturnings in the literary, as well as in the political world, since the year 1789, to be much concerned now about the ready-made judgments of these nice and correct gentlemen of the pharmacopæia. Let them even count their packets, and take their powders regularly. None but a most wanton and mischievous person would attempt to disturb the composure of their stomachs by a dose of Coleridge or Carlyle. Let them continue, in the midst of these stormy times, to sit apart in their neatly-varnished cabinets, dealing forth, for recreation, at intervals, stout, puffy blasts against such questionable men as he with whom we have here to do—"a fool—an affected puppy—a blown-up bundle of conceited verbosity—a genius sublimely unintelligible—a metaphysician—a GERMAN!"—'Tis both a shorter and an easier method at all times to live down than to write down merely negative criticism of this kind. We shall, therefore, for the sake of ourselves, and those of our readers who are not too wise to ask questions, try in what fashion we can answer this one;—*What are we to make of Thomas Carlyle?*

Thomas Carlyle, in the common use of the English language, is not a poet. Much less does he look like a philosopher—as philosophers, calm, cool, and reasoning, are wont to be; a critic, though he has criticised a great deal, you cannot call him in the common sense at all; to science he has no pretence, one of the most unscientific men of decided grasp perhaps that breathes; political economy and statistics he hates; law he declares to be a mere SHAM; at legislation certainly he aims, and that on a great scale; but legislation, he says expressly, is not his business, and he has no business to intermeddle with it. What, then, shall we make of him? He is a preacher, a preacher out of the pulpit,—a prophet perhaps; for in these respectable days, when no man can preach or prophesy in the regular pulpits who cannot squeeze his thoughts into the orthodox dialect of the Thirty-nine Articles, or The Confession of Faith,—a thinker of power and originality, a soul burdened with a moral message to its fellow-souls—a heart from the fiery center of Nature shot direct, as some one phrases it, literally "raging with humanity." Such an one, though meant by nature for occupying a pulpit, finding the entrance into the churches as they now are, guarded by grim comminatory clauses, and barricaded by thorny formulas, which he cannot swallow, necessarily becomes a wandering prophet, a preacher of the wilderness, whose house is where he can find shelter, and whose dinner must often be brought to him by ravens: what, since the invention of printing, we call a prophet no longer, but only a writer of books, a literary man of a very strange and eccentric character. Such a preacher, such a prophet is Thomas Carlyle; and if you do not take up "Past and Present" in this serious acceptation, you had better throw it down. The book is not written for you. People do not go to church merely or mainly to be amused. "ERNST IST DAS LEBEN." Life is a very serious thing: and we live, unquestionably, in very serious times. Mr. Carlyle (who has more of Schiller than of Goethe in him, though he is always talking of the latter) has written this motto, from the earnest German poet, upon the portico of his temple. Enter seriously with the real intent to worship, and assuredly you will find something worthy to be worshipped; for here also, amid many outlandish and fantastic imps, "here also there are GODS."

But what kind of Gods?—what sort of a sermon?—and what is the text?—The Gods, we are afraid, are strange Gods, very German-looking Gods, not English at all. The sermon is a very strange sermon, couched in a very strange dialect, half ancient Hebrew, and half modern Teutonic, rushing strangely into all places which vulgar sermons are strangely careful to eschew; orthodox only in one point, that it deals somewhat largely in a certain sweeping facility of denunciations; and the text is twofold; one from a book that we ought all to know something about—a very good text, but one very difficult to preach on to any practical purpose in this country— "THE LOVE OF MONEY IS THE ROOT OF ALL EVIL;" and the other, also a very good text, from the proverbial philosophy of some pious old monk-"LABORARE EST ORARE"— "*Working is the best praying.*"—Labour, free labour, and the just wages of labour; labour, not for the material love of cold metals basely bright, but for the love of God, and of your fellow-men, for the love of mere labour, if you can find nothing better; this is the sum and substance of Thomas Carlyle's new book, and the drift of his new sermon: and if you will only not be too hasty to take offence at grotesque peculiarities,—if you will bear in mind charitably, that the most comely cavaliers in the days of romance used constantly to be escorted by the most ugly and misshapen dwarfs,—then, after reading to the end, you are like to confess with us, that, though somewhat too long, and too much crammed with eager iterations, it is, nevertheless, on the whole, a very good book, a very sound and (not to speak it profanely) Evangelical discourse.

But Mr. Carlyle is more than a preacher. He is a prophet also. A prophet is not essentially different from a preacher; he is only different in degree. Prophesying is preaching in its highest power. Preaching is a common thing—too common, and too cheap by far now-a-days—a thing to be heard decently on Sunday, (by all respectable persons as least,) that it may be decently forgotten on Monday; but prophecy is only for great occasions, for stirring eras, when self-renovating Time is pregnant with some new birth; such as the era of the preaching of Christianity, the era of the Reformation, the era of the French Revolution, of which last era, this present year, 1843, in Great Britain, is a part. We may be mistaken: every man may be mistaken; but we think we can mark with the finger distinctly three men who, in their whole aspect and character, deserve to be esteemed the mighty literary (as opposed to scientific or legislative) prophets of the great revolutionary change which is even now working itself out in this troubled isle. The men we mean are, Percy Bysshe Shelley, Samuel Taylor Coleridge, and Thomas Carlyle. Don't think it strange that these so different intellects in some respects, are here named together. It is the cast and character of the men, the tone of their mind, their position in relation to the age, of which we speak. No matter that Coleridge was outwardly connected with that political party whose office it is to maintain the present by explaining the past, rather than to interpret the future by creating the present: inwardly he did not belong to them: therefore, also, some of the less wise of them have already begun publicly to proclaim him a heretic. No matter either that of these three men whom we call preëminently prophets, the two who are gone had the function of verse, the one who remains has not; their vocation of preaching, of prophesying is the same. Do you not feel it? Is there not something serious and weighty, as if of a prophet-burden—something solemn, awful, and soul-compelling in the apparition, in the utterances of these men? Do you not see how they stand forth each of them, apart from the busy throng of British actualities, and in a dialect each of his own, testify solemnly against the various idol-worships of the age—the worship of Mammon and Materialism in all its portentous extent, of false glory, and of vain shows, of gilded coaches, and of sounding names, of titled idleness and mitred stupidity? This you must feel, this you must see in them, or you see and feel nothing at all in the matter. This you must see and feel specially in Thomas Carlyle; and yet, again, specially in this new book of his; than which a more solemn sermon in some respects, and terrible prophecy, has never been thundered into British ears.

There is one thing which, from the days of Cassandra downwards, has been characteristic of all prophetic utterances, that they are wont to be delivered in a language which, to the common ear, is not easy to be understood. This unintelligibility, in the case of true prophets, arises, in a great measure, not so much from any intellectual peculiarity on the part of the preacher, as from a moral incapacity on the part of the hearers. "Ears have they, but they hear not." They cannot understand, chiefly because they will not understand. At the same time, even prophets of the highest class are seldom altogether without blame in the matter of the proverbial obscurity with which they are wont to involve their oracles. Possibly, in some points of view, this obscurity cannot be altogether avoided; but it should always be guarded against. Unhappily of all modern prophets, there is none who lies open to the charge of having involved himself in needless obscurity, so manifestly as Thomas Carlyle. We must, therefore, speak more particularly of this matter, as much for the sake of the public, as for the sake of Mr. Carlyle himself perhaps. How does this obscurity of the prophetic diction arise in the general case, and why is Mr. Carlyle in particular more obscure than his brethren? Consider what language is. It is the general system of audible, and (by help of writing) visible symbols, whereby reasonable souls have agreed to express that general stock of ideas which one reasonable soul has in common with another; the common currency of thought, so to speak. But it is also another, and a no less important thing. It is that particular body of audible symbols which each particular soul moulds and shapes out for itself to express that particular system of ideas, so and so arranged, and so and so coloured, that belongs to it as an individual, and to no other; at least to none in exactly the same combination, and to exactly the same degree. Now, there are two kinds of style: the style of common men, and the style of uncommon men. Of these two kinds, you will plainly see that the former will necessarily be altogether composed of the common currency of thought; while the latter will always bear upon it a distinct image and superscription, to be deciphered perfectly only by spirits kindred to the coiner. And the more uncommon and original a man is, the more uncommon, original, and, to the common man, unintelligible will be his style. This is a universal rule applicable to all writers and speakers; but there is something more than this in the case of the prophet. He is a man who has not merely more of the individual to imprint upon his language than common men, but his whole habits of thought and manner of life tend to withdraw him (inconveniently we must say) from that public, or mass of common men, to whom it is his vocation to preach. John the Baptist was not the only prophet who showed himself fond of solitude and the wilderness. They must all be educated in that school. They must talk much with themselves, with God, and with the devil too, sometimes. Is it, then, strange at all,—is it not rather quite natural, that, with a gigantic soul, struggling with strong throes continually to shape the world to its likeness despotically, and not slavishly receive a likeness from the world, and communing daily in solitary places with spirits rather than with men,—the prophet should unconsciously (the wicked world says affectedly) form to himself a style of utterance only half understood at times by those common mortals to whom it is addressed? 'Tis a pity this prophetic obscurity—a great pity; but let not money-making men, with glib eloquence discoursing largely of the great material Trimurti, CORN, COIN, and CURRENCY,—let not prim "Dandiacal bodies," expert masters of small-talk, and of large oaths,—let not nice, critical gentlemen, with a fluent array of vituperatory and laudatory phrases, from the most recent or the most ancient dictionary of Aesthetics,—let not exact, scientific men, painfully grinding out, to name the most musical things in nature, the most dissonant jargon in art,—let not damnatory, sacerdotal men, systematically deafening their own ears, and other peoples' with an "inane tumult of unintelligent and unintelligible hearsays,"—let not the wholesale dealers in these kinds, or in any other kind of authorized slang, be too ready to be found declaiming against the unauthorized slang of Thomas Carlyle, the literary prophet. Let us be charitable,—let us be considerate. We all deal in slang, more or less. The only difference is, that the prophet deals in a new and strange slang known only to himself, and not yet become the property of any legitimate corporation of men. This charity the prophet has a right to expect from us. He is not the less bound, however, to get rid of his slang as quickly as he can. Is there not offence enough in the matter, with adding a new stumbling-block in the manner? Men who are capable only of small things will lay hold of the tags of your style, and incommode the free movement of your apostleship seriously. Do not be afraid to harm your mighty mission by being as little singular as possible in small things. A more original, a more powerful, a more racy style, than Mr. Carlyle's, the English language has not to show; but its faults—O what faults! Was not the English language made to be understood by English men? It may be true—it is true to a certain extent—that the preachers of German things, in England, at the present day, are forced to Germanize their English, just as the Greek of the New Testament was necessarily Hebraized by the first preachers of Christianity; but Mr. Carlyle does not give himself any reasonable pains to temper the harsh edge of this disagreeable necessity. He will not even condescend to explain; he merely alludes. He tumbles and tosses, plunges and plashes, spouts and plays capriciously, a huge, strange, leviathan of literature is his wild German ocean at large, and seems nothing concerned to think, that of those who behold the portentous phenomenon, for twenty that will wonder and gaze, only one will be edified; as if the mission of a great prophet were to open the outward eyes of men merely, and not rather their understandings and their hearts. The god who exults thus inconsiderately in the strangeness of his own Avatar, had need to see well to it, that the children of men may not mistake him here and there (innocently enough) for a posture-maker and a buffoon.

We hope no reasonable admirer of Mr. Carlyle will consider us as having spoken too largely, or too severely on this merely external matter of style. There are some men in whom a vicious style of writing is so ingrained, that you cannot hope to reform them by criticism any more than you can teach the gnarled oak not to delight in tortuosity. There are also in Mr. Carlyle's style some peculiarities which, though they may be more nearly allied to fault than excellence, no man that loves natural vigour more than a conventional classicality, would wish to see removed. But there are other peculiarities, again, which are mere adventitious tricks, which do not belong to Mr. Carlyle's nature essentially; as any one may satisfy himself, by comparing the earlier productions of this writer's pen with the later. These tricks and juggleries of German phrase, partly of metaphysical, partly of merely grammatical peculiarity, our direct clear-seeing, steady-marching, hard-hitting, English tongue will not away with. Besides, John Bull, as Mr. Carlyle has very clearly discerned, is a great respecter of use and wont in all things, and will have law and custom to reign supreme, to a certain extent, over language as well as over the Church. Let this author, therefore, who, though of German training, has evidently not walked the streets of London with his eyes shut, only condescend to untwist a few of these foolish Teutonic tassels that he so studiously appends to his English speech: let him take, then, some historical theme worthy of his strength—Oliver Cromwell, say, Martin Luther, or Napoleon: let him leave the story as much as possible to tell itself, and not swamp it, as he did the French Revolution, in monstrous self-repeating convolutions and contortions of German phrase and German philosophy;—*so*, we predict he is strong enough to plant himself proudly upon the very top-pinnacle of British authorship; otherwise, he is secure only of a conspicuous niche in that already too crowded gallery of the "Eccentricities of Genius."

In order to understand rightly Mr. Carlyle's sermon, of which we shall now proceed to give some extracts, the reader will first consider, and mark distinctly, the preacher's position, intellectual and moral, in reference to the present age. We live in an age of railroads, and steam-coaches, patent coffee-percolators, and block-pavements. Plato knew nothing of these things: Immanuel Kant, 2000 years after him, not much more. Between Arkwright, with his sounding host of spinning jennies, and Hesiod, with his caroling troop of Heathen gods and goddesses, what a leap! Such a leap there is between Thomas Carlyle's "Past and Present," and the last edition of Adam Smith, or any other book of these days (of which there are so many) that deals mainly in material facts and figures. Mr. Carlyle is the most thorough, the most earnest, the most despotic of all modern spiritualists. He is a burning-hot, heavy-hammering, practical English Platonist; not one of your old serene metaphysical vapourers, placid mathematical visionaries there at Alexandria. Marching with a visible glory in his countenance, from the base of the double-peaked Parnassus in Germany, upon the one summit of which sits Goethe, and on the other Jean Paul Richter;—marching resolutely forth, with a burden in his breast, as from some modern sacred Sinai, he dashes wildly into the midst of our Utilitarian stir here in Britain, and startles the ears of the money-changers, and the pleasure-hunters, and the idlers and hypocrites in high places, with the ominous cry heard of old from the wilderness, "Repent, I say unto you. Repent! Repent, or ye shall all certainly perish!"—Is Thomas Carlyle's prophetic cry in season, or out of season at the present hour? We think it is altogether in season. Who can deny that we English are idol-worshippers of Mammon more than any people upon the earth? It is not a broad, day-staring truth which our many faithful church-goings, and constant cries of "Church in danger!" do not disprove at all, but rather prove in many ways? Who can deny that pampered idleness lolls with us in high places, and honest labour starves? Who can believe that these things shall be upon God's earth, and no prophet be sent to testify against them? Thomas Carlyle is not the first who has lifted up his voice against these things; neither will he be the last. Let us therefore receive him honourably, as a God-sent prophet, and thank Heaven for him. Adam Smith, and Ricardos, and M'Cullochs, we have enough in every shop: they are prophets, too, after their fashion; and whoso denounces them is not wise. But there is an older and a more venerable gospel than that of political economy, of which Mr. Carlyle is one of the most notable modern missionaries; and among other definitions of wealth in these mercantile times,—in this mechanical age,—in this money-making country,—there was need of a strong and an earnest voice to call out loudly in every street this one also—"THE WEALTH OF A MAN IS THE NUMBER OF THINGS WHICH HE LOVES AND BLESSES, WHICH HE IS LOVED AND BLESSED BY." There was need of a prophet to preach the old gospel of Christ, "THE KINGDOM OF HEAVEN IS WITHIN YOU," somewhere out of the pulpit,—a gospel altogether contrary to that now preached in the pulpit by the Puseyites. . . .

[Extracts from Book I]

Such is the evil: we have known it, we have felt it in manifold ways—rising Hydra-headed against all attempts to subdue it—only too sadly. But where, and what is the remedy? Here, we have no doubt, Mr. Carlyle will disappoint many an inquirer, as he did in his precursor of this book, the "Chartism;" but Mr. Carlyle is true to his vocation. The remedies which he proposes are not legislative or legal remedies at all: he points at such, indeed, but he does not project them. The remedies which he proposes are the remedies which a preacher and a prophet only can propose—the same remedies that are proposed in the New Testament, in the Sermon on the Mount. Begin, he says, with examining yourself: see that your heart be in the right place. Be sure that you actually do wish to do something for the love of your brother's soul, and not for the love of your own purse. So setting out, you will find plenty of things to do: otherwise, unprovided with the motives of an honest love, you can only prove yourself a busy bungler; and there are too many such already. This is a favourite text with Mr. Carlyle; and no doubt he is right. Look at the thousandfold futile fruitless "tongue-fence" that goes on every day there in Parliament, and you will certainly see that the want of honest will to do, is the main cause why so little is done. . . .

The vain expectation of good from details of legislation, without a true and a loving heart, being thus summarily cut off, Mr. Carlyle proceeds to protest in his strong speech against that evil which, while it subsists to its present extent, is the grand obstacle to all improvement, namely, the Love of Money, or, as he phrases it, the *Gospel of Mammonism.* . . .

Here is a prophet's blast, indeed! containing much, doubtless, that is true, and something also that is not true. 'Tis a strong word that, *"Two centuries of Atheistic government!"* and too like the sweeping condemnations that we are accustomed to hear from Puseyite pulpits. We wish Mr. Carlyle would avoid such damnatory paradoxes. Even in the mouths of earnest prophesying men, these things have something puerile in them, and, worse than puerile, pernicious.

We do not stay to inquire whether the love of money is to be rooted out of the heart of man by putting a veto on "fair competition," and suppressing "cash-payment." Mr. Carlyle may settle these things (which may require a little more study than he, perhaps, has hitherto bestowed on them) with the political economists, with the bankers, and bill-brokers, and with Robert Owen. We proceed to the second great plague of England, which, after the gospel of Mammonism, must, according to Mr. Carlyle, imperatively be swept from its habitation on British soil, otherwise we are ruined,—it is the gospel of titled luxury and idleness, the plague of the UNWORKING ARISTOCRACY, of men holding land in a country, and doing no duty to the country, except, indeed, it be—as Mr. Carlyle delights to iterate—the duty of shooting partridges, and dilettantizing at legislation. . . .

But the grand theme of this book remains. To balance these false gospels of "Mammonism" and "Do-nothing Aristocracy," we have the true gospel of Labour, and the just wages of Labour. Let the working man hear that, and amid his sooty toil rejoice. He is the only hero, in Mr. Carlyle's estimation—the only noble. . . .

Mr. Carlyle's book is full of pictures dark enough, of complaints loud enough, and blasts strong enough of earnest, indignant appeal. But there is faith also, (as a prophet can never exist without that,) and a triumphant outlook into the boundless conquests that the "Chivalry of Labour," million-handed, under its thousand captains of the "Gifted," is yet destined to achieve on the earth. . . .

THE TIMES

6 October 1843, 3-4.

ANON.

We owe some apology to the public for having suffered a work from Mr. Carlyle's pen to remain so long on our hands unnoticed. We might plead in our defence the pressure of more important subjects during the Parliamentary session, did not the author himself supply us with a still better excuse. "Literature," says Mr. Carlyle, "when noble, is not easy, but only when ignoble." We admit the justice of the remark, but at the same time are inclined to think that the difficulty of literature presses sometimes as severely upon the reader as upon the writer of books; and we know of few writers with whom one is more likely to share this honour than Mr. Carlyle. For ourselves, we are free to confess that the difficulty of understanding Mr. Carlyle rather increases upon us than vanishes upon a closer acquaintance with him, and we therefore trust our title to *"nobleness"* is complete.

Mr. Carlyle has long been known as an original and powerful writer, and of all his works, the volume before us may perhaps be considered, as it was doubtless intended by its author to be, the most characteristic performance. He seems to have been desirous of figuring as a solecism in the literary world, and has spared no pains to secure for himself this distinction. His present work is a kind of commentary upon his former lectures on "Hero Worship" and "Chartism;" the same characters, with sundry new personages, are again brought before us; the same idea, or rather set of ideas, prevails throughout; the same vague and unsatisfactory notions about "heroism" are to be found in every part of it. In poetical language, it may be called an epic upon "work;" for to this point all the writer's conclusions tend. In his capacity as an author, Mr. Carlyle has given a practical illustration of his theory. His "work" has evidently been to read German, and to engraft upon the English language, not only the sentiments, but the style of his favourite authors. We do not quarrel with him for this. Every man who wishes to give a *personal* character to his writings, must clothe them in a style of his own. It is perfectly natural for him to do so, and the best style for him is that which comes to him most naturally. It is best, moreover, not only for himself, but for his readers. It is to a certain extent a key to his real thoughts and character. Scarcely any two men think exactly alike; and Mr. Carlyle no doubt *writes* in the style in which he has been accustomed to *think*. The style of Addison would suit him as little as it would have suited Dr. Johnson. His own style is the best *for himself*, and for his readers. It helps to teach us not only what he thinks, but what he is. We do not say that this furnishes any apology for those hideous Anglo-German and Anglo-Latin compounds with which Mr. Carlyle's writings abound. Peculiarity of style is one thing, an affected phraseology quite another.

But if Mr. Carlyle's style be singular, the view which he takes of literature in general is not less so. The greatest of heathen philosophers has recorded his belief that the world would never be well governed till either Kings became philosophers, or philosophers Kings. Mr. Carlyle has improved upon the sentiment, and has in a former work laid it down as a matter of positive certainty that the age is approaching in which this great desideratum will be realized. He has even gone further, and, not content with the triumph of *philosophy* (written or unwritten) over mere unintellectual monarchies, has appropriated the prediction in favour of book-writers—amongst whom he himself is not to be forgotten. "I say," says he, "of all priesthoods, aristocracies, governing classes, at present extant in the world, there is no class comparable for importance to that priesthood of the writers of books."* Well said, Mr. Carlyle! Once get this admitted, and we shall make our fortunes, and of course take care of our publishers. "Let us look at the Chinese; they have found out the way to govern—they make their *literati* their rulers. We do not say with what degree of success, yet still the very attempt is *precious*. What can we do better than copy them? Let us be governed by a library, or a philosophical institution—a far easier and cheaper system than cabinets and boards of trade!" Perhaps this is not exactly what Mr. Carlyle means. He does not intend to do without cabinets and boards of trade, only they must consist of book-writers. Nay, but what have we to do with the writers? We have got their books, we do not require *them*. Of what use are books except to teach us how to govern, and do this thing and that? What more do we need? We fear, after all, that Mr. Carlyle's plan of governing by book-writers will not be found to answer even to themselves.

But, in truth, there is a vastly greater difference between writing and acting than Mr. Carlyle seems to imagine. "Literature," says a very acute thinker of the present day, "is almost in its essence unreal; for it is the exhibition of thought disjoined from practice. Its very home is supposed to be ease and retirement, and when it does more than speak or write it is accused of transgressing its bounds. This indeed constitutes what is considered its true dignity and honour, viz., its abstraction from the actual affairs of life; its security from the world's currents and vicissitudes; its saying without doing. . . . Hence mere literary men are able to say strong things against the opinions of their age, whether religious or political, without offence; because no one thinks they mean anything by them. They are not expected to go forward to act upon them, and mere words hurt no one." However, we will do Mr. Carlyle the justice to say, that his examples of great Kings, or heroes, as he calls them, do not altogether illustrate his principle of book-writing supremacy; being seldom, whatever their other qualities, men of letters, much less book-writers. In spite of himself, Mr. Carlyle cannot help separating fact from theory, even in his most choice illustrations. Cromwell, whom he considers the *beau ideal* of all heroes that ever have lived or are to live in this world, was certainly not a literary character; nor have we yet heard of the palm of Minerva being conceded to Mahomet—another denizen of Mr. Carlyle's temple of fame. And yet he seems to think Burns a very ill-used man, because Great Britain did not rise as one man to make him Prime Minister or King!

John Knox and Burns (Mr. Carlyle has a truly Scottish predilection for his own countrymen) were the two greatest heroes of their respective ages. *Antagonism* is our author's leading idea; a man must have knocked down something in order to win his favour. No matter what that is—churches or kings—things sacred or profane— no matter what he sets up in their place—something he must pull down, or he can be no hero of Mr. Carlyle. John Knox and Mahomet (we have no objection to class them in the same category) compete for the palm of heroship with Luther and Cromwell; while these are placed in most Catholic juxtaposition with Anselm and Becket. It would be invidious to mention living heroes, else we might venture to suggest Mr. O'Connell as an addition to Mr. Carlyle's next list. He, too, has done some work, good or bad.

But leaving these speculations, let us proceed to consider the more immediate subject of the present volume—the past and present condition of England. . . .

The progress of the manufacturing system—the impediments thrown in its way by the Corn Laws—the moral evils which have marred its effects upon the labouring classes—the avarice of master manufacturers, the idleness of landlords—the hardships of the New Poor Law—these are the materials with which Mr. Carlyle has to deal.

The task is doubtless no easy one, and the manner in which our author executes it is, we fear, a conclusive proof of the incompetence of a mere man of letters to grapple with the terrible realities which hover around and threaten destruction to our social system. The science of politics in the present day is widely different from the theories of heathen philosophers. It is eminently a *practical* science. Every man endued with a well-regulated mind, and enlightened by a sound education, is more or less able to judge of the rectitude and justice of any prescribed line of politics. If he is not, the fault lies more in his own deficiency of moral perception, than in any abstruseness of the science of politics itself. "It is as hard," said Lord Bacon, "to be a true politician as to be truly moral." With the code of Christian morals, and the experience of past ages, before us, the difficulty ought to consist, not in the speculative, but in the practical part of politics. The secret cause, indeed, of decay in all States has been the dissolution of the bond between public and private morality. No State can long exist which has ceased to feel confidence in its own laws and institutions; no laws or institutions can long inspire confidence which are not founded on the basis of immutable morality. To apply the science of morals to that of politics—to follow what is *true*, not what is *expedient*—this is the great problem, on the solution of which depend all our hopes of national continuance. "This universe," says Mr. Carlyle, "has its laws. If we walk according to the law, the law-maker will befriend us; if not, not. Alas! By no Reform Bill, ballot-box, five point Charter—by no boxes or bills or charters, can you perform this alchymy. Given a world of knaves, to produce an honesty from their united action! It is a distillation, once for all, not possible."

All very true, this. But still we are as far as ever from the point. What *are* the laws of the universe? If the world has gone wrong, what is the best way of setting it right again? Above all, what is the statesman's business in the matter? How is he to meet, counteract, and overthrow the evils of which philosophers tell him? His business is to act with the materials that are given him, not to speculate about the laws of the universe, about which he can know but little, and is not concerned to know much. Let a man be ever so much a philosopher, in the literary sense of the word, he is not a whit nearer the mark, unless he have genius as well as knowledge—unless he have the faculty of applying to every-day politics the philosophic maxims with which his mind is stored. Philosophy is but a lamp, which, however useful and necessary in itself, will never supply a man with either hands or materials to work with.

An instance of Mr. Carlyle's *unpractical* character soon presents itself. He finds it to be one of the laws of the universe (though most men would be content with a smaller range) that those who would not work should not eat; and discovering, or fancying that he discovered, that this truth was first publicly recognized by the New Poor Law, he took it for granted that that law must be a good thing, or at least that the old law was a bad thing. In his lectures on Chartism he puffed that atrocious measure as "a protection of the thrifty labourer against the thriftless and dissolute," not perceiving that while the New Poor Law was founded on the principle of punishing those who could not get work for themselves, it had the effect at the same time of reducing the wages of those who could. We are glad, however, to see that in the present volume Mr. Carlyle draws in his horns a bit when descanting on the New Poor Law, and never speaks of it but with censure.

We could mention many other anomalies in Mr. Carlyle's philosophy, which lead us to hope that his age of book-writing Governments may be still far distant; but as we wish to part on good terms with a writer, whose works, however eccentric, are always amusing, we shall conclude with a few remarks on that part of his volume on which we are ready to bestow unqualified praise. Mr. Carlyle's great power consists in depicting the past, not in reaching forward to the future. His genius is not *creative*, but displays itself in grouping and throwing light upon the different characters portrayed in his compositions. He has a wonderful facility of seeing his way through the intricacies of historical events, in reducing them to their proper shape and proportion, in tracing their causes, and developing the successive changes to which they have given birth. His work on the French Revolution is, in this respect, unrivalled; and we must apply the same remark to that portion of the volume before us which is devoted to old historical recollections. This is a kind of running commentary upon a singular chronicle lately published by the Camden Society, entitled *Chronicles of Jocelin of Brakelond*, a monk of St. Edmundsbury. . . .

[The remainder of the article is taken up with excerpts from Book II of *Past and Present*.]

[*Lecture V., on Hero Worship.]

"Carlyle's *Past and Present*: A Prophecy"

SOUTH ATLANTIC QUARTERLY

21 (January 1922): 30-40.

STANLEY T. WILLIAMS

One day when Mr. Arthur Henderson was stating in no uncertain terms what would be acceptable to the British Labor Party, a member of the audience was moved to quote to his neighbor a sentence from Carlyle's *Past and Present*: "Some 'Chivalry of Labour,' some noble humanity and practical divineness of labour, will yet be realized on this earth." Recent strikes, then, had made the Labor Party "chivalrous," if not "divine;" the speaker's tone was that of complacence, of realized prophecy. "Chivalrous" and "divine" are not the adjectives applied by all men to the Labor Party; but every faction would admit one other epithet, that of *powerful*. Every history of industrialism, of socialism, or merely of political history indicates the growth of the Labor Party; its progress since 1843, the date of the appearance of *Past and Present*, has been almost incalculable. Curiously enough Carlyle's book ends with a section called *Horoscope*, a somewhat incoherent and passionate effort to read the future of labor in the light of the past and his own present-day England. *Past and Present* deals as much with the unknown future as with the known past. Carlyle dogmatizes on the twelfth century, but he speculates concerning the twentieth.

Horoscope is a protracted oracle. Carlyle was oppressed by the industrial tyranny of the forties; and he prophesied the eventual emancipation of the working-man. Nebulous, repetitive, and rhapsodical in style, even as the ancient Delphic oracles, *Horoscope* has, nevertheless, "blest islets of the intelligible" which are pertinent today. For example, "an actual * * * industrial aristocracy, real not imaginary aristocracy, is indispensable and indubitable for us;" or "we shall again have * * * instead of mammon-feudalism and unsold cotton shirts and preservation of the game, noble just industrialism;" or "a question arises here: whether in some ulterior, perhaps some far distant stage of this 'Chivalry of Labour,' your master-worker may not find it possible, and needful, to grant his workers permanent *interest* in his enterprise and theirs?"

Past and Present abounds in such prevision. Carlyle's neology has become our terminology: "Cash-payment;" "gospel of mammonism;" "captains of industry." Though these phrases were created by Carlyle, they are now, as Mr. Frederick Harrison says, household words.

This aspect of Carlyle's genius is especially noticeable in *Past and Present*. It has been the cause of many references to him as a prophet, a seer, and a Jeremiah. But Mr. R. H. Hutton warns us against attributing to Carlyle a definite "message."

Carlyle was, Mr. Hutton maintains, always negative; his thought centered upon the *simulacra* of his time; he was a specialist in the diseases of the commonwealth. This is certainly true. Carlyle was not a prophet either in the mystical sense—a Tiresias who saw truly but with "what labour oh, what pain!"—nor according to the modern notion of a prophet an inspired leader who bestows upon his people new philosophies. But Carlyle's imagination, flaming in a few fields of thought, in some ways illumined the future. Carlyle really *foresaw* the rise of the Labor Party, though, of course, he did not guess its extent. And *Past and Present* is an example of this power.

Past and Present is a piercing glance into the feudal age, and a no less acute critique upon contemporary England. The book is enriched by Carlyle's wisdom, and ennobled by his most eloquent and most untrammelled manner. Mr. John Morley, re-reading it in 1891, exclaimed: "What energy, what inexhaustible vigour, what incomparable humor, what substantial justice of insight, and what sublimity of phrase and image!" Of these qualities and of the high originality of design much has been written, yet in 1921 something yet remains to be said concerning the relation of Carlyle's present to our own.

A student of political history once told me that the social disorders of the thirties and forties had never seemed real to him until he read *Past and Present*. When Carlyle pushed across the table to his mother the manuscript of the *French Revolution* he cried: "Never has a book come more *flamingly* from the heart of a man." His comment might have included *Past and Present*. Yet, in spite of the apparently careless fervor of the book, the method used in its composition was that of the literary artist. Over the historian's account of the Manchester insurrection we nod; over Carlyle's, even today, we instinctively clench our fists. For here "persons influence us, voices melt us, looks subdue us, deeds inflame us." Manchester is become, derisively, "Peterloo." The riot becomes in Carlyle's pages a series of stirring images: "Woolwich grapeshot will sweep clear all the streets;" "there lie poor sallow work-worn weavers, and complain no more now." Tennyson hints mildly at some misery connected with "spirit, alum, and chalk;" Carlyle tells one unforgettable anecdote; that of the parents found guilty of poisoning three children to defraud a burial society of 38s, due upon the death of each child. This was a story likely to make some impression even upon the British Philistine; resignation to human suffering did not seem so easy; it seemed a parallel to Carlyle's relentless descriptions of the tanneries at Meudon with their human skins. Concrete, personal detail is characteristic of Carlyle's literary method in *Past and Present*.

Such detail is not always ghastly. To emphasize the talkiness of parliament Carlyle says much of "oceans of horse-hair, continents of parchment;" to accentuate the sin of indifference he relates sardonically the history of the men of the dead sea, who "listened with real tedium to Moses, with light grinning, or with splenetic sniffs and sneers." *Past and Present* is crammed with detail, yet the central purpose of the book is maintained; like a single strand strung with brilliant beads of allusion, of anecdote, of minute detail.

One phase of Carlyle's use of detail is imaginative allusion. As a reader Carlyle had despoiled all literature; he once boasted that while at Craigenputtock he had read everything; and *Past and Present* is a mosaic of allusion. Sometimes an allusion—such as the Behemoth of Chaos—caps a sentence, and is not employed again. More often the illustration echoes through the book: "The day's wages of John Milton's day's work, named *Paradise Lost* and Milton's *Works*, were Ten Pounds, paid by installments, and a rather close escape upon the gallows." An ingenious variation is the use of a myth to point the idea of a chapter or a succession of chapters. Thus *Midas* and *The Sphinx* are chapter captions; in each case there is constructed an elaborate application to England. In the first the "baleful fiat of enchantment" prevents the conversion of the nation's wealth into prosperity; and in the second, England, since she has failed to answer the spiritual questions of life, is being torn to pieces. It is impossible to exaggerate the multiplicity of Carlyle's allusions and examples. *Horoscope*, in particular, is like a stream bearing the *membra disiecta* of literature and history: Columbus, Thersites, Mahomet, Cromwell, Wallace, Igdrasil, Byron and Pilate, King John, Hydra-Coil, Jotuns, Rhadamanthus, Burns and Kilkenny Cats!" "The Iliad and Lakenheath eels!" The writer's juxtaposition is hardly closer than Carlyle's. Such an inundation at first stimulates, then fatigues, but the total effect is that of eloquence and brilliance of manner.

Carlyle's allusions are most pungent when fictitious. He refers solemnly to personages who were without being until they sprang full-formed from his own brain. Who, pray, are Colacorde, Blusterowski and Schnüspel? It is entertaining to know that Schnüspel, the distinguished novelist, is Charles Dickens, but it is as pleasant to know that we cannot label Colacorde and Blusterowski. Their flavour lies not in who they are, but in what they connote. Every aviary has birds whose ludicrousness is surpassed only by their absurd self-esteem. Like them Blusterowski is a grotesque, and grotesques Carlyle loved. Jabesh Windbag is perfect without analysis; so is Sauerteig of the *Houndsditch Indicator*, and Bobus Higgins, "sausage-maker on the great scale." In the matter of elections, says Carlyle, "what can the incorruptiblest *Bobuses* elect, if it be not some Bobissimus?" No one would give readily these Carlylean gargoyles.

All other stylistic devices known to Carlyle are commandeered in *Past and Present* for his attack on the strongholds of English apathy. The book has an amazing exuberance of feeling and expression. Nowhere is it more evident that Carlyle thinks and writes with his whole body. Through four long parts he belabors, unwearying, the numbskulls of his generation. His hyperbole is excessive, but he convinces by his honesty, and by the profusion of his illustration, comment, and exhortation; for these qualities are the essence of *Past and Present*, differentiating it from the commonplace pamphlets of the time.

If the style of *Past and Present* is unique, the underlying conception of the book is no less so. One illusion of a materialistic present is a sense of superiority to the past. A popular form of Victorian complacency was loud felicitation over the escape from feudalism. Carlyle tried to show, as did Ruskin later, that in some respects the present was worse than the past. An examination of certain aspects of twelfth century life would prove this. With imagination as his guide Carlyle turned to the fact of the twelfth century as described in a manuscript. The structure of his book followed logically. The *Proem* gives the clue to his purpose; to paint with all his skill a true picture of social conditions in England. The second book, *The Ancient Monk*, indicates twelfth century England's freedom from these evils. The third part, *The Modern Worker*, a development of ideas suggested in the *Proem,* is a relentless contrast between the nineteenth and twelfth centuries. *Horoscope*, the fourth part, is concentrated Carlylean foreboding. Throughout *Past and Present* every lesson for the present is pointed by an experience from the past; a method at variance with modern radicalism which adorns its precepts by morals from an unknown future. In reversion to the past Carlyle outdoes the most conservative historians. "The past," he once remarked, "is a dim, indubitable fact; the Future, too, is one, only *dimmer.*"

The part of *Past and Present* called *The Ancient Monk* is based literally on a "dim, indubitable fact," a manuscript of the twelfth century, *Chronica Jocelini de Brakelonda, de rebus gestis Samsonis Abbatis.* * * * Portions of this part are merely interlineations of the original. Carlyle's picture of Bury St. Edmund's, then, is not romance, but reality, fortified by authority and scholarship. *The Ancient Monk* commands respect because it is truthful in both letter and spirit.

The most obvious danger in using the *Chronica* was pedantry. Carlyle was addressing not German scholars, but English business men. The practical value of his book would not be enhanced by Latin syntax, however erudite. But if heaviness was the English reader's *bete noir*, it was also Carlyle's. He avoids the shoal of pedantry by never forgetting how near it is and how dangerous; and by ridiculing unceasingly the foibles of bastard learning. "I have traced," said an acquaintance of mine triumphantly, "the ancient expression 'cold feet' as far as the early Piedmontese dialect." "That superb change," exclaimed another, "of m to n in the early provencal." "My thesis," declared a third, "deals with the cells in the hind legs of grasshoppers." Darwin once stated that of all minds that he knew Carlyle's was least fitted for scientific enquiry. Certainly no one was ever more scornful of the idiosyncrasies of scholarship. He never tires of scoring pedantry. Whenever he refers to the *Chronica* he jeers: "Giant Pedantry will step in with its huge *Dugdale* and other enormous *Monasticons* under its arm!" Or he indulges in a burlesque pedantic note on "Beodric" and "Weorth." Or, still more frequently, he lifts above all such researches the notice: "Dry Rubbish Shot Here."

If Carlyle's Scylla was pedantry then his Charybdis was dilettantism; and from this reef, too, he resolutely steers his course. Englishmen were interested in the middle ages—Scott's novels had been a powerful influence—but their interest was colored by the rosy mist of romance. The twelfth and thirteenth centuries were one vast field of the cloth of gold, on which played at life crusaders, Paladine, troubadours, true-hearted knights and fair-haired maidens. "How glorious," thought the Victorian, and later read with a shock of disapproval more accurate tales of blood, lust, and mediaeval social conditions. Carlyle despised this fool as heartily as he did the pedant. This reader, he declared, believed without effort that the ring found in the river Trent belonged to the Countess of Leicester. Why not, if it happened in the age of chivalry?

Carlyle achieves a *via media*. In his attitude towards the past he is never pedant, and never dilettante. The twelfth century is not dry rubbish, nor is it a glowing canvas of color. In Carlyle's hands it becomes fact made vivid by imagination. The election of Abbot Samson is a beautiful illustration of Carlyle's method, especially if compared with the original. "And now there remains on our list two only, Samson Subsacrista and the Prior. Which of these two? It were hard to say—by Monks who may get themselves foot-gyved and thrown into limbo for speaking! We humbly request that the Bishop of Winchester and Geoffrey the Chancellor may again enter, and help us to decide. 'Which do you want?' asks the bishop. Venerable Dennis made a speech, commending the persons of the Prior and Samson; but always in the corner of his discourse, *in angulo sui sermonis*, brought Samson in. 'Either of them is good,' said venerable Dennis, almost trembling; 'but we would have the better, if it pleased God.' 'Which of the two *do* you want?' inquires the Bishop pointedly. 'Samson!' answered Dennis: 'Samson!' echoed all of the rest that durst speak or echo anything." Jocelyn's record reads: *Et responsum est precise a pluribus et a majori parte, 'Volumus Samsonem,' nullo reclamante.* "The total effect of this method is an amazing sense of the reality of the life at Bury St. Edmund's. "Let us know always," reiterates Carlyle, "that it *was* a world, and not a void infinite of gray haze with fantasms swimming in it." And again: "That it is a *fact* and no dream, that we see it there, and gaze into the very eyes of it. Smoke rises daily from those culinary chimney-throats; there are living human beings there, who chant, loud-braying, their matins, nones, vespers."

Carlyle has thus visualized for his readers a society which may be compared, point for point, with that of the nineteenth century. None so actual has been done by other social idealists. The dreamy Utopias of Sir Thomas More, of William Morris, or of Samuel Butler, or of the many others do not warrant practical discussion. They belong to romance. But this twelfth century, if limited, was real; it merited consideration in the fifties; perhaps it does now. Carlyle's next step is to contrast relentlessly the two social orders, Bury St. Edmund's and Victorian England. "How silent * * * lie all cotton trades and such like; not a steeple chimney yet got on end from sea to sea." Landlord Edmund had no complaints from his tenants; or partridge seasons; or Corn Bills, or sliding scales.

Why should he have had? Society was in its childhood. Here Carlyle is merely picturesque. But in the vital points of contrast he is stimulating. The points are three, the old familiar fetiches of Carlyle, government, religion and leadership. Carlyle is not reticent concerning his horror of them as they are in the nineteenth century, and his worship of them as they were in the twelfth century. One sees at once that Bury St. Edmund's under Abbot Samson is a tiny corner of a Carlylean social heaven. Here at least was a segment of a working feudal aristocracy. Here was a government untainted by *laissez-faire*; one that took care of its people. The business of a government, Carlyle was wont to shriek, is to govern. Even a Gurth is entitled to his parings. Give the negro plenty of "sweet-pumpkin" and govern *him*. This is well-known Carlylese, repeated a thousand times in *Past and Present*. Abbot Samson ruled and cared for those under him; among his people were no Chartisms or Manchester insurrections. Let the nineteenth century ponder on this sequence of cause and effect; a government that governs and a contented people.

Yet still more remarkable was a religion with faith. The religion of Carlyle's era has been described as one which church members would be amazed to hear doubted, or see practiced. Ruskin's famous threnody in *Modern Painters*, on the death of faith is a typical nineteenth century lament. "My heart was lightened," writes Clough, "when I said 'Christ is not risen.'" "We have forgotten God," is Carlyle's oft-repeated cry. But the faith of Abbot Samson is like that of the Apostles, silent, unquestioning. Carlyle notes that under Samson there were no "spectral Puseyisms or Methodisms." "Methodism with its eyes on its own navel." Introspective religions were unborn. Here were religious men who *believed*. Let the nineteenth century meditate also on this.

But, after all, the third point of contrast is most striking, leadership at Bury St. Edmund's. Carlyle did not expect either the British government or the British religion to change *instanter*; he did not suggest institutional revolution. But he did believe that the kind of leadership in state and church could be altered, if light was vouchsafed the British people; what he did suggest was spiritual revolution. Real leaders could be selected. Thus the greatest contrast between the twelfth and nineteenth centuries was not in institutions but in men. Abbot Samson is plainly balanced against George III. The twelfth century worships a Samson or a St. Edmund, the nineteenth a defender of the faith who is deaf, sightless and insane, or Dickens, a distinguished novelist, or Hudson, a railroad engineer. The test of leadership in one century is worth, in the other the ballot box.

For this is clearly the old doctrine of "the hero," Carlyle's only and faint constructive theory. We are to find "the hero," that wisest and best, that blend of vigor, silence, obedience, loyalty, with his surplusage of spiritual force, that—it must be said—*ignis fatuus*! In this romantic, political, economic tract called *Past and Present* Carlyle would persuade the nineteenth century that in the twelfth century the rainbow's end was reached, "the hero" was found.

He did not persuade the nineteenth century. In spite of admiration for *Past and Present* the nineteenth century was never convinced that Carlyle's notion of "the hero" was a practical remedy. Carlyle as a political critic is one person; Carlyle as a constructive political theorist is another. Vivid and beautiful as *The Ancient Monk* is, a child could impugn its practical application. One palpable falseness of analogy is that Samson's community was considerably fewer in numbers than the twenty-seven millions of Englishmen for whom *Past and Present* was written. There were other fractions of a feudal aristocratic society coeval with Samson's régime whose history would make different reading from that of Bury St. Edmund's. Moreover,

Carlyle seems to suggest that the individualistic religious growth of seven centuries can be forgotten. Can the nineteenth century believe, as did the monks of St. Edmund, in a heaven like that of Thomas A. Kempis? What Carlyle calls "diseased introspection" is an inevitable by-product of the thought of Luther, Wycliffe and Wesley, and of the scientific revelations of the nineteenth century. The perplexity is at least honest; not so much could be said of a return to blind mediaeval faith. We ought, it is true, to find better leaders or "heroes;" democracy is probably not the last stage of economic process, the ballot box may be a *faute de mieux*. Yet we cannot select our leaders as the Bishop of Winchester did Samson. There is hardly a detail of Samson's household management which is transferable to our own.

In fact, Carlyle cannot tell us what to do. Never expect him to do so. What he can do is to tell us, in the most profound sense, what is the matter. This service *Past and Present* performs in 1921 as it did in 1843. Throughout the century it was praised. "There is nothing like it," wrote Clough. Its eloquence was partly responsible for Kingsley's novel, *Yeast*. It roused thousands of Englishmen from inertia to a fresh consideration of social conditions. The very pessimism of the book stung critics out of their complacency. What if Carlyle did, as Henry James said, "scold like" an angry governess. He made men look about them more thoughtfully. "I hope," Carlyle wrote his mother, "it will be a rather useful kind of book. It goes rather in a fiery strain about the present condition of men in general, and the strange pass they are coming to; and I calculate it may awaken here and there a slumbering blockhead to rub his eyes and consider what he is about in God's creation." This was the sum of the matter; a word from Carlyle was a call to action. There is no surrender to *laissez-faire*. "Ay, by God, Donald, we must help them to man it!" He seems to say: "Ich bin ein Mensch begoren. Und das muss ein Kämpfer sein." Every sentence in *Past and Present* is a plea against acquiescence. As Ruskin declares: "What can you say of Carlyle but that he was born in the clouds and struck by the lightning?"

Today Carlyle's idealism seems like the frantic arguments of a man attempting to prove established facts. No better idea of the change in social thought can be had than by realizing that the reforms desired by Carlyle were then considered visionary. Imagine a place now for factory inspectors; for protection against typhus; or for organization of labor. Yet these are but a few of the changes urged by Carlyle, as if he were a minority of one; now they are *faits accomplis*. Of the laborers of England he asks: "Where are they to find a supportable existence," or "*cash-payment* is not the sole relation of human beings!" Such reforms as insurance for workingmen, model tenements for families, the right to strike, hardly occur to Carlyle as present issues. Yet these are the commonplaces of today. And these were to come by action of the state; not through "Morrison's Pills," as Carlyle dubbed opportunist legislation, but through thoughtful constructive government. State supervision of insurance, of railroads, and factories have arrived in a manner exceeding Carlyle's wildest dreams.

Indeed what the modern reader feels about the advance of labor since 1843 is that a new *Past and Present* is needed. No longer is it so necessary to denounce the gospels of mammonism, dilettantism, of oppression of workmen, of extortion by capital. The boot is on the other leg. Labor's emancipation is more complete than even Carlyle would have guessed likely. Possibly a book proclaiming the rights of the employer would be as pertinent today as was *Past and Present* in 1843. During the war there appeared in an English newspaper, in adjacent columns, accounts of the imprisonment of trivial offenders, and also of the release of notorious strike leaders. The union of all labor parties of the world, without respect to nationalism, is possible. In the newspapers of today appears the notice of a strike which will hold motionless every industrial activity in the British Isles. Carlyle's pious allusion to the land belonging to "the Almighty God, and to all His children of men that have ever worked well on it" is now an acknowledged principle among some millions of Communists, though indeed there is no certainty that God is included, or the test of working on the land required by this extraordinary party. The wheel has come full circle. In three-quarters of a century men shrink not from the gospel of mammonism, but from the gospel of bolshevism.

Carlyle, as has been said, was not, in any supernatural sense, a prophet. Yet, apart from the mood of monition ever natural to him there is vision in his thoughts of the future of workingmen. The French Revolution was to him a continual memento; he honestly feared that some similar fate would befall the industrial leaders of England. When he speaks of England "very ominously, shuddering reeling, on the cliff's edge!" he is more than rhetorical. He saw clearly that things would change with "the millions who rejoiced in potatoes." Of his insistence upon the spiritual truths which underlay the necessity for such changes much might be said. Who can deny that Carlyle is in some degree responsible for governments whose "business is to govern"? He was a leader in the battle against *laissez-faire*. It is enough to notice once more the significance of *The Modern Worker* as a knife-edge of economic progress. Contrast the condition of labor mirrored there with its status today. But more than this, *Past and Present* is, in some respects, a prophecy.

"Refractions of *Past and Present*"

CARLYLE PAST AND PRESENT

Ed. K. J. Fielding and Rodger L. Tarr. (New York: Barnes and Noble; London: Vision, 1976): 96-111.

G. ROBERT STANGE

In spite of the sledgehammered preachments, the brilliant tableaux, the amiable flights of humour, Carlyle is difficult to know. One is in the habit of looking for a definable "positions", a reconciliation of opposites, but this atheistical Calvinist will not reconcile the contradictions of his thought or the opposed tendencies of his art; his work is a constant dialectic, an almost reckless play of antithetical forces. The couplings, too numerous to list, can be found in any of his works: a passion for the past confronts journalistic contemporaneity; respect for the plodding accumulation of historical fact somehow lives with the wildest flights of fantastic artistry; contempt for the values of bourgeois society is made to lead to a systematic celebration of Captains of Industry. The whole business can be very irritating—as well as very charming. The clash of opposites produces a continual release of energy, a reassuring sense of life.

The special virtue of *Past and Present* rests, I think, in its accommodation of inherent oppositions to its structure and very language. As an example of Carlyle's historical method it is not as impressive as *The French Revolution*, and as a purely literary work not as affecting and ingenious as *Sartor Resartus*; but as an example of the range of Carlyle's interests, of the intersection of his literary and historical methods, I find it the most appealing—the most central of his works. If we consider it as a special kind of book, it turns out to be three things: an essay in "anti-history", a stylistic *tour de force*, and a tract for the times. To be orderly we must consider the work under these three heads, but it soon becomes clear that in every respect the distinction and power of *Past and Present* are in its exploitation of a stylistic idea.

I

Bracketed by the amateur zeal of the Camden Society (founded in 1838) and the austere precision of Bishop Stubbs' *Constitutional History* (published in 1874), *Past and Present* represents an important stage in the interpretation of the Middle Ages. The celebrated second book, "The Ancient Monk", is in form no more than a highly selective re-telling of *Chronica Jocelini de Brakelonda*, which had been published in 1840 as the thirteenth volume of the Camden Society publications. Detailed studies have been made, both of Carlyle's use of the chronicle and of his historical method.[1] It may not be necessary to repeat that, according to the received opinions of a later day—of the views, let us say, represented by the practice of Sir Lewis Namier—Carlyle was not writing history at all. What has not been sufficiently remarked is the degree to which he himself was aware of and even tended to exploit his anti-historical impulses. His approach to the twelfth century "world" of St Edmundsbury Monastery is resolutely modern; the choice of a medieval subject was, in 1843, very modish, and Carlyle's method was to maintain a double focus on his historical material. "Read it here", he tells his audience, "with ancient yet with modern eyes".[2] There is no attempt at the "objectivity" of more recent historians; we are never "immersed" in the past; neither events, institutions nor persons are given the quiddity of their thirteenth-century existence. There is, in fact, a stubborn avoidance of almost all the qualities of modern historical method, and yet "The Ancient Monk" continues to hold the reader's interest. If it does not give us an insight into the historical past, what—we must ask—does it do?

The answer might be that the finest achievement of Book II is in its expression of a sense of *process*. The modern writer is insistently before us, reading the old chronicle, reacting to it, moralizing on it, extending its meanings. He offers his readers a personal vision, dramatizes for them the way in which a committed, intellectually active man apprehends the materials of his art. Book II lives as a continuing reflection not on historiography, but on the possibility of our knowing the past. This open-ended form, the sense that expression is a process that never is completed, is part of the impulse of Romanticism which infused nineteenth century art. Carlyle's affinities, even when writing history, are with Browning and Dickens rather than with the elder Hallam or Stubbs. The protagonist of Book II is not, I would suggest, Abbot Samson, but Carlyle himself. Our attention is stimulated, our sympathies aroused by the writer's struggle to communicate to us the meaning he has found in Jocelyn's faded chronicle: out of the activity of expressing a historical insight Carlyle draws dramatic tension. This method of involving the reader in the creative process can be seen in the poetry of Browning and G. M. Hopkins. Hopkins, particularly, could make his subject the effort to realize a poetic insight, and by dramatizing the very act of writing poetry give to personal, ostensibly lyrical sensation an air of dramatic action:

> But how shall I . . . make me a room there:
> Reach me a. . . . Fancy, come faster—
> Strike you the sight of it? look at it loom there. . . .[3]

One effect of the dramatic impulse in both poetry and prose is to make the scene the module of construction. And indeed Carlyle as dramaturge often makes his effect by a succession of vivid pictures. This aspect of his writing was commented on from the beginning. Henry James, Sr, for example, remarked that Carlyle was not essentially a man of ideas; picturesqueness, he felt, was "the one key to his intellectual favour"; in order to sympathize he needed "visual contact".[4] And Carlyle himself insisted that it was an "indispensable condition" that the historian "*see* the things transacted, and picture them wholly as if they stood before our eyes".[5]

That Carlyle was faithful to this principle in writing *Past and Present* is affirmed by the most cursory consideration—either of the book itself or of one's recollections of it. Perhaps the most memorable episode of Book II is "The Election", the subject of Chapter VIII. It is worth noting how its climactic episode is conceived:

> What a Hall,—not imaginary in the least, but entirely real and indisputable, though so extremely dim to us; sunk in the deep distances of Night! The Winchester Manorhouse has fled bodily, like a Dream of the old Night; not Dryasdust himself can shew a wreck of it. House and people, royal and episcopal, lords and varlets, where are they? Why *there*, I say, Seven Centuries off; sunk *so* far in the Night, there they *are*; peep through the blankets of the old Night, and thou wilt see! King Henry himself is visibly there; a vivid, noble-looking man, with grizzled beard, in glittering uncertain costume; with earls round him, and bishops, and dignitaries, in the like. The Hall is large, and has for one thing an altar near it,—chapel and altar adjoining it; but what gilt seats, carved tables, carpeting of rush-cloth, what arras-hangings, and huge fire of logs:—alas, it has Human Life in it; and is not that the grand miracle, in what hangings or costume soever?— (*CW* 10:79-80)

So far the author has given us a static setting, the paragraph that follows brings in the characters; they perform their actions and the scene is concluded as abruptly as if a curtain were lowered.

The literary skill represented by this galaxy of set pieces is stunning, but it is questionable whether they conduce to historical understanding. I think the only way the defender of Carlyle can answer the charge that he was a bad historian is to affirm that he was not a historian at all. He shows, in fact, none of the characteristics that mark serious historians of the most diverse schools. Not being, as James remarked, a man of ideas, he is not at all interested in making ideational patterns out of history; but he is equally unconcerned with either the forms or social effects of institutions. And unlike even the Romantic historians he is not attentive to the interaction of the private and public life—an obliquity which seems at first especially strange in view of the persistence of Carlyle's concept of the hero. However, I think it is the very supremacy of the heroic ideal that annihilates a concern for the complex interpretation of the individual life and the outer, public world. In Carlyle's view the heroic individual *makes* his universe: "The clear-beaming eyesight of Abbot Samson", for example, "is like *Fiat lux* in that inorganic waste whirlpool; penetrates gradually to all nooks, and of the chaos makes a *kosmos* or ordered world!" (*CW* 10:92). Elsewhere it is suggested that the "singular shape of a Man" and the "shape of a Time" are the same (*CW* 10:126), a view which hardly allows for the study of that web of influences and reactions which some of the more penetrating historians have undertaken. For Carlyle the individuals who are worth writing about exist as discrete beings; all that matters in either past or present is the agon of the individual soul.

Such views, I repeat, make for bad history, but, in Carlyle's case, for intensely effective art. What he is interested in *Past and Present* is, after all, not the Middle Ages, nor historical method, nor mind or thought, but an image, sensually evoked, of the past.

II

As a work of art *Past and Present* is a triumphant expression of the organic principle, an aesthetic tenet that Carlyle had encountered first in the work of the German critics, and then in the less admired redactions of Coleridge. By the 1830's, however, this notion had become so much a part of Romantic art that its metaphorical foundation was quite forgotten. Coleridge had said, "such as life is, such is the form", and the writers and artists of the new school were not inclined to doubt that in form all genuine art resembled a natural organism—even though such identification would be logically no more valid than the conception of the universe as a machine, or of a poem as an architectonic structure. But from the assumption that the reciprocal connection between art and nature was *real*, that true art was, in fact, *alive*, all other aspects of the organic principle developed. Abstraction, logical pattern, artistic rules are obviously to be contemned. In a truly organic creation there can be no distinction between form and content—an article of faith that led to the more elaborately figurative notion that in a work of art, as in the universe, the smallest part reflects the structure of the whole, and the other way around. A frequent means of illustrating this pleasing relationship was the leaf which repeats in small the structure of the tree. And since art is a natural process, always becoming, never being, it must reflect the dialectic of growth, and incorporate what were called the elementary opposites of existence. Such basic antitheses as the one and the many, odd and even, light and dark, right and left, provided a natural pattern for art.

A reader familiar with Carlyle will have observed that even this brief summary of the organic principle elicits some of his characteristic procedures. For example, a tree was one of the most commonly used symbols of natural growth and of the unity of disparate elements. In *Past and Present* Carlyle heightens this motif and by recurrent statement makes of the Life-tree Igdrasil the emblem of his book. It is first mentioned in the peroration of Book I:

> For the Present holds in it both the whole Past and the whole Future;—as the LIFE-TREE IGDRASIL, wide-waving, many-toned, has its roots down deep in the Death-kingdoms, among the oldest dead dust of men, and with its boughs reaches always beyond the stars; and in all times and places is one and the same Life-tree! (*CW* 10:38)

And again, toward the end of Book II there is an invocation of

> ... The Life-tree Igdrasil, which waves round thee in this hour, whereof thou in this hour art portion, has its roots down deep in the oldest Death-Kingdoms; and grows; the Three Nornas, or *Times*, Past, Present, Future, watering it from the Sacred Well! (*CW* 10:129)

The last mention, almost an exact repetition, comes in the first chapter of the last book, "Horoscope".

The tree symbol which in poetry has stood for the unification of body, soul and spirit (*viz.* Tennyson's "Hesperides" and Yeats's "Among School Children") represents for Carlyle the unity of time and natural order. Since the three *Nornas* are also the tenses by which language is organized, syntax embodies the essential condition of being; the written work is made of living stuff, and like the life-tree has its roots among the dead dust of the past, grows in the present and reaches to the stars of the future ("Horoscope").

The whole book, as its title suggests, is based on a pattern of oppositions. The two experienced aspects of time, the known present and the past that the writer makes known to us, determine the ordering of the sections—a formal arrangement which suggests the penetration of the present by the values of the past, an act of realization which might bring about a better future. The large antithesis of the title is played out in a series of variations: smaller contrasts between law and anarchy, man and phantasm, heaven and hell, valetism and heroism, idleness and work, facts and semblances, jargon and genuine speech. Individual phrases and sentences tend to incorporate contraries: "Brief brawling Day, with its noisy phantasms, its poor paper-crowns tinsel-gilt, is gone; and divine everlasting Night, with her star-diadems, with her silences and her veracities, is come!" (*CW* 10:156). Such continual oppositions are the mechanics of Carlyle's style; we move through his writing from one "wondrous Dualism" (*CW* 10:44) to another. The technique seems at first to resemble eighteenth-century antithetical prose, but the effect of Carlyle's method is altogether different. A writer like Gibbon, for example, holds the two elements of his sentences in a witty and pleasing balance. Each sentence—it is not extreme to say—is an image of reason, the syntax weighs the pro and the con, leads the well-conducted mind by normal, rational procedures to the truth. As aesthetic structures Gibbon's antithetical periods are analogous to the ordered symmetries of eighteenth-century architecture. But in Carlyle's binary constructions there is no symmetry; the play of contraries is varied and dynamic, rudely jolting us into some new awareness. Often one element of an opposition is meant to annihilate the other: "It is very strange, the degree to which these truisms are forgotten in our days; how, in the ever-whirling chaos of Formulas, we have quietly lost sight of Fact" (*CW* 10:176). Or: "Observe, too, that this is all a modern affair; belongs not to the old heroic times, but to these dastard new times" (*CW* 10:156). Elsewhere the oppositions are fused: "O Mr. Bull, I look in that surly face of thine with a mixture of pity and laughter, yet also with wonder and veneration" (*CW* 10:160). Most characteristically, however, Carlyle's phrases seem designed to show how one term of an antithesis contains its opposite: "The cloudy-browed, thick-soled, opaque Practicality, with no logic utterance, in silence mainly, with here and there a low grunt or growl, has in him what transcends all logic—utterance: A Congruity with the Unuttered" (*CW* 10:159). The puns here are clever, but they lead to an illuminating paradox; the "cloudy-browed, thick-soled" Man of Practice is "dumb" in the proper Carlylean way, but he may have his head in the very heavens and be more durable of soul than his opposite number, the Man of Theory. The resolution of this sentence does not yield that pleasure in paradox that is a grace of Augustan prose; there is instead a rather solemn affirmation—opacity and silence are ultimately the only clear speech; the gross and earthy are the ethereal—statements such as this are closer to parable than they are to wit writing. Again and again one discovers that Carlyle's sentences re-enact the movement of discovery through transcendence.

Whereas the antithetical periods of Gibbon and other Augustan writers are discrete, each figuring a well-balanced world view, Carlyle's are part of a larger analogical structure. The sentence mirrors the chapter, the chapter the book. The architectural parallel to this style would be the Gothic of Abbot Samson's day, the aesthetic of which Carlyle could have found in Goethe's famous panegyric of Abbot Erwin, architect of Strasbourg Cathedral.[6]

The image of the world projected by Carlyle's prose is of continual becoming, of ideas and things always being born out of their opposites. The sense of experience that Carlyle's writing leaves us with is suggested by Vico's term, "the coincidence of contraries". In shaping a work like *Past and Present* Carlyle would want his antitheses to be dictated by nature rather than by what seemed to him the mechanical rationalism of Augustan prose. It was his task to find a "living" form in which the relation between contraries is as that of the trunk of a tree to its flower, or of life to the death from which it has sprung.

The prose-texture of the non-historical sections of *Past and Present* has the density of good poetry. In a brief essay it is impossible to perform the kind of sentence by sentence analysis that such writing demands, yet by looking at the skeleton of imagery in a representative chapter it might be possible to suggest what rewards further study could bring. "Phenomena" is the first chapter of the third book, "The Modern Worker". The title picks up a minor but persistent motif in the first and second books, and Carlyle here prepares to work out the various implications of the word. It derives—we are meant to know—from the Greek verb which means "appear" or "show". In philosophical usage phenomena are objects known through the senses rather than through thought or intuition, and phenomenalism is the theory that there is no knowledge or existence outside the phenomenal world. In science phenomenology is the description of objects without interpretation, explanation or evaluation. In ordinary usage a phenomenon is simply any observable fact or event. As one or another meaning of the word is developed, all its connotations remain present as overtones.

After an abrupt, Browningesque beginning, the text of the chapter is set forth in the second paragraph: "We have quietly closed our eyes to the eternal Substance of things, and opened them only to the Shows and Shams of things". The author then goes on to present, with phenomenological detachment, three appearances or shows, all occurring in the present but belonging to different epochs of history; each example is a procession which has lost all meaning, and in the conclusion all three are whirled together into one phantasmagoric rush toward the devouring gulf. Earlier in his book Carlyle had given a preliminary statement of this theme:

> What sight is more pathetic than that of poor multitudes of persons met to gaze at King's Progresses, Lord Mayors' Shows, and other gilt-gingerbread phenomena of the worshipful sort, in these times; each so eager to worship; each with a dim fatal sense of disappointment, finding that he cannot rightly here! (*CW* 10:55)

More ominously, and more than once, he had alluded to the destination of these processions: "We are rushing swiftly on the road to destruction; every hour bringing us nearer, until it be, in some measure, done" (*CW* 10:30). The streets over which these emblematic progresses proceed are both the "broad way" of the New Testament and a "life road" advancing "incessantly" toward "the firm-land's end" (*CW* 10:143).

The first of the "Phantasms riding with huge clatter along the streets, from end to end of our existence" (*CW* 10:137) is the rheumatic Pope, who, finding it laborious to kneel in his car in the procession on Corpus-Christi Day, has had constructed a "stuffed rump" or cloaked figure inside which he can sit with his hands and head extended, and so bless the Roman population.[7] The construction in which the "poor amphibious Pope" sits is merely a prop for what Carlyle calls "the Scenic Theory of Worship" and this bit of tourist lore comes to image the decay of the living, medieval Catholicism extolled in Book II. The Pope's frankness and wholeheartedness, which the author claims to admire, are employed in "Worshipping by stage-machinery; as if there were now, and could again be, in Nature no other" (*CW* 10:139).

The next degraded symbol, or "Phantasm walking the streets", appears in London rather than Rome, and resumes in one ludicrous image the fatuity of a decadent aristocracy:

> The Champion of England, cased in iron or tin, rides into Westminster Hall, "being lifted into his saddle with little assistance", and there asks, If in the four quarters of the world, under the cope of Heaven, is any man or demon that dare question the right of this King? Under the cope of Heaven no man makes intelligible answer,—as several men ought already to have done. Does not this Champion too know the world; that it is a huge Imposture and bottomless Inanity, thatched over with bright cloth and other ingenious tissues? Him let us leave there, questioning all men and demons. (*CW* 10:140-41)

The final phenomenon is an empty symbol of the bourgeois world, the "great Hat seven-feet high, which now perambulates London streets" advertising the products of a hatter in the Strand. Carlyle's comment on this achievement of English Puffery can stand as a final judgment on the social utility of modern advertising:

> The Hatter in the Strand of London, instead of making better felt-hats than another, mounts a huge lath-and-plaster Hat, seven-feet high, upon wheels; sends a man to drive it through the

streets; hoping to be saved *thereby*. He has not attempted to *make* better hats, as he was appointed by the Universe to do, and as with this ingenuity of his he could very probably have done; but his whole industry is turned to *persuade* us that he has made such (*CW* 10:141).

The three symbols of passing phenomena bring into focus a cluster of allusions that have appeared in earlier sections of *Past and Present*; but further, their congruity with each other enhances their meaning. Each example, available to any reader of the daily press, represents with factual precision a great ruling institution, two of which are beyond reconstruction, a third which may yet regain its value by honest work. All involve the use of an integument or artificial covering, a schema which—as *Sartor Resartus* sufficiently demonstrates—expresses a view not only of appearance and reality, but of truth and falsehood, and ultimately of the transcendental as opposed to the phenomenal world. Each artifice moves to the plaudits of the crowd, and each is hollow. But the most characteristic trick of Carlyle's humour is the fact that, though the symbols display themselves in the streets around us, they seem to belong to a mad, surreal world. In the conclusion to "Phenomena" the Pope, the Champion of England and the great Hat are swept up, along with other "unveracities", in a phantasmagoric procession that resembles some vision of Hieronymus Bosch. This is no longer merely a crowd-pleasing progress through the streets of Rome or London, but a whole population advancing "toward the *firm-land's end*". The overtones now evoke the rush of the Gadarene swine, the frenzied procession of the lemmings:

> ... the seven-feet Hat, and all things upwards to the very Champion cased in tin, begin to reel and flounder,—in Manchester Insurrections, Chartisms, Sliding-scales; the Law of Gravitation not forgetting to act. You advance incessantly towards the land's end; you are, literally enough, "consuming the way". Step after step, Twenty-seven Million unconscious men;—till you are *at* the land's end: till there is not Faithfulness enough among you any more; and the next step now is lifted *not* over land, but into air, over ocean-deeps and roaring abysses:—unless perhaps the Law of Gravitation have forgotten to act? (*CW* 10:144)

Even the kind of superficial account of Carlyle's prose that I have given suggests that, though his attitudes are essentially "Victorian", he belongs to a distinctive tradition. His literary structures are conceived in a very different way from those of Newman and Arnold, or even from those of his disciple Ruskin. A prose so densely allusive, organized according to an elaborate scheme of interwoven symbols, fiercely magnifying for satiric purposes the impedimenta of everyday life, finds itself on a line which extends—in English literature—from Swift to Joyce. If *A Tale of a Tub* is one of the ancestors of *Past and Present*, *Ulysses* is certainly its legitimate heir.

III

Considered as a social tract *Past and Present* turns out to have had an unexpectedly large influence. It has been used by thinkers on both the left and the right, and ultimately it appears to have succeeded by the force of its style, rather than by the weight of its social facts or the cogency of its arguments. The aspect of the book's influence which has been least commented on is its effect outside England. Within a year after its publication in April 1843, *Past and Present* had been treated to a review by Emerson and an extensive interpretation in German by Friedrich Engels.

It would be hard to conceive anything more perfervid than Emerson's essay in the *Dial*. For him the book is not only a "new poem", an "Iliad of English woes", but, "In its first aspect it is a political tract, and since Burke, since Milton, we have had nothing to compare with it".[8] Emerson seems determined to make the book all things to all men: "Every reader shall carry away something".[9] And though he comments on the disproportion of Carlyle's picture, "the habitual exaggeration of the tone",[10] he concludes that Carlyle's is the first style to express the richness of the modern world, the only "magnificent" style of his time.

Emerson's conceit that *Past and Present* was Carlyle's "poem" on England, and the *French Revolution* his poem on France became received opinion in the United States. As far as Carlylean attitudes were applied to a developing industrial society, they were derived from *Past and Present*. The great vision of Bury St Edmunds and of medieval organicism seems to have interested American readers only as "literature", but the social myth of Captains of Industry may be said to have found its natural home in the United States. In other quarters, particularly in the vague traditions of populist thought, the denunciation of a system in which the "cash-payment nexus" was the sole bond of human society became a part of the everyday vocabulary. It is worth noting, however, that this influence is purely rhetorical. Carlyle imposed in the most powerful way an attitude, a general receptiveness; he most emphatically did not communicate a connected set of ideas, or—much less—a system of thought. His singularity in this respect is felt if one compares his influence in America with that of John Mill, or even Ruskin. To his journal Emerson confided a remark about *Past and Present* which he kept out of his review; he observed that what Carlyle was "doing now for England & Europe" was "rhetoricizing the conspicuous objects".[11] It is a shrewd and quite complete definition.

Engels' admiration for Carlyle is less well known than Emerson's, but he may have spread the fame of *Past and Present* wider than any other commentator. His article, "*Die Lage Englands*; 'Past and Present' by Thomas Carlyle", was written in January 1844 and published immediately in the short-lived *Deutsch-Französische Jahrbücher* which Marx had initiated in Paris.[12] The essay, which has never been translated into English, is extraordinarily interesting; it is not only the first product of Engels' association with Marx, but—as its title suggests—is a kind of preliminary sketch for Engels' own book, *Die Lage der arbeitenden Klasses in England*, which was published in Leipzig in 1845, but did not reach the English public until 1892.[13] One of the commentators on Marxist thought says that the young Engels "saw the English industrial situation . . . through the eyes of Thomas Carlyle".[14] In the light of Engels' first-hand experience of the factory system in Manchester and his close association with working-class people in England, the claim is hyperbolic; but it seems fair to regard Engels' book as one of the most important results of Carlyle's influence on other writers.

The degree of respect Engels shows for Carlyle's social views, and the warmth of his admiration for what he calls this "wonderfully beautiful" book come as a surprise from a writer whose political astringency and polemical fierceness are famous. It is revealing of Engels' own character that he begins his discussion by emphasizing the living, human quality of Carlyle's writing. Of all the books and pamphlets that have appeared in recent years, he finds Carlyle's the only one that strikes a humane note or expresses an essentially humanitarian point of view.[15] Carlyle is identified for Engels' continental readers as an interpreter of German literature, and is then placed politically—in a way that Disraeli might have appreciated—as being by origin a Tory, a party to which he always stands closer than he does to the Whigs. "So much is certain", Engels bitterly adds, "a Whig could never have written a book that was half so human as *Past and Present*".[16]

Though Engels tells his readers that he is simply going to proceed in an orderly way through the four parts of Carlyle's book, and then begins with long quotations from the first chapter, he manages to create the impression that the book is purely a social tract. He skips, for example, from the middle of the first book to the second chapter of the third, ignoring the whole medieval section. It is not, I think, that Engels wishes to conceal Carlyle's medievalism, or his religiosity, and to re-make him into a socialist critic, but rather that he is eager to give his readers the *usable* Carlyle, to translate a devastating vision of English industrial society. Addressing himself to the reactionary elements of Carlyle's thought, he points out that what Carlyle means by "atheism" is not disbelief in a personal God, but "disbelief in an inner essence of being (*Wesenhaftigheit*), in the infinity of the universe, disbelief in inner reason (*Vernunft*), a despair of the human spirit and of truth". His struggle is not against disbelief in the revelations of the Bible, but against that "most terrible of unbeliefs, unbelief in the Bible of World-history".[17] Though Engels' interpretation errs in making Carlyle sound rationalist and humanistic, it seems to me to be closer to the truth than the views of those commentators who have insisted on Carlyle's theological bent, and evoked his vision of God. Nietzsche's remark that Carlyle was "an English atheist who made it a point of honour not to be one" has the virtue of avoiding by paradox both extremes of misinterpretation, but Engels' enthusiastic praise of the "humane" Carlyle affirms a side of the man that we may too often overlook.

Carlyle's yearning for an "Aristocracy of Talent" and his belief in Hero-worship are simply brushed aside by Engels as he moves into an extended interpretation of Carlyle as a pantheist, and indeed a *German* pantheist.[18] He relates his views to those of Goethe and accurately places him as "mehr schellingisch als hegelisch".[19] Having located Carlyle on ground where Engels feels at home he is then able to employ against him his own newly-forged ideological weapons. He attacks Carlyle and the whole tribe of German pantheists for their belief that a new religion could reconstitute a decaying society and a universe that has been deprived of meaning. Engels draws his arguments from the writings of Feuerbach, whose *Grundsätze der Philosophie der Zukunft* had been published in 1843, and of Bruno Bauer, both of whom he and Marx were shortly to attack with zeal.

Engels' discussion is, of course, an oversimplification, since it ignores the Calvinistic bases of Carlyle's views and implies that by taking a proper turn here and there he would emerge as a rational social critic. However, if the young Engels did not manage to penetrate in his definitions to the paradoxical heart of Carlyle's *Weltanschauung* where the forms of Calvinist belief, German metaphysics and a fierce social indignation play out their continual dialectic, he at least discussed Carlyle's work with a seriousness and sophistication that is not found anywhere else in the forties and fifties. There was not, to my knowledge, any British writer who considered Carlyle's work in so wide a philosophical context, and gave it such serious and informed attention.

But what is most admirable in Engels' essay is his reminder to us that as a social tract *Past and Present* is not merely an occasional pamphlet, but still an active, usable document, drawing on many currents of thought and belief. Engels need not have relied on Carlyle for his information about the condition of England. As his subsequent book shows, he had collected a great deal of data on his own, and by 1843 several writers had described "the perilous state of the land". The English book which has sometimes been associated with *Past and Present*, R. B. Seeley's *The Perils of the Nation; An Appeal to the Legislature, the Clergy, and the Higher and Middle Classes* (London, 1843), demonstrates how necessary literary art may be even to the communication of social statistics. Seeley's four-hundred-odd pages are marked by knowledge and deep (Evangelical) earnestness. His view of England is as dark as Carlyle's; for him England is "one vast mass of superficial splendour, covering a body of festering misery and discontent . . . however capital may have prospered, *the nation*, in a most important point, *has declined and decayed*".[20] Seeley quotes remarks made in the Commons by Buller and Lord Ashley (later Lord Shaftesbury), he refers to reports of the Commissioners of Enquiry and passes on a great deal of useful information about conditions of housing and sanitary regulations. But all of Seeley's shocking facts do not, somehow, startle or move us. His concern and obvious rectitude conduce finally to a kind of nagging dullness. Engels sums it all up when he insists that only Carlyle's book strikes the "menschliche Saiten". It is not just the note of humanity, it is the note of life. And it is this resonance, rather than the scope of his political views or the adequacy of his social documentation that gives Carlyle's tract for his times an indestructible energy.

NOTES

[1] Grace J. Calder, *The Writing of "Past and Present"* (New Haven: Yale UP, 1949) contains a great deal of valuable information. A. M. D. Hughes' edition of the work (Oxford UP, 1918) has an informative introduction and full annotation. [The Strouse critical edition of *Past and Present* edited by Clyde de L. Ryals, Joel Brattin, and D. J. Trela is now being prepared—eds.]

[2] *Past and Present, Centenary Edition of the Collected Works.* Ed. H. D. Traill. (London: Chapman, 1898): 10:107. Hereafter cited in text by volume and page.

[3] "The Wreck of the Deutschland", stanza 28.

[4] See "Some Personal Recollections of Carlyle", *The Literary Remains of Henry James*. Ed. William James (Boston: J. R. Osgood, 1885): 429, 425. A more extended study of this aspect of Carlyle is C. R. Sanders, "The Victorian Rembrandt: Carlyle's Portraits of His Contemporaries", *Bulletin of the John Rylands Library* 39 (1957): 521-57.

[5] *Collected Letters of Thomas Carlyle and Jane Welsh Carlyle*, 24 vols. Ed. Charles R. Sanders, K. J. Fielding, and Clyde de L. Ryals, et al. (Durham: Duke UP, 1970-): 7:52.

[6] Goethe's essay, "Von deutscher Baukunst", was published in 1773 under the auspices of Herder, and is the most important early statement of the spiritual beauties of "Gothic" architecture—a term which Goethe consciously rescued from disrepute. See *Gedenkausgabe der Werke, Briefe und Gespräche*, Ernst Beutler, ed., 24 vols. (Zurich, 1949-50), *Schriften zur Kunst*, 13:16-26.

[7] A number of travellers to Rome seem to have commented on this ingenious contrivance. Henry Crabb Robinson saw a Corpus Christi procession in 1830 and described with some wonder the artful chair by which the Pope "acts kneeling". *Diary, Reminiscences and Correspondence of Henry Crabb Robinson*. Ed. T. Sadler. (London, 1869) 2:469-70.

[8] *Past and Present* in *Natural History of the Intellect*, in *The Complete Works of Ralph Waldo Emerson*. Ed. Edward W. Emerson. (Boston and New York, 1904): 12:379. The original essay appeared in *The Dial* 4 (July 1843): 96-102.

[9] *Natural History* 12:380.

[10] *Natural History* 12:386.

[11] *Journals and Miscellaneous Notebooks of Ralph Waldo Emerson*, W. H. Gilman and J. E. Parsons, eds. (Cambridge: Harvard UP, 1970): 8:408.

[12] See Karl Marx and Friedrich Engels, *Werke* (Berlin, 1957): 525-49.

[13] *The Condition of the Working Classes in England in 1844* (London, 1892) is a translation of a new continental edition published in Stuttgart in the same year.

[14] Peter Demetz, *Marx, Engels and the Poets* (U of Chicago P, 1967): 37.

[15] *Werke* 525.

[16] *Werke* 528.

[17] *Werke* 539.

[18] *Werke* 542.

[19] *Werke* 543. A much fuller discussion of Engels and Carlyle is to be found in Steven Marcus's *Engels, Manchester and the Working Class* (New York: Random House, 1974): 102-12.

[20] Seeley xvii, xxxviii-ix.

A BIBLIOGRAPHY OF SUGGESTED READINGS*

SARTOR RESARTUS

Nineteenth-Century Reviews

[William Maginn]. "Thomas Carlyle." *Fraser's Magazine* 7 (1833): 706.

Sun 1 April 1834: 2.

Athenaeum 424 (12 December 1835): 931.

[Everett, Alexander H.]. "Thomas Carlyle." *North American Review* 41 (October 1835): 454-82.

F[rothingham], N[athaniel] L. *Christian Examiner* 21 (September 1836): 74-84.

Knickerbocker Magazine 9 (April 1837): 432.

Southern Literary Journal 1 (March 1837): 1-8.

Metropolitan Magazine 23 (September 1838): 1-5.

Monthly Review 147 (September 1838): 54-66.

Tait's Edinburgh Magazine 5 (September 1838): 611-12.

Democratic Review 23 (August 1848): 139-49.

[Barrett, Joseph H.]. *American Whig Review* 9 (February 1849): 121-34.

Contemporary Criticism

Scott, J. W. "Carlyle's *Sartor Resartus*." *University of California Chronicle* 24 (1922), 153-61, 337-46, 427-39.

Chrisman, Lewis H. "*Sartor Resartus*." *Methodist Review* 108 (1925): 193-208.

Liljegren, S. B. "The Origin of *Sartor Resartus*." *Palaestra*, no. 148 (1925): 400-33.

Paterson, W. P. "Books That Have Influenced Our Epoch: Carlyle's *Sartor Resartus.*" *Expository Times* 41 (1929): 32-38.

Dunn, Waldo H. "The Centennial of *Sartor Resartus.*" *London Quarterly Review* 155 (1931): 39-51.

Holmberg, A. O. *David Hume in Carlyle's "Sartor Resartus".* Lund: Gleerups, 1934.

Wrigley, F. "The Centenary of *Sartor Resartus.*" *Congregational Quarterly* 12 (1934): 53-56.

Eckloff, L. *Bild und Wirklichkeit bei Thomas Carlyle. Eine Untersuchung des bildlichen Ausdrucks in Carlyles "Sartor Resartus."* Königsberg, Ger.: Ost-Europa, 1936.

Smith, Fred M. "Whitman's Debt to Carlyle's *Sartor Resartus.*" *Modern Language Quarterly* 3 (1942): 51-65.

Maynard, T. "*Sartor Resartus.*" *Commonweal* 52 (1952): 43-44.

Rinehart, Keith. "Carlyle's *Sartor Resartus.*" *Explicator* 9 (1953): item 32.

Moore, Carlisle. "*Sartor Resartus* and the Problem of Carlyle's 'Conversion.'" *PMLA* 70 (1955): 662-81.

___. "The Persistence of Carlyle's 'Everlasting Yea.'" *Modern Philology* 54 (1957): 187-96.

Sanders, Charles R. "The Question of Carlyle's 'Conversion.'" *Victorian Newsletter* no. 10 (1956): 10-12.

Cooper, Bernice. "A Comparison of *Quintus Fixlein* and *Sartor Resartus.*" *Transactions of the Wisconsin Academy of Sciences, Arts, and Letters* 48 (1958): 253-72.

Toole, William B. "Carlyle's *Sartor Resartus*, II, ix." *Explicator* 17 (1959): item 65.

Witte, William. "Carlyle's Conversion." *The Era of Goethe: Essays Presented to James Boyd.* Oxford, Eng.: Blackwell, 1959. 179-93.

Deneau, Daniel P. "Relationship of Style and Device in *Sartor Resartus.*" *Victorian Newsletter* no. 17 (1960): 17-20.

Lindberg, John. "The Artistic Unity of *Sartor Resartus.*" *Victorian Newsletter* no. 17 (1960), 20-23.

Agnihotri, Surendra H. "The Philosophy of Clothes as Revealed in *Sartor Resartus.*" *Aryan Path* 32 (1961): 219-24.

Malin, James C. "Carlyle's Philosophy of Clothes and Swedenborg's." *Scandinavian Studies* 33 (1961): 155-68.

Metzger, Lore. "*Sartor Resartus*: A Victorian *Faust.*" *Comparative Literature* 13 (1961): 316-31.

Deen, Leonard W. "Irrational Form in *Sartor Resartus.*" *Texas Studies in Language and Literature* 5 (1963): 438-51.

Plard, Henri. "Le 'Sartor Resartus' de Carlyle et Jean Paul." *Etudes Germaniques* 28 (1963): 114-28.

Ryan, Alvin S. "The Attitude Towards the Reader in Carlyle's *Sartor Resartus.*" *Victorian Newsletter* no. 23 (1963): 15-16.

Levine, George. "*Sartor Resartus* and the Balance of Fiction." *Victorian Studies* 8 (1964): 131-60.

Sanders, Charles R. "The Byron Closed in *Sartor Resartus.*" *Studies in Romanticism* 3 (1964): 77-108.

Tennyson, G. B. "'The true Shekinah is man.'" *American Notes and Queries* 3 (1964): 58.

Ryan, Alvan S. "Carlyle, Jeffrey, and the 'Helotage' Chapter of *Sartor Resartus.*" *Victorian Newsletter* 27 (1965): 30-32.

Tennyson, G. B. *"Sartor" Called "Resartus."* Princeton, NJ: Princeton UP, 1965.

Bertolotti, D. S. "Mark Twain Revisits the Tailor." *Mark Twain Journal* 13 (1967): 18-19.

D'Avanzo, Mario L. "'The Cassock' and Carlyle's 'Church Clothes.'" *Emerson Society Quarterly* 50 (1968): 74-76.

McMaster, Rowland D. "Criticism of Civilization in the Structure of *Sartor Resartus.*" *University of Toronto Quarterly* 37 (1968): 268-80.

Dunn, Richard J. "David Copperfield's Carlylean Retailoring." *Dickens the Craftsman.* Ed. Robert Partlow. Carbondale: Southern Illinois UP, 1970. 95-114.

Christensen, Allan C. "A Dickensian Hero Retailored: The Carlylean Apprenticeship of Martin Chuzzlewit." *Studies in the Novel* 3 (1971): 18-25.

Clubbe, John. "John Carlyle in Germany and the Genesis of *Sartor Resartus.*" *Romantic and Victorian: Studies in Memory of William H. Marshall.* Rutherford, NJ: Fairleigh Dickenson UP, 1971. 264-89.

Reed, Walter J. "The Pattern of Conversion in *Sartor Resartus.*" *Journal of English Literary History* 38 (1971): 411-31.

Brantlinger, Patrick. "'Teufelsdröckh' Resartus." *English Language Notes* 9 (1972): 191-93.

Brookes, Gerry H. *The Rhetorical Form of "Sartor Resartus."* Berkeley, CA: U of California P, 1972.

Dilthy, Wilhelm, and (Trans. Murray Baumgarten and Evelyn Kanes). "*Sartor Resartus*: Philosophical Conflict, Positive and Negative Eras, and Personal Resolution." *Clio* 1 (1972): 40-60.

Sigman, Joseph T. "'Diabolico-Angelical Indifference': The Image of Polarity in *Sartor Resartus.*" *Southern Review* (Australia) 5 (1972): 207-24.

Hafter, Monroe Z. "*El diablo mundo* in the Light of Carlyle's *Sartor Resartus.*" *Revista Hispánica Moderna: Columbia University Hispanic Studies* 37 (1972-73): 46-55.

Brantlinger, Patrick. "'Romance,' 'Biography,' and the Making of *Sartor Resartus.*" *Philological Quarterly* 52 (1973): 108-18.

Dibble, Jerry A. "Carlyle's 'British Reader' and the Structure of *Sartor Resartus.*" *Texas Studies in Language and Literature* 16 (1974): 293-304.

Franke, Wolfgang. "Another Derivation of 'Teufelsdröckh.'" *Notes and Queries* 21 (1974): 339-40.

Sigman, Joseph T. "Adam-Kadmon, Nifl, Muspel, and the Biblical Symbolism of *Sartor Resartus.*" *Journal of English Literary History* 41 (1974): 233-56.

Wilson, John R. "*Sartor Resartus*: A Study in the Paradox of Despair." *Christianity and Literature* 23 (1974): 9-27.

Blondel, Jacques. "Vision et ironie dans *Sartor Resartus.*" *Confluents* no. 2 (1975): 3-11.

Fontaney, Pierre. "Message et muflerie dans *Sartor Resartus.*" *Confluents* no. 1 (1975): 177-85.

Landow, George P. "'Swim or Drown': Carlyle's World of Shipwrecks, Castaways, and Stranded Voyagers." *Studies in English Literature* 15 (1975): 641-55.

Clubbe, John. "Carlyle on *Sartor Resartus.*" *Carlyle Past and Present.* Ed. K. J. Fielding and Rodger L. Tarr. London: Vision, 1976. 51-60.

Edwards, Janet R. "Carlyle and the Fictions of Belief: *Sartor Resartus* to *Past and Present.*" *Carlyle and His Contemporaries.* Ed. John Clubbe. Durham, NC: Duke UP, 1976. 91-111.

Pickering, Sam. "*Sartor Resartus*, Thomas Carlyle, and the Novel." *Research Studies* 44 (1976): 208-16.

Franklin, Stephen L. "The Editor as Reconstructor: Carlyle's Historical View as a Shaping Force in the Fiction of *Sartor Resartus.*" *Ball State University Forum* 18.3 (1977): 32-39.

Janssen, Winnifred. "The Science of Things in General: Method or Madness?" *Dutch Quarterly Review* 7 (1977): 23-44.

Dibble, Jerry A. *The Pythia's Drunken Song: Thomas Carlyle's "Sartor Resartus" and the Style Problem in German Idealistic Philosophy.* The Hague: Nijhoff, 1978.

Haney, Janice L. "'Shadow-Hunting': Romantic Irony, *Sartor Resartus*, and Victorian Romanticism." *Studies in Romanticism* 17 (1978): 307-33.

Tarr, Rodger L. "Dorothea's 'Resartus' and the Palingenetic Impulse of *Middlemarch*." *Texas Studies in Literature and Language* 20 (1978): 107-18.

Glassman, Peter. "' "His Beautiful Edifice, of a Person" ': *Sartor Resartus*." *Prose Studies* 2 (1979): 25-40.

Dale, Peter Allan. "*Sartor Resartus* and the Inverse Sublime: The Art of Humorous Destruction." *Allegory, Myth, and Symbol*. Ed. M. W. Bloomfield. Harvard English Studies 9. Cambridge: Harvard UP, 1981. 293-312.

Vijn, J. P. *Carlyle and Jean Paul: Their Spiritual Optics*. Amsterdam, Neth.: Benjamins, 1982.

Baker, Lee C. R. "The Old Clothesman Transformed: Thomas Carlyle's Radical Vision." *Victorians Institute Journal* 11 (1982-1983): 45-51.

Waterston, Elizabeth. "Past and Present Selves: Patterns in *Sartor Resartus*." *Thomas Carlyle 1981: Papers Given at the International Thomas Carlyle Centenary Symposium*. Ed. H. W. Drescher. Scottish Studies 1. Frankfurt: Lang, 1983. 111-24.

Earest, James D. "The Influence of Thomas Carlyle on the Early Novels of Miguel de Unamuno." *Kentucky Philological Association Bulletin* (1984): 25-35.

Baker, Lee C. R. "The Open Secret of *Sartor Resartus*: Carlyle's Method of Converting His Reader." *Studies in Philology* 83.2 (1986): 218-35.

Vanden Bossche, Chris R. "Desire and Deferral of Closure in Carlyle's *Sartor Resartus* and *The French Revolution*." *Journal of Narrative Technique* 16.1 (1986): 72-78.

Beirnard, Charles A. "Rebelling from the Right Siade: Thomas Carlyle's Struggle Against the Dominant Nineteenth-Century Rhetoric." *Studies in Scottish Literature* 22 (1987): 142-56.

Kelly, Mary Ann. "*Daniel Deronda* and Carlyle's Clothes Philosophy." *Journal of English and Germanic Philology* 86.4 (1987): 515-30.

Komarova, E. G. "Rol' ironii v romane T. Karleilia 'Sartor Resartus.'" *Vestnik Leningradskogo Universiteta* (Russian) 4 (1987): 79-81.

Timko, Michael. "Carlyle's Asafoetidaic Vision." *Prose Studies* 10:3 (1987): 270-82.

apRoberts, Ruth. *The Ancient Dialect: Thomas Carlyle and Comparative Religion*. Berkeley, CA: U of California P, 1988.

Howells, Bernard. "Heroïsme, dandysme et la 'Philosophie du costume': Note sur Baudelaire et Carlyle." *Revista di Litterature Moderne e Comparate* 41.2 (1988): 131-51.

Sharma, T. R. "The *Gita* and the Theme of Conversion in Carlyle's *Sartor Resartus*." *The Influence of "Bhagavadgita on Literature Written in English*. Ed. T. R. Sharma. Meerut, India: Shalabh, 1988. 37-48.

Sieminski, Greg. "Suited for Satire: Butler's Re-Tailoring of *Sartor Resartus* in *The Way of All Flesh.*" *English Literature in Transition (1880-1920)* 31.1 (1988): 29-37.

Stowell, Sheila. "Teufelsdröckh as Devil's Dust." *Carlyle Newsletter* 9 (1988): 31-33.

Miller, J. Hillis. "'Hieroglyphical Truth' in *Sartor Resartus*: Carlyle and the Language of Parable." *Victorian Perspectives: Six Essays.* Eds. J. Clubbe and J. Meckier. Newark: U of Delaware P, 1989. 1-20.

Rosenberg, John D. "Carlyle and Historical Narration." *Carlyle Annual* 10 (1989): 14-20.

Davis, Dale W. "Symbolizing the Supernatural in Carlyle's *Sartor Resartus.*" *University of Mississippi Studies in English* 8 (1990): 92-96.

Hughes, Linda K. "Sartor Redivivus: Or, Retailoring Carlyle for the Undergraduate Classroom." *Victorian Newsletter* 78 (1990): 29-32.

Tarr, Rodger L. "The Manuscript Chronology of *Sartor Resartus*: Some Speculations." *Carlyle Annual* 11 (1990): 97-104.

Hijiya, Yukihito. "*Sartor Resartus*: A Philosophy of a Mystic." *Carlyle Society Papers.* Ed. Ian Campbell. Edinburgh: Carlyle Society, 1992. 41-50.

Hruschka, John. "Carlyle's Rabbinical Hero: Teufelsdröckh and the Midrashic Tradition." *Carlyle Annual* 13 (1992-93): 101-08.

Rundle, Vivienne. "'Devising New Means': *Sartor Resartus* and the Devoted Reader." *Victorian Newsletter* 82 (1992): 13-22.

Elfenbein, Andrew. "The Sorrows of Carlyle: Byronism and the Philosophic Critic." *Victorian Literature and Culture.* Ed. John Maynard, et al. Nework, NY: AMS, 1993. 147-67.

Choi, Byong-hyon. "*Sartor Resartus*: Carlyle's Metaphor and Message." *Journal of English Language and Literature* 40.3 (1994): 461-73.

Felluga, D. Franco. "The Critic's New Clothes: *Sartor Resartus* as 'Cold Carnival.'" *Criticism* 37.4 (1995): 583-99.

THE FRENCH REVOLUTION

Nineteenth-Century Reviews

Examiner 1546-1548 (17 September-1 October 1837): 596-98, 629-30.

Literary Gazette 1062 (27 May 1837): 330-32.

Monthly Repository 11 (September 1837): 219-20.

Monthly Review 11 (August 1837): 543-48.

Southern Rose 6 (25 November 1837): 174.

A. [John S. Mill]. *London and Westminster Review* 27 (July 1837): 17-53.

[Morgan, Lady Sydney]. *Athenaeum* 499 (20 May 1837): 353-55.

[Thackeray, William M.]. *Times* 3 August 1837: 6.

Wilson, John]. *Blackwood's Edinburgh Magazine* 42 (November 1837): 592-93.

American Monthly Magazine 5 (March 1838): 290.

Christian Examiner 23 (January 1838): 386-87.

New Yorker 4 (10 March 1838): 813.

Southern Rose 6 (14 April 1838): 174.

B[artol], C. A. *Christian Examiner* 24 (July 1838): 345-62.

[Channing, W. H.]. *Boston Quarterly Review* 1 (October 1838): 407-17.

New York Review 5 (July 1839): 109-35.

[Prescott, William H] *North American Review* 49 (October 1839): 342.

Little's Museum of Foreign Literature 90 (December 1840): 385-94.

M[azzini], J[oseph]. *Monthly Chronicle* 5 (January 1840): 71-84.

[Merivale, Herman]. *Edinburgh Review* 71 (July 1840): 411-45.

American Biblical Repository 7 (January 1842): 233-34.

Democratic Review 19 (December 1846): 491.

Graham's Magazine 30 (January 1847): 83.

Contemporary Criticism

Hilles, Frederick W. "'Mother of Dead Dogs' from 'History of the French Revolution.'" *Modern Language Notes* 42 (1927): 506-08.

Harrold, Charles F. "Translated Passages from Carlyle's *The French Revolution*." *Journal of English and Germanic Philology* 27 (1928): 51-66.

___. "Carlyle's General Method in *The French Revolution*." *PMLA* 43 (1928): 1150-69.

Hirst, W. A. "The Manuscript of Carlyle's *The French Revolution*." *Nineteenth Century and After* 123 (1938): 93-98.

Young, Louise M. *Carlyle and the Art of History*. Philadelphia, PA: U of Pennsylvania P, 1939.

Lea, Frank A. "Carlyle and the French Revolution." *Adelphi* 18 (1941): 20-24, 36-38.

Wellek, René. "Carlyle and the Philosophy of History." *Philological Quarterly* 23 (1944): 55-65.

Blair, Walter. "*The French Revolution* and *Huckleberry Finn.*" *Modern Philology* 55 (1957): 21-35.

Ben-Israel, Hedva. "Carlyle and the French Revolution." *Historical Journal* 1 (1958): 115-35.

Cobban, Alfred. "Carlyle's *French Revolution.*" *History* 48 (1963): 306-16.

Lea, Frank A. "Carlyle and the French Revolution." *Listener* 72 (1964): 421-23.

Sharrock, Roger. "Carlyle and the Sense of History." *Essays and Studies* 19 (1966): 74-91.

Kusch, Robert W. "The Eighteenth Century as 'Decaying Organism' in Carlyle's *The French Revolution.*" *Anglia* 89 (1971): 456-70.

Leicester, H. M. "The Dialectic of Romantic Historiography: Prospect and Retrospect in *The French Revolution.*" *Victorian Studies* 15 (1971): 5-17.

Tarr, Rodger L. "Thomas Carlyle's Growing Radicalism: The Social Context of *The French Revolution.*" *Costerus* 1 (1974): 113-26.

Clubbe, John. "Epic Heroes in *The French Revolution.*" *Thomas Carlyle 1981: Papers Given at the International Thomas Carlyle Centenary Symposium.* Ed. H. W. Drescher. Scottish Studies 1. Frankfurt: Lang, 1983. 165-85.

MacKay, Carol H. "The Rhetoric of Soliloquy in *The French Revolution* and *A Tale of Two Cities.*" *Dickens Studies Annual* 12 (1983): 197-207.

Timko, Michael. "Splendid Impressions and Picturesque Means: Dickens, Carlyle, and the French Revolution." *Dickens Studies Annual* 12 (1983): 177-95.

Vanden Bossche, Chris R. "Prophetic Closure and Disclosing Narrative: *The French Revolution* and *A Tale of Two Cities.*" *Dickens Studies Annual* 12 (1983): 209-21.

Buckett, Anna. "History as Verbal Construct: Strategies of Composition and Rhetoric in the Histories of the French Revolution by Carlyle, Scott, and Mignet." *Revista Canaria de Estudios Ingleses* 9 (1984): 55-69.

Clubbe, John. "Carlyle as Epic Historian." *Victorian Literature and Society.* Ed. James R. Kincaid. Columbus, OH: Ohio State UP, 1984. 119-45.

Culviner, Thomas. "Heroes and Hero-Worship: Not So Simple in *The French Revolution.*" *Victorian Institutes Journal* 13 (1985): 83-96.

Rosenberg, John. *Carlyle and the Burden of History.* Cambridge, MA: Harvard UP, 1985.

Lloyd, Tom. "Madame Roland and Schiller's Aesthetics: Carlyle's 'The French Revolution.'" *Prose Studies* 9.3 (1986): 39-53.

Cumming, Mark. "Allegory and Phantasmagory in *The French Revolution*." *Journal of English and Germanic Philology* 86.3 (1987): 332-47.

Ryals, Clyde de L. "Carlyle's *The French Revolution*: A 'True Fiction.'" *Journal of English Literary History* 54.4 (1987): 925-40.

Cumming, Mark. *A Disimprisoned Epic: Form and Vision in Carlyle's "French Revolution."* Philadelphia, PA: U of Pennsylvania P, 1988.

Daleski, H. M. "Imagining Revolution: The Eye of History and of Fiction." *Journal of Narrative Technique* 18.1 (1988): 61-72.

Furness, N. A. "Two Views of the French Revolution: Georg Buchner's *Dantons Tod* and Thomas Carlyle's *The French Revolution*: A History." *The Carlyle Society Papers, Session 1987-88*. Edinburgh: Carlyle Society, 1988.

Tarr, Rodger L. "Carlyle's *The French Revolution*: A Hitherto Unavailable Manuscript Fragment." *Carlyle Newsletter* 9 (1988): 33-36.

Halladay, Jean R. "*Sartor Resartus* Revisited: Carlylean Echoes in Crane's *The Red Badge of Courage*." *Nineteenth Century Prose* 16.1 (1988-1989): 23-33.

Sorensen, David. "Carlyle, Knox, and the *French Revolution*: Lecture Delivered to the Carlyle Society of Edinburgh, October 15, 1988." *The Carlyle Society Papers, Session 1988-89*. Edinburgh: Carlyle Society, 1989.

Ryals, Clyde de L. "Carlyle's *The French Revolution*: A True History." *A World of Possibilities: Romantic Irony in Victorian Literature*. Columbus, OH: Ohio State UP, 1990. 17-33.

Sorensen, David. "Carlyle, Macaulay, and the 'Dignity of History.'" *Carlyle Annual* 11 (1990): 41-52.

Sørensen, Knud. "Carlyle and Dickens on the French Revolution: A Stylistic Study." *Dolphin* 19 (1990): 134-45.

Parker, Noël. "La Dynamique de l'histoire dans le style de *The French Revolution* de Thomas Carlyle." *Après 89 la révolution modèle ou repoussoir*. Eds. L. Domergue and G. Lamoine. Toulouse: PU du Mirail, 1991. 199-211.

Sorensen, David. "Carlyle, Gibbon, and the 'Miraculous Thing of History.'" *Carlyle Annual* 12 (1991): 33-43.

Cumming, Mark. "'Such a Figure Drew Priam's Curtains!': Carlyle's Epic History of the French Revolution." *Representing the French Revolution: Literature, Historiography, and Art*. Ed. J. A. W. Heffernan. Hanover, NH: UP of New England, for Dartmouth College, 1992. 63-77.

HEROES AND HERO-WORSHIP

Nineteenth-Century Reviews

New Yorker 11.6 (24 April 1841): 93.

New York Review 9 (July 1841): 266.

"Carlyle's Lectures." *Tait's Edinburgh Magazine* 8 (June 1841): 379-83.

[Barrett, Joseph H.]. *Monthly Review* 155 (May 1841): 1-21.

D. *Arcturus* 1 (May 1841): 354-62.

[Fuller, Margaret]. *Dial* 2 (July 1841): 131-33.

H., J. A. *Monthly Magazine* 93 (April 1841): 391-412.

[Thomson, William]. *Christian Remembrancer* 3 (March 1842): 341-53.

___. *Christian Remembrancer* 6 (August 1843): 121-43.

Democratic Review 19 (December 1846): 490.

Biblical Review 3 (March 1847): 183-86.

American Whig Review 9 (April 1849): 339-44.

Contemporary Criticism

Lehman, Benjamin H. *Carlyle's Theory of the Hero*. Durham, NC: Duke UP, 1928.

Bentley, Eric R. "Modern Hero-Worship: Notes on Carlyle, Nietzsche, and Stefan George." *Sewanee Review* 52 (1944): 441-56.

___. *A Century of Hero-Worship*. Philadelphia, PA: Lippincott, 1944.

DeLaura, David J. "Ishmael as Prophet: *Heroes and Hero-Worship* and the Self-Expressive Basis of Carlyle's Art." *Texas Studies in Language and Literature* 11 (1969): 705-32.

Donovan, Robert A. "Carlyle and the Climate of Hero Worship." *University of Toronto Quarterly* 42 (1973): 122-41.

Hafter, Monroe Z. "Heroism in Alas and Carlyle's *On Heroes*." *Malcolm Lowery Newsletter* 95 (1980): 312-34.

Sonstroem, David. "The Double Vortex in Carlyle's *On Heroes and Hero Worship*." *Philological Quarterly* 59.4 (1980): 531-40.

Buckler, William E. "The Aesthetic of Seeing/The Morality of Being: Carlyle's Grand and Simple Insight into the Humanness of Heroism." *Prose Studies* 4.3 (1981): 287-300.

Campbell, Ian. "On *Heroes*." *Le Mythe du héros*. Ed. N. J. Rigaud. Aix-en-Provence, Fr.: Université de Provence, 1982. 147-64.

Ousby, Ian. "Carlyle, Thackeray, and Victorian Heroism." *Yearbook of English Studies* 12 (1982): 152-68.

Bidney, Martin. "Diminishing Epiphanies of Odin: Carlyle's Reveries of Primal Fire." *Modern Language Quarterly* 44.1 (1983): 51-64.

Haws, Charles H. "Carlyle's Concept of History in *Heroes and Hero Worship*." *Thomas Carlyle 1981: Papers Given at the International Thomas Carlyle Centenary Symposium*. Ed. H. W. Drescher. Scottish Studies 1. Frankfurt: Lang, 1983. 153-63.

Pratt, Branwen B. "Carlyle and Dickens: Heroes and Hero Worshippers." *Dickens Studies Annual* 12 (1983): 233-46.

Deledalle-Rhodes, Janice. "Carlyle et l'Islam—une mise au point." *Mythes, Croyances et Religions dans le Monde Anglo-Saxon* 2 (1984): 79-90.

Culviner, Thomas. "Heroes and Hero Worship: Not So Simple in *The French Revolution*." *Victorians Institute Journal* 13 (1985): 83-86.

Goldberg, Michael, intro. *On Heroes, Hero-Worship, and the Heroic in History*. Berkeley, CA: U of California P, 1993.

Timko, Michael. "Thomas Carlyle: Chaotic Man, Inarticulate Hero." *Carlyle Studies Annual* 14 (1994): 55-69.

PAST AND PRESENT

Nineteenth-Century Reviews

Examiner 1839 (April 1843): 259-61.

Graham's Magazine 23 (June 1843): 58.

Magazine of Domestic Economy and Family Review 1 (June 1843): 561-64.

Monthly Review 161 (May 1843): 190-203.

Tait's Edinburgh Magazine 10 (June 1843): 341-48.

Times 6 October 1843: 3-4.

E., R. B. *Thoughts on Thomas Carlyle; or, A Commentary on "Past and Present."* London: Ward, 1843.

[Emerson, Ralph W.]. *Dial* 4 (July 1843): 96-102.

Maurice, F[Frederick D]. "On the Tendency of Mr. Carlyle's Writings." *Christian Remembrancer* 6 (October 1843): 451-61.

[Morgan, Lady Sydney]. *Athenaeum* 811-812 (13 May-20 May 1843): 453-54, 480-81.

[Renouf, Peter L.]. *Dublin Review* 15 (August 1843): 182-200.

[Smith, William H.]. *Blackwood's Edinburgh Magazine* 54 (July 1843): 121-38.
[Richardson, Merrill]. *New Englander* 2 (January 1844): 25-39.

Smith, J. T. *American Biblical Repository* 12 (October 1844): 317-52.

Contemporary Criticism

Chrisman, Lewis H. "*Past and Present.*" *Methodist Review of Literature* 110 (1927): 713-27.

Anon. "[Gabriel Wells] Gives Carlyle Draft to British Museum." *New York Times* 20 July 1928: 6.

G[ibson], J. P. "Carlyle's *Past and Present.*" *British Museum Quarterly* 3 (1928): 75-76.

Calder, Grace J. "Carlyle's *Past and Present.*" *Yale University Library Gazette* 6 (1931): 33-35.

Rowse, A. L. "The Message of *Past and Present.*" *New Statesman and Nation* 25 (1943): 370.

Calder, Grace J. *The Writing of "Past and Present."* New Haven, CT: Yale UP, 1949.

Fain, John T. "Word Echoes in *Past and Present.*" no. 8 (1955): 5-6.

Levine, Richard A. "Carlyle as a Poet: The Phoenix Image in 'Organic Filaments.'" *Victorian Newsletter* no. 25 (1964): 18-20.

Marrs, Edwin W. "Dating the Writings of *Past and Present.*" *Notes and Queries* 14 (1967): 370-71.

Brock, D. Heyward. "The Portrait of Abbot Sampson in *Past and Present*: Carlyle and Jocelin of Brakelond." *English Miscellany* 23 (1972): 149-65.

Hopwood, Alison L. "Carlyle and Conrad: *Past and Present* and *Heart of Darkness.*" *Review of English Studies* 23 (1972): 162-72.

Tarr, Rodger L. "Dickens' Debt to Carlyle's Justice Metaphor in *The Chimes.*" *Nineteenth-Century Fiction* 27 (1972): 208-15.

Altick, Richard D. "*Past and Present*: Topicality as Technique." *Carlyle and His Contemporaries*. Ed. John Clubbe. Durham, NC: Duke UP, 1976. 112-28.

Smith, Julia A. "Thomas Arnold and the Genesis of *Past and Present.*" *Arnoldian* 3.2 (1976): 14-16.

Stange, G. Robert. "Refractions of *Past and Present.*" *Carlyle Past and Present.* Ed. K. J. Fielding and Rodger L. Tarr, 1976. 96-111.

Buckler, William E. ""*Past and Present* as Literary Experience: An Essay in the Epistemological Imagination." *Prose Studies* 1.3 (1978): 5-25.

Jann, Rosemary. "The Condition of England Past and Present: Thomas Carlyle and the Middle Ages." *Studies in Medievalism* 1.1 (1979): 15-31.

Georgianna, Linda. "Carlyle and Jocelin of Brakelond: A Chronicle Rechronicled." *Browning Institute Studies* 8 (1980): 103-27.

Smith, Julia. "The Structure of *Past and Present*: Contrast, Infinity and the Meaning of Repetition." *Conference of College Teachers of English Studies* 47 (1982): 20-24.

Keating, Peter. "Backward or Forward? Carlyle's *Past and Present*." *Thomas Carlyle 1981: Papers Given at the International Thomas Carlyle Centenary Symposium.* Ed. H. W. Drescher. Scottish Studies 1. Frankfurt: Lang, 1983. 207-22.

Childers, Joseph W. "Carlyle's *Past and Present*, History, and a Question of Hermeneutics." *CLIO* 13.3 (1984): 247-58.

Hirsch, Gordon. "History Writing in Carlyle's *Past and Present*." *Prose Studies* 7.3 (1984): 225-31.

Malone, C. "Voices of the Ages: The Editor and His Texts in *Past and Present*." *Carlyle Annual* 10 (1989): 41-49.

Tarr, Rodger L. "Carlyle's *Past and Present*: A Hitherto Unavailable Manuscript Fragment." *Carlyle Annual* 10 (1989): 85-86.

Lawson, R. Bland. "The 'Condition of England Question': *Past and Present* and *Bleak House*." *Victorian Newsletter* 79 (1991): 24-27.

Beckett, Ruth. "*Past and Present*: Carlyle and Ruskin on Scott and Victorian Medievalism." *Scott in Carnival: Selected Papers from the 4th International Scott Conference, Edinburgh, 1991.* Eds. J. H. Alexander and D. Hewitt. Aberdeen: Association for Scottish Literary Studies, 1993. 512-22.

Ulrich, John M. "'A Labor of Death and A Labor Against Death': Translating the Corpse of History in Carlyle's *Past and Present*." *Carlyle Studies Annual* 15 (1995): 33-47.

*This bibliography was prepared by Rodger L. Tarr from his *Thomas Carlyle: A Bibliography of English-Language Criticism* (Charlottesville, VA: U of Virginia P, 1976) and from his forthcoming entry on the Carlyles for *CBEL3*. Certain items are from Tarr's *Thomas Carlyle: A Descriptive Bibliography* (Pittsburgh, PA: U of Pittsburgh P, 1989).

INDEX

About the Editors

D. J. TRELA is Associate Professor of English and Director of the School of Liberal Studies at Roosevelt University.

RODGER L. TARR is University Distinguished Professor at Illinois State University.

ISBN 0-313-29107-1

90000>